Crossed o

Praise for this book

'Meghji skilfully unveils the layers of this complex society with candour and a warm curiosity. It makes you want to get on the next flight to Bolivia.'

Noo Saro-Wiwa, author of Looking for Transwonderland

'Shafik Meghji is a natural travel writer with a ready mastery of history, anecdote and atmosphere, and Crossed off the Map is the best sort of travel book – an informed and informative portrait of Bolivia that doubles as a vicarious journey for readers on an epic scale, through high mountains, across the altiplano and into deep tropical forests.'

Tim Hannigan, author of The Travel Writing Tribe

'Crossed off the Map is an amazing book. I've discovered so much more of my own country through it. It makes you realise the wonder of Bolivia.'

Sergio Mendoza, journalist for La Nube and Bloomberg News

'A thoroughly engrossing and informative look at a clearly underappreciated part of the world. I now want to read it all again … and explore Bolivia for myself.'

Lyn Hughes, founding editor of Wanderlust

'Following in the footsteps of everyone from Che Guevara, conquistadors and colonialists, to Inca pilgrims and even dinosaurs, Meghji is a wonderful travelling companion, bringing to life a Bolivia rarely seen in such bright and beautiful light.'

Monisha Rajesh, author of Around the World in 80 Trains

About the author

Shafik Meghji is an award-winning travel writer, journalist and author based in South London. Specialising in Latin America and South Asia, he has co-authored more than 40 guidebooks for Rough Guides and DK Eyewitness, and writes for BBC Travel, Wanderlust and Lonely Planet, among others. He is a member of the British Guild of Travel Writers and a fellow of the Royal Geographical Society. shafikmeghji.com

Crossed off the Map
Travels in Bolivia

Shafik Meghji

Published by Practical Action Publishing Ltd
and Latin America Bureau
Practical Action Publishing Ltd
27a Albert Street Rugby,
Warwickshire, CV21 2SG, UK
www.practicalactionpublishing.org

Latin America Bureau (Research & Action) Ltd
Enfield House, Castle Street, Clun, Shropshire, SY7 8JU, UK
www.lab.org.uk

ISBN 978-1-90901-425-1 Paperback
ISBN 978-1-90901-426-8 Hardback
ISBN 978-1-90901-427-5 Electronic PDF

Since 1974, Practical Action Publishing has published and disseminated books
and information in support of international development work throughout
the world. Practical Action Publishing is a trading name of Practical Action
Publishing Ltd (Company Reg. No. 1159018), the wholly owned publishing
company of Practical Action. Practical Action Publishing trades only in support
of its parent charity objectives and any profits are covenanted back to Practical
Action (Charity Reg. No. 247257, Group VAT Registration No. 880 9924 76).

Latin America Bureau (Research and Action) Limited is a UK registered
charity (no. 1113039). Since 1977 LAB has been publishing books, news,
analysis and information about Latin America, reporting consistently from
the perspective of the region's poor, oppressed or marginalized communities,
and social movements. In 2015 LAB entered into a publishing partnership
with Practical Action Publishing.

Meghji, S. (2022) *Crossed off the Map: Travels in Bolivia*, Rugby, UK: Practical
Action Publishing <http://dx.doi.org/10.3362/9781909014275>.

Typeset by vPrompt eServices, India

Contents

Acknowledgements

A huge thanks to everyone at the Latin America Bureau and Practical Action Publishing for helping to make this book a reality, in particular my editor Nick Caistor, Alistair Clark, Mike Gatehouse, Sue Branford, Rebecca Wilson, Clare Tawney, Chloe Callan-Foster, Rosanna Denning and Jenny Peebles.

Thanks also to the many friends and colleagues who read various drafts and provided feedback and encouragement, including Nick Hilborne, Nick Edwards, James McConnachie, Sergio Mendoza, Noo Saro-Wiwa, Tim Hannigan, Lyn Hughes and Monisha Rajesh.

For their insight, advice, recommendations, contacts, and help with research trips, I want to thank Lyliam Gonzalez, Miriam and Efrem Hinojosa, Frank Reinkens, Daniela Röthlisberger, Sylvain Truchot, Janette Simbron, Bibiana Garside, Luis Arturo, and the teams at Chalalán and La Paz on Foot.

Thanks also to my *Rough Guide to Bolivia* editors and co-authors, Mani Ramaswamy, Daniel Jacobs, Stephen Keeling, Ann-Marie-Shaw, Alice Park and Claire Saunders; Diana Jarvis for an excellent map; Elizabeth Haylett Clark at the Society of Authors; Chloe Currens at the Penguin Random House WriteNow scheme; and Jess Hartley and Nick Bland for their companionship on the road.

Most of all, I want to thank Jean, Nizar and Nina Meghji for their unfailing encouragement (and expert proofreading skills); and Sioned Jones for her love, support and a wonderful journey across the *altiplano* and the Yungas.

Prologue

Bolivia does not exist

In 1867, so the story goes, Mariano Melgarejo, the 15th president of Bolivia, asked the British ambassador to pay respects to his latest mistress. When the request was haughtily declined, Melgarejo, whose time in office was marked by brutality and political miscalculation, took great offence. The ambassador was swiftly apprehended, stripped naked, tied to an ass – facing the rear, naturally – and paraded around the main square of La Paz, before being kicked out of the country.

When news of the incident reached Queen Victoria, she angrily ordered the Royal Navy to bombard the Bolivian city. After being politely told that La Paz was located high in the Andes, 400 km from the Pacific coast, she called for a map of South America. When one was produced, Queen Victoria took it and crossed out the country's name. Bolivia, she declared, does not exist.

***

This apocryphal story is known as the 'black legend'. It appears to have been first recounted in a book published in Chile, which has always had a fraught relationship with Bolivia, in the 1870s. There are several versions of this tall tale: in one the British ambassador is punished for refusing to talk to Melgarajo's donkey; in another for declining a glass of *chicha*, a lightly alcoholic maize beer whose fermentation process traditionally involves human saliva. The date of the incident, identity of the protagonists, and nature of the dispute change from telling to telling.

But although the 'black legend' may not be true, it sometimes seems as if Bolivia really was crossed off the map. Despite being twice the size of France, sharing borders with Brazil, Argentina, Chile, Peru and Paraguay, and lying right in the heart of South America, Bolivia tends to be overshadowed by its neighbours. It rarely makes more than a fleeting appearance in the international media, and the coverage it does receive typically focuses on political scandals and environmental disasters.

Tourist numbers have more than doubled over the last decade. Before the Covid-19 pandemic around 1.2 million foreigners were visiting every year, including 100,000 from English-speaking countries. Bolivia is now a firm fixture on the 'Gringo Trail', the backpacking circuit around South America, but most travellers stick to a handful of destinations – the shimmering Uyuni salt flat, majestic Lake Titicaca, the beautifully preserved city of Sucre. Few venture much beyond the Andean region or have anything more than a passing knowledge of Bolivian history, which is perhaps not their fault given that, beyond academic titles, English-language books about the country are few and far between. Travel writers tend to hurry through Bolivia en route to somewhere else, and there has not been a major travelogue dedicated solely to the country in many years.

Yet this is only a recent phenomenon. Between the 16th and early 20th centuries, an array of conquistadors, colonialists, adventurers, missionaries, treasure hunters, revolutionaries, explorers, entrepreneurs, diplomats, soldiers, scientists, and bandits flocked to Bolivia from across the globe. They produced books, reports, letters, and diaries containing stories that once read are impossible to get out of your head. For as improbable as it may seem to many beyond its borders, Bolivia helped to shape the modern world.

***

I heard about the 'black legend' on my first visit to South America in 2004. At that point Bolivia wasn't really on my radar: the plan was to head to Rio de Janeiro for *carnaval*, before flying to Peru and hiking the Inca Trail to Machu Picchu. But one hedonistic month in Brazil rolled into another and my funds ran perilously low. Flights to Peru were prohibitively expensive and I realised with some trepidation that the only option was an arduous 4,100-km journey across the continent on wheezing buses and trundling trains. At the time, Bolivia felt like an obstacle to me, a huge chunk of the map dividing central Brazil from southern Peru, and I resolved to travel through it as quickly as possible.

But after crossing the border at the steamy town of Puerto Quijarro, my perspective swiftly began to change. A train, the *Ferrobús*, carried me west through the lakes, swamps, forests, and seasonally flooded plains of the Pantanal, the world's largest tropical wetlands, home to anacondas, caimans, jaguars and hundreds of species of birds. A short way into the journey, a wiry man in his sixties leaned over to introduce himself. Services on this route, he told me, were once known as 'Death Trains', thanks to their transportation of yellow fever victims in the 1950s, several fatal derailments, and the alarming tendency of some inebriated passengers to clamber onto the carriage roofs before toppling off the sides. 'But that's all in the past,' he said with a smile.

Fifteen hours later, after a broken night's sleep, we pulled into the stiflingly hot city of Santa Cruz de la Sierra. On my first morning in Bolivia, I encountered in quick succession straight-backed, dungaree-wearing Mennonites chatting in Low German, Japanese-Bolivian farmers shopping for tractor parts, *campesinos* carrying bundles that looked heavy enough to crush them, and tough youths in blacked-out 4x4s. In the main plaza I sat on a bench and watched a cacophonous band of protesters bang pots and pans outside the 19th-century cathedral, while a shaggy-haired sloth hung from the branches of a towering tree. Santa Cruz felt like nowhere else I had visited: I was hooked.

Over the following weeks I veered off course, travelling to the Andes and the Amazon via the world's highest city, most dangerous road, and largest salt flat. I met so-called 'witches' in bowler hats and miners who toiled in near-medieval conditions and offered libations to statues of devilish figures. Locals told me about revolutionary movements, utopian societies built in the wilderness, ancient sites hidden away in the jungle, clocks that ran backwards, and pink river dolphins. They also spoke about Bolivia's interactions with its neighbours and the wider world – fragments of history largely forgotten beyond the country's borders. I learned that Bolivia was once home to one of the richest cities on Earth, helped to kickstart the process of globalisation, irrevocably changed the fortunes of Europe and Asia, and played host to everyone from Che Guevara to Butch Cassidy, rubber barons to drug traffickers.

Time ran out and I reluctantly headed on to Peru. But Bolivia took hold of my imagination and has never quite let go. Back home in London, I searched in vain for a contemporary English-language book to give me a greater insight into this country of 12 million people. My fledgling career as a sports reporter suddenly felt rather tame and I started to write about travel for a living. I always planned to return to Bolivia, but circumstances intervened. My work took me to Kathmandu and Kampala, Easter Island and Estonia, Paris and Patagonia. I wrote guidebooks, articles and blog posts, and eventually moved from Brixton to Buenos Aires. But I never made it back to Bolivia.

Six and half years passed, disturbingly quickly, until I received a speculative email on a cold and rainy November morning in 2010. The author of *The Rough Guide to Bolivia* had just pulled out: would I be interested in co-authoring the next edition? I jumped at the chance.

***

Throughout the following decade, working on the guidebook allowed me to spend extended periods of time in Bolivia. I returned repeatedly and explored the country in far greater depth than would otherwise have been possible. Over the course of several editions, I travelled to virtually every region, in the process checking out hundreds of guesthouses, hostels, and hotels, visiting innumerable national parks, museums, galleries, and historic sites, eating dozens of plates of *pique a lo macho*, and losing many days of my life on buses, trains, planes, taxis, and trucks. Moreover, I was able to spend time with countless Bolivians who were gracious enough to show me round, share their knowledge and experiences, and put up with a steady barrage of questions. My research trips also coincided with a particularly dramatic period of the country's history. Under the administration of Evo Morales, who in 2006 became Bolivia's first indigenous president, the economy grew at unprecedented rates, millions were lifted out of extreme poverty, and great cultural changes rippled through society.

Gradually the idea for this book began to develop. The initial plan was to write a straight-forward travelogue about a culturally rich, geographically diverse country that had influenced the world in profound and unexpected ways over the past 500 years. But as I got to know Bolivia better I felt the urge to widen my focus. It became increasingly clear that the country stands on the front line of many of the touchstone issues of the 21st century. There was a populist president who overturned the established political order. The country has untapped reserves of a resource vital for global tech. Waves of mass migration have seen the movement of more than a quarter of the population. After centuries of oppression, indigenous Bolivians have started to gain greater political, economic, and cultural power. Ambitious development projects promise great riches, but threaten some of the most biodiverse places on Earth. The intensifying climate crisis has shrunk glaciers, caused major droughts, and transformed Bolivia's second-biggest lake into a dust-bowl. There was a contested election, political crisis, and right-wing backlash. And that's without mentioning the 'war on drugs', a burst of rapid urbanisation or the growth of an innovative new architectural movement.

In many ways, it felt as the future had already arrived in Bolivia, so I expanded the scope of the book. As well as exploring the country's turbulent history, I wanted to provide a snapshot of some of the contemporary challenges it faces, while attempting to avoid the pitfalls and prejudices that too often characterise non-Bolivian – and particularly western – writing about the country. I also aimed to share the views, opinions, and experiences of some of the Bolivians I have met over the years who rarely get a hearing in the English-language media (I've changed some of their names in the book for reasons of privacy or security). They showed me places I would otherwise have missed, were generous with their stories and expertise, patient with my incessant questions and note-taking, and forgiving of my misconceptions and misunderstandings. This book would not have been possible without them.

CHAPTER 1

Before Bolivia

Indigenous cultures: Llanos de Moxos,
Tiwanaku, and Lake Titicaca

It didn't take long to find the skull. Barely an hour after leaving Puerto
Ballivián, a scruffy little Amazonian port in the Llanos de Moxos, the
Reina de Enin shuddered to a halt on a placid stretch of the chocolatey
brown Ibare River. A brilliant yellow butterfly fluttered across the deck
of the weather-beaten red-and-green catamaran, which resembled
a Mississippi paddle steamer that had fallen on hard times. Two
fishermen paddled by in a wooden canoe, their wake unsettling a
saucer-sized turtle resting on a floating branch. As I clambered out of
the *Reina de Enin* and into an idling motorboat, kingfishers, egrets, and
crested oropendolas – black birds with striking blue irises and bright
yellow tails – flashed overhead.

The riverbanks were dense green walls, but my guide Eduardo located
a barely perceptible opening and navigated us into a narrow channel.
It felt like entering a cave. The thick canopy blocked out the sunlight
and a stagnant odour wafted out of the opaque black water. Spindly
ficus trees spread sinuous creeper-draped branches across our route.
Eduardo moved to the front of the boat and knelt down, wielding a
paddle in one hand and a machete in the other. Flying insects swarmed
over us, nipping at patches of exposed flesh. A woodpecker tapped
away repetitively. During the rainy season, the water level rises by one
and a half metres or more, which makes for a much smoother journey,
Eduardo explained, as we bumped over semi-submerged logs. At the
height of the dry season, by contrast, the water recedes so much that
boats are no longer necessary on the route we were taking – you can
simply walk along it.

After 20 minutes we emerged from the gloom into a sunny lagoon
filled with water lilies. Herons, storks, and cormorants perched on
the shoreline, and a three-toed sloth clung to an overhanging branch;
although clumsy and lethargic on the land, they are surprisingly
agile swimmers, Eduardo informed me. On the far side of the lagoon
was a dome-shaped hill or *loma*, roughly 10 m in height and lightly
covered with trees. At first glance, it looked natural, a mere wrinkle

in the landscape. Yet the *loma* was man-made, one of an estimated 20,000 earthworks built by a little-known culture a thousand years or more ago.

We landed at the base of the hill and I stepped onto a muddy beach, expecting to sink. Instead there was a crunch under foot: the ground was covered by thousands of grey- and terracotta-coloured pottery fragments, from chips the size of a fingernail to chunks larger than a dinner plate. I attempted to tip-toe around them, but they were impossible to avoid. These potsherds were not merely waste, Eduardo told me, they were used as building materials to stabilise and expand the *lomas*.

Most of the earthworks in the Llanos de Moxos have been swallowed up by the forest, but the family who lived on this one had cleared and cultivated the land. At the top of the hill, which was roughly the size of a football pitch, were two slightly ramshackle huts, a pigsty, and a rusted 1950s motorbike lying on its side; the nearest road was many kilometres away. A skeletal mongrel raised its head briefly at our approach, but soon returned to its nap. An even skinnier cat, its ribcage almost visible, showed more interest, sniffing excitedly at our boots. No one else was home; Eduardo, a friend of the family, thought they were probably out fishing. Behind the huts was a grove of fruit trees: pomelo, mango, cacao, and lemon. The skins of two caimans and the hollowed-out carcass of an armadillo were draped across the lower branches, like clothes on a washing line.

At the far side of the hill a narrow causeway led to another *loma*. This one – like most *lomas* today – was unoccupied and, as a result, thickly covered with near-impenetrable foliage. 'Before the 1990s, there was not much information about this ancient culture,' said Eduardo. 'We didn't learn about it in school or even at university. Now we have much more information. We know they built these hills to be safe in the rainy season. They usually had one hill per family. The *lomas* are generally between 5 and 20 m high; this one, for sure, was once at least 10 m higher than it is today, but has been eroded. And all over these hills you can find pieces of pottery.'

As we looked around I spotted a pair of virtually intact pots poking out of the soil. More emerge every year, rising to the surface during the rainy season, like daffodils in the spring. Eduardo shook his head: 'This is nothing.' He led me to a patch of earth marked out with twigs. In the centre was the neck of another half-buried pot, jutting out at a 45-degree angle. I glanced into it and saw a jawbone with an almost complete set of yellow-brown teeth grimacing back at me. The teeth were child-sized and, although discoloured, remarkably well preserved. They were also profoundly unnerving. 'I found this urn last week,' said Eduardo. 'Sometimes you find them with whole bodies inside.'

Alongside the pottery, the ground around us was strewn with rubbish: plastic bottles and packets, old sandals, scraps of paper and card, chewed-up bits of rubber, rusted strips of metal, and disintegrating blocks of polystyrene. Seasonal flooding, erosion, and rainfall were gradually blending the modern detritus with the ancient relics, incorporating some of the resulting mixture into the hill and dispersing the rest through the surrounding waterways. Perhaps, I thought, in another thousand years, visitors will sift through the Coke bottles and Lays packets and marvel at the long-forgotten culture that produced such treasures.

As we walked back to the motorboat, I lagged behind. When no one was looking, I guiltily slipped a couple of pottery fragments, their ribbed sides worn smooth over the centuries, into my pocket.

***

The Bolivian Amazon confounds expectations about the country, its people and, in particular, its history before the arrival of the Spanish. Bolivia is regularly described as an 'Andean' country, but the north of the country, representing more than a third of the total landmass, lies within the Amazon basin, wedged between Brazil to the north and east and Peru to the west. The eastern part of the Bolivian Amazon takes its name from a great meandering river, the Beni. The western side of the Beni region largely resembles the Amazon of popular imagination: Andean foothills gradually collapsing into dense tropical rainforest. East of here, by contrast, stretch the Llanos de Moxos (or Mojos), some 120,000 sq km – an area almost the size of England – of tropical savannah veined with rivers, streams, and waterways. During the wet season, which generally lasts from December to May, as much as 60 per cent of the region is flooded, thanks to torrential rainfall and snow-melt from the Andes.

Today, the Llanos de Moxos is sparsely populated and dominated by vast cattle ranches. But the region has been inhabited for some 10,000 years, initially by hunter-gatherer communities. In approximately 1000 BCE, more complex societies started to develop. When we think of Latin America's ancient cultures, images of Inca temples and Maya pyramids typically spring to mind. The societies of the Llanos de Moxos were quite different. In response to a highly challenging environment – sharply fluctuating water levels, poor-quality soil, and a lack of domesticated animals and sources of stone – they built thousands of earthwork structures across an area that may have been as large as 200 sq km. The earthworks included canals, causeways, aqueducts, levees, irrigation ditches, raised fields, reservoirs, and dykes, as well as *lomas*.

The earthworks were multi-functional: *lomas* were used as homes for the elites, as fields for crops such as yucca and maize, for religious ceremonies, and as burial grounds. The largest villages in the region were home to 2,000 people or more. According to archaeologist Clark L. Erickson, author of *Amazonia: The Historical Archaeology of a Domesticated Landscape*, constructing the earthworks involved 'mass movement of soils, transformation of local topography, soil enrichment, and change in vegetation composition'.

Artificial canals and causeways provided transport and communication links and helped not only to mitigate the damage from the seasonal floods, but actively manage the water levels. Lagoons – some spanning up to 10 sq km – and weirs were created to aid fishing. Other earthwork formations were designed to drive wild animals on to designated patches of dry land, where they could be more easily hunted. This hydraulic engineering was not merely functional: Erickson argues the earthworks also acted as 'boundary and territorial markers, and as monumental ritual and political statements'. Their scale can only really be appreciated from the air, where the serpentine bends, straight-sided squares and rectangles, sharp zigzags and near-perfect circles look like geometric patterns printed on a giant green canvas. Alongside the earthworks, the societies also produced pottery, much of it finely decorated.

Academic interest in the Moxos sites is relatively recent. The first excavations were carried out in the 1910s by Swedish archaeologist Erland Nordenskiöld, but the extent of the earthworks only started to become apparent half a century later. Today, many in the Beni credit a Texan, Kenneth Lee, with playing a key role in increasing understanding of the Moxos culture. Lee, an engineer and geologist working for Shell, travelled to the region in the late 1950s in search of oil. As he flew over it in a helicopter, he noticed a number of geographical features that looked suspiciously man-made and decided to investigate further. Lee was captivated and ended up dedicating the rest of his life to studying this lost culture, a commitment that earned him the nickname '*el gringo querido del Beni*' – 'the beloved gringo of the Beni'.

The museum that now bears his name receives few visitors. It is located a couple of kilometres north of Trinidad, the capital of the Beni, the only city in the Bolivian Amazon, and – as I was later to learn – a hub of the brutal 19th and early 20th-century rubber industry. Beyond the faded sign and bumpy driveway was a replica *loma* that looked like a nondescript hillock, as well as representations of artificial lagoons and raised fields. The front door of the museum was locked, but I eventually found someone to let me in. On display were musical instruments and wooden masks, the latter depicting stylised but realistic human faces, in contrast to the supernatural imagery more commonly found in artworks from Bolivia's ancient Andean societies. There was also an incredible range of ceramics: bowls, plates, urns, and other vessels of various sizes and shapes were finely decorated with geometric patterns, notably 'S' shapes and lines of zigzags.

The museum, however, has only limited capacity and more and more potential exhibits turn up each year. One Trinidad resident told me that during a recent flood a river near her home burst its banks and washed a cache of pottery onto her land, including several intact pots and bowls. 'I told the authorities, but they weren't interested, so I've kept them,' she said. 'Many people in Trinidad have bits of pottery in their homes or gardens. I sometimes use them as plant pots.'

***

The earthworks challenge the idea that the Amazon prior to 1492 was some kind of untouched wilderness and elegantly rebut the notion complex societies could not have developed in the region before the arrival of Europeans. These views were initially shaped by the accounts of the conquistadors, who encountered communities devastated by infectious diseases brought to the continent by the Spanish and Portuguese to which they had no immunity.

One of several parts of the Amazon with sizeable indigenous populations, the Llanos de Moxos paints a more nuanced and intriguing picture. Its archaeological sites suggest the region was home to far more people – perhaps as many as a million, according to some estimates – and far more complex societies than previously assumed. Moreover, for a thousand years or more, these societies sculpted, tamed, and exploited the landscapes around them, creating – to quote Charles C. Mann, author of *1491: The Americas Before Columbus* – 'one of the largest, strangest, and most ecologically rich artificial environments on the planet'.

Today, although most of the abandoned earthworks have been reclaimed by the forest, a few around Trinidad have been repurposed. A half-hour drive northwest of the city took me to Loma Suárez, a lumpy grass mound named after a notorious rubber baron. Here I killed a couple of hours as I waited for a boat to take me to Chuchini, a nature reserve built on another *loma* 5 km further north. Nearby, at a small port set on a double bend of the Ibare River, two men loaded gas canisters onto a rusted, patched-together boat named the *Mary Celeste*, ahead of what looked an optimistic 500-km journey north to the town of Guayaramerín on the Bolivian-Brazilian border. The Chuchini motorboat, thankfully, was rather more modern. On board were 25 strikingly blond young North Americans from Salt Lake City, Utah. They were members of a Mormon organisation, Humanitarian Experiences for Youth, and were in Bolivia for a fortnight of proselytising and school-building, their guide explained. One young boy, however, had rather more adventurous plans. 'We're going to eat monkey brains – unless the piranhas eat us first,' he told me excitedly.

We set off at noon, the children oohing and aahing as Efrem, whose family owns and runs Chuchini, pointed out colourful birds and lurking caimans. After a quarter of an hour we turned off the Ibare onto a narrow Moxeño-built channel fringed with reeds and spindly trees. Almost immediately the engine ground to a halt and the boat jolted into the bank, the impact showering us with twigs, leaves and ants. The conversation on board quietened noticeably, even after the pilot got us going again. Eventually we pulled into a shimmering lagoon overlooked by a squat green hill ringed with trees and patrolled by a pair of dogs yapping excitedly at our arrival.

After distributing the young Mormons to their rooms, Miriam, Efrem's wife, showed me round the *loma*. The flat, grassy summit contained several accommodation blocks, a semi-open dining room, a football pitch, and a playground. A series of walking trails led off into the surrounding rainforest, which echoed with birdsong. The reserve was created in 1973 after Efrem's parents learned of the area's archaeological and environmental significance. More than 1,500 Moxeño artefacts have since been excavated from the site. 'The name 'Chuchini' means "Den of the Jaguar",' Miriam explained, 'one of around 100 mammal species you find here. There are also more than 200 species of birds.'

The family's foresight protected the area from the deforestation, poaching, ranching, commercial agriculture, and fishing that has destroyed much of the Beni, particularly the area around Trinidad. Today, the reserve relies on tourism and volunteers. Trinidadians come for the day to swim in the lagoon, lounge in a hammock, or stroll along the jungle trails. Foreign travellers tend to stay longer and often take part in volunteer programmes. A qualified vet, Efrem oversees a small wildlife rehabilitation centre. Among his patients were a group of racoon-like coatis, several monkeys, and a pair of handsome toucans, their orange-and-yellow beaks so unnaturally bright I initially mistook them for plastic models.

After a lunch of *pique a lo macho*, a gut-busting combo of steak strips, chips, onions, peppers, boiled eggs, and chilli sauce, Efrem took me round his one-room museum. It was packed with items excavated from the reserve, most of them in remarkably good condition. Two large pots contained human remains, including a full set of adult teeth. Others were decorated with inter-connected lines and geometric patterns that some archaeologists have speculated might represent ancient maps. 'If you look at some of the earthworks from the sky they look like human or animal figures,' said Efrem. 'Like the Nazca Lines in Peru.'

Alongside the pots were vaguely human figurines. I was captivated by two in particular. One was the torso of a woman who appeared to be wearing a spotted bikini. The other was a one-legged man with a protruding belly button, prominent nipples and narrow, almond-shaped eyes. 'Some people claim these are "Asian" features and even that the Moxos civilization had an Asian origin,' said Efrem, raising a sceptical eyebrow at a doggedly persistent form of ignorance, whose holders find themselves unable to credit ancient indigenous cultures with the ability to produce anything of sophistication, and instead tout outlandish theories of foreign – or even extraterrestrial – assistance.

***

Overnight I got a first-hand insight into the extreme climatic conditions of the Llanos de Moxos. The generator stopped at 11.30 p.m., the fan shut down and the heat steadily ramped up. All the windows were open, but the night was perfectly still. I lay in bed like a starfish, my body on fire. Over the previous days, I'd acquired rings of swollen, overlapping mosquito bites around my ankle bones and up my calves. There were also bites across my shoulder blades, stomach and chest, plus several on my earlobes, one in my left armpit, and a particularly ferocious trio on my upper right thigh. A total of 53. Cold showers and erroneously titled 'jungle-strength' bite cream provided only the briefest of respites. It took all the will power I possessed not to scratch them as I lay for hours, desperately willing sleep.

I must have drifted off at some point because an almighty rainstorm woke me at 6 a.m. Gale-force winds howled through the trees and my room shook so violently that my glasses and phone toppled off the bedside table. It was the result of a *surazo*, Miriam told later me over breakfast, a frigid wind that periodically blows up from Antarctica, over Patagonia and across the heart of Bolivia between May and August, plunging temperatures and resulting in great downpours. As she spoke, I felt a fresh sense of respect for the inhabitants of the Llanos de Moxos, ancient and present-day, who had not only carved out an existence here but managed to flourish.

A motorboat arrived at 8 a.m. to take me back to Loma Suárez. There was nowhere to shelter and the warmest item of clothing I had was a light-weight running jacket. Within moments of setting off across the gunboat-grey lagoon, I was drenched. Overnight hundreds of water lilies had choked the canal; they soon got tangled in the outboard motor, forcing us to paddle through a carpet of green. By the time we reached the open waters of the Ibare, the rain was coming down in sheets. The motor kicked back into life and we picked up pace. Raindrops felt like hailstones as they drove into my face. I was soaked and frozen. Eventually, we reached Loma Suárez, I climbed up the bank, adding a thick layer of mud to my sodden clothes.

Balanced precariously on a *moto-taxi*, unable to feel my fingers, we roared off along a road that had more potholes than tarmac. Swirling gusts of wind almost blew us over and we narrowly avoided a head-on crash with a careering jeep.

***

As the earthwork builders flourished in the Llanos de Moxos, one of the most influential ancient societies in South America was developing in a very different environment 300 km to the west. Tiwanaku (or Tiahuanaco) was one of the first great Andean empires, but is little known today outside of Bolivia and archaeological circles, obscured by the long shadow of the Inca who succeeded it. Originating around 1000 BCE, the society was based around a grand city, also known as Tiwanaku, set at almost 3,900 m above sea level. At its height, the Tiwanaku empire dominated a vast area spanning much of modern-day Bolivia, southern Peru, north-east Argentina, and northern Chile.

I travelled to the ancient capital, 75 km west of the city of La Paz, with Carlos, who wasted no time in telling me that he was 'the premier guide in Bolivia' and spoke fluent English, French, German, Portuguese, and Greek, as well as Spanish and Aymara, the language of one of Bolivia's major indigenous groups. Standing a little over one and a half metres, resolutely rotund, and wearing a sun hat with ear flaps, he wielded a walking stick like a sword, jabbing furiously to reinforce his arguments and swishing at anyone who dared to interrupt him.

As we drove across the *altiplano*, the high plateau that divides the eastern and western chains of the Andes, Carlos said: 'If you want to understand Bolivia, you have to visit Tiwanaku.' Outside, the golden-green plains were inhabited by a few lonely herds of cows, sheep and llamas, and some semi-derelict homesteads and small-holdings. Beyond were undulating brown-green hills and further north the jagged, mist-shrouded mountains of the Cordillera Real, the 'Royal Range'. A stream of trucks roared past, heading to and from the Peruvian border. Dozens of little shrines with white crosses lay by the side of the road, tributes to deceased drivers. Eventually a wonky road sign indicated the turn-off for Tiwanaku. 'Tiwanaku was the mother culture of the Andes,' said Carlos, 'influencing civilisations as far away as Colombia.' In its heyday, roughly between 500 and 900 CE, the capital city is believed to have had a population of around 30,000, with tens of thousands more in the surrounding countryside. Some archaeologists argue these figures are too conservative and that it may have been home to as many as 115,000 people, with another quarter of a million in its hinterland. The city boasted pyramids, palaces and other buildings, running water, and an enclosed sewerage system. It also produced intricate pottery, radiated religious beliefs far beyond its boundaries, and drew thousands of pilgrims from across the Andes.

Tiwanaku was also the hub of an extensive trade network that included fish from the Pacific, llamas and potatoes from the *altiplano*, and grains from the fertile plains around nearby Lake Titicaca. There were probably also links with the earthwork-builders of the Llanos de Moxos: stone axes found in the latter, an area with no natural sources of the rocks necessary to make these items, are believed to have originated from the Tiwanaku empire.

The oldest surviving account of Tiwanaku is from a conquistador, Pedro de Cieza de León, who travelled through the region in the middle of the 16th century. By this stage the site was abandoned and in ruins, yet it was still a mesmerising place. In his four-part *Chronicles of Peru*, de Cieza de León described a hill 'made by the hands of man, on great foundations of stone' and stone idols 'so large they seem like small giants'. He continues:

[There] are stones of such enormous size that it causes wonder to think of them, and to reflect how human force can have sufficed to move them to the place where we see them ... [To] the westward, there are other ancient remains, among them many doorways, with their jambs, lintels, and thresholds, all of one stone ... from these great doorways there came out other still larger stones, upon which the doorways were formed, some of them thirty feet broad, fifteen or more long, and six in thickness. The whole of this, with the doorway and its jambs and lintel, was all one single stone. The work is one of grandeur and magnificence, when well considered. For myself I fail to understand with what instruments or tools it can have been done ...

It is asserted that these edifices were commenced before the time of the [Inca], and I have heard ... the [Inca] built their grand edifices at Cuzco on the plan which they had observed at the wall near these ruins. They even say that the first [Inca leaders] thought of establishing their court at Tiahuanaco. Another remarkable thing is, that in all this district there are no quarries whence the numerous stones can have been brought, the carrying of which must have required many people.

***

You now need an active imagination to bring the site to life. Only a fraction of it has been excavated and many of the larger buildings are little more than piles of ochre-red rubble. Even the roof of the museum, built only a few years ago, appeared on the verge of collapse. A woman wearing a blue shawl and a straw hat half-heartedly attempted to sell me a bag of popcorn, while fluffy tan-and-beige alpacas nibbled at the grass. The authorities displayed a limited sense of humour: a sign near the ticket booth warned that dancing, music, and 'playing' were strictly banned.

I was midway up a hill before realising it was actually the remains of a seven-tiered pyramid. Close by 175 stone heads protruded at regular intervals from the ancient brick walls of a sunken pit. Each face was different, offering up expressions of blank acceptance, deep knowledge, and sheer terror. The pit is believed to have been a temple, Carlos explained, with the heads representing the deities of the ethnic groups conquered by the expansionist Tiwanaku. It was a potent symbol of domination: we have you and your gods.

Opposite was a stone portico, the Gateway of the Sun, entrance to a much larger complex with uncannily straight walls, the Kalasasaya, the religious heart of Tiwanaku and former home of the ruling emperors. Above the gateway was the supreme creator god, Thunupa (known to the Inca as Viracocha): 24 rays shot out from his face and severed heads dangled from his hands. It was made from perfectly cut stone blocks and, Carlos told me, it remained unclear how the craftsmen managed to be so precise without the benefit of modern techniques and tools.

In some ways the most impressive sight came at the end of my visit: a modest stone block balanced precariously on a chunk of wood. Known as the 'megaphone', it had a spiral-shaped hole running through the centre that mimicked the design of the human inner ear and amplified sound in a similar fashion. We took turns to whisper into it, our voices booming out of the other side. I wondered aloud how the people of Tiwanaku could have worked out how to do this. 'They probably would have chopped off people's ears and studied them,' said Carlos matter-of-factly.

We stopped for lunch at the cheerful Hotel Tihuanaco: quinoa soup, fried chicken, and a lurid pink yoghurt of indeterminate flavour. Photos of past diners, including former Venezuelan president Hugo Chávez and King Juan Carlos I of Spain were pinned to the wall. As we ate I tried to rebuild the ruins in my mind and conjure up an image of Tiwanaku at its peak. The task was complicated by the fact that many archaeologists believe the city was deliberately left unfinished. '[It was] always partly in ruins – intrinsically so, because the fallen walls bequeathed on Tiwanaku the authority of the past,' wrote Mann. An ancient branding strategy, in other words: rather than exercising brute force, the city managed to dominate a spider-web of client states by successfully marketing itself as a religious and cultural hub.

Good PR, however, only gets you so far. Around 1000 CE the region suffered a climate crisis: there was a long-term decline in rainfall, a succession of severe droughts lasting decades, and waves of punishing dust storms. These periods were punctuated by equally devastating floods. Some climatologists believe a supercharged version of the El Niño climate pattern – a so-called 'mega-Niño' – was to blame. Within half a century Tiwanaku's population died off or dispersed and the culture collapsed. 'The geography around Tiwanaku at that time was completely different to how it is now. There were 50 to 60 years without rain, Lake Titicaca shrank, and many, many people died. It was the end of days,' said Carlos.

The Spanish continued where the climate left off. Conquistadors looted the site, stripping away the gold and finest statuary, destroying most of the religious idols and using the stones to construct churches and mansions. Centuries later the Bolivian authorities almost finished the job. When Hiram Bingham, the US academic and senator misleadingly credited with 'discovering' Machu Picchu, visited Tiwanaku in the early 1900s he noted '500 trainloads of stone' had been taken from the site over the previous decade to build 'bridges and warehouses' for the La Paz-Guaqui railway line.

Even today, despite being a UNESCO World Heritage Site, Tiwanaku is relatively poorly protected, with erosion a particular problem. This is surprising given the site's significance in modern Bolivia. The Tiwanaku empire was made up of a patchwork of ethnic and cultural groups; academics have raised doubts about the links between it and the region's present-day Aymara inhabitants. According to Jédu Sagárnaga, an archaeologist and anthropologist at the Universidad Mayor de San Andrés in La Paz, Tiwanaku and the Aymara are 'completely different things'. The Aymara are 'groups [who] arrived from the north of Chile ... they [had] very different world views and cultures,' he said in the 2018 film *Cholet*. Nevertheless, many Aymara people strongly identify with Tiwanaku. The site is a great source of pride for a people long-subjected to oppression and prejudice, as well as a place of deep religious significance. On the eve of the winter solstice, religious figures known as *yatiris*, thousands of local pilgrims, and a scattering of new age travellers from around the globe gather amid the ruins to celebrate the start of the Aymara new year.

Moreover, the idea of Tiwanaku as a spiritual homeland of the Aymara people has become an important political symbol. When he won the 2006 presidential election, Evo Morales staged an elaborate inauguration ceremony at the site, explicitly linking his reign with that of the historic empire. In a piece of political theatre of which the original rulers of Tiwanaku would have heartedly approved, the country's first indigenous president wore a copy of a pre-Inca priestly tunic, underwent purification rituals carried out by a *yatiri*, made offerings to Pachamama (Mother Earth), and, in his bare feet, delivered a speech from the Kalasasaya to many thousands of his supporters.

This ceremony was repeated each time Morales won re-election. In his 2015 inauguration speech, he said: 'For more than 500 years we have suffered darkness, hate, racism, discrimination and individualism ... Despite so much suffering and massacre, we never gave up, we never accepted defeat; we knew that our victory would come.'

The link between Morales and Tiwanaku continued in his controversial presidential palace, a $34-million 29-storey skyscraper in downtown La Paz, which was completed in 2018. As well as a top-floor suite spanning more than a 1,000 sq m and boasting a sauna, jacuzzi, and massage room, the palace features numerous elements of Tiwanaku iconography.

Morales though was far from the first political leader in the Andes to harness the symbolic power of Tiwanaku – the Inca were at it centuries earlier. 'Tiwanaku was the cradle of the Inca culture,' said Carlos, as we left the site. 'The Quechua-speaking Inca learned so much from it. They adopted Tiwanaku's five sacred animals: condor, llama, puma, snake, and fish. These animals are still sacred to both the Aymara and the Quechua today.' In his book *Ancient Tiwanaku*, anthropologist John Wayne Janusek goes further, arguing the 'Inca venerated Tiwanaku as their mythical homeland'.

***

The links between the Tiwanaku and the Inca are particularly evident at Lake Titicaca. From La Paz, I caught a bus from the Cemetery District, which felt a rather ominous point of departure. We headed northeast across the *altiplano* towards Wiñay Marka, a branch of Lake Titicaca.

Its waters were perfectly smooth, with clumps of reedy islands just offshore and Peru visible in the distance. At the village of Huatajata, locals sat outside restaurants, tucking into platefuls of barbecued trout, drinking beer, and studiously ignoring the ever-darkening clouds.

Just beyond was the Estrecho de Tiquina, a narrow channel separating the rest of Bolivia from a ragged peninsula to the west. Here we filed out of the bus and onto a motor launch for the short crossing. The bus itself was manoeuvred onto a wooden barge that listed alarmingly to one side, barely staying above the water line. A few years previously, the driver told me, a similar vessel carrying a bus-load of passengers had sunk mid-crossing. After safely reaching the opposite bank, the bus continued north-west towards the tip of the peninsula. Eventually the gleaming blue of the main body of the lake and then the town of Copacabana – which predates its more famous namesake in Rio de Janeiro – came into view. I got off at Plaza Sucre, collected my backpack and headed to the shore.

There were no samba beats on the original Copacabana Beach. No beach volleyball players. No bronzed sunbathers lounging on the sand. In fact, there was very little sand at all: the 'beach' was a stretch of hard-baked mud interspersed with intermittent, balding patches of grass. A flotilla of swan- and duck-shaped pedalos was banked up at one end, next to an upturned kayak and several aged rowing boats, rotting wood and rusty metal held together by peeling paint. A faded yellow-and-blue 'Copacabana Tours' sign pointed directly into the freezing water.

Offshore, besides a motor launch, was a modern knock-up of a traditional reed boat, which have been used on the lake for centuries. Made of tightly-bound yellowy-brown totora fibres and curling up into tips at the bow and the stern, it vaguely resembled a banana. In 1970, local boat-makers constructed a larger sea-going version, the *Ra II*, for Norwegian ethnographer-explorer Thor Heyerdahl, who transported it to Morocco and from there used it to sail to the Caribbean in an attempt to prove transatlantic travel was possible using ancient technology. On the Peruvian side of the lake, totora reeds have been used to construct more than a hundred floating islands on which members of the indigenous Uros community live.

Rising up above the northern end of the beach was a steep hill, Cerro Calvario. Fourteen Stations of the Cross marked the route to the summit, just visible against the darkening sky. Beyond was an undulating row of green hills topped with a single, unbroken line of trees, like a trimmed Mohican haircut. Just off the beach was a line of interchangeable, unimaginatively titled food stalls ('Kiosco No 1', 'Kiosco No 2', and so on). Each one had plastic tables, the odd stray dog or pigeon loitering nearby, and virtually identical trout-based menus. (Trout were introduced to the lake by the government in the 1930s and soon flourished, albeit at the expense of the native fish species.)

Copacabana (from the Aymara phrase *cota cawuaña*, which loosely translates as 'to overlook the lake') may be an underwhelming beach, but the body of water it faces more than compensates. Some 3,810 m above sea level, Lake Titicaca is a giant, glinting sapphire between the eastern and western chains of the Andes. Spanning 8,300 sq km, it is the world's largest high-altitude lake and is divided – roughly one-third to two thirds, respectively – between Bolivia and Peru (locals joke that Peru got the 'Titi' and left them with the 'caca').

More than 250 m deep in places and fed by 27 rivers, Lake Titicaca has long been a spiritual centre. It is surrounded by the ruins of temples, shrines, ritual baths, and ceremonial buildings, some of which pre-date both the Inca and Tiwanaku. The most significant sites, though, are in the lake itself. Some 12 km north-west of Copacabana and visible from the beach on a clear day is Isla del Sol (Island of the Sun). Five hundred years ago, this island and its smaller neighbour, Isla de la Luna (Island of the Moon), were of immense religious significance throughout the Andean world, revered as the birthplace of the sun and the moon.

The Tiwanaku empire built the first religious structures on Isla del Sol, and Titicaca was similarly significant for the Aymara kingdoms that later dominated the region. But from the 15th century, the Inca weaved the lake and its islands into their own creation myths, transforming Titicaca into a place of religious pilgrimage for people across the Andes. As with the ancient cultures in the Llanos de Moxos and Tiwanaku, the Inca did not develop an alphabetic written language, so the earliest surviving accounts of their society come from the conquistadors, who were not exactly impartial observers. (The Inca did, however, use a system of bright, knotted cords known as *khipus* or *quipus* to count and record numbers and data. Some researchers argue this system may also have been used to record stories and legends.) One of the earliest Spanish accounts of the Inca belief system – of which there are many different versions – comes from a Galician explorer, mariner, geographer, cosmographer and adventurer.

Born in 1532, Pedro Sarmiento de Gamboa spent more than 20 years travelling round Mexico, Peru, the Strait of Magellan, and the south Pacific. He suffered a few setbacks along the way, including twice falling foul of the Inquisition in Peru: the first time, in 1564, was for possessing 'magic ink' that made his love letters irresistible to women, as well as a pair of 'magic rings'; the second, in 1575, was for having 'magical' amulets. He was found guilty on both occasions; his punishments included attending mass at Lima cathedral naked and with a lit taper in his hand.

In between these bouts of unpleasantness, he was commissioned by the Viceroy of Peru to write a history of the Inca. The imaginatively-titled result, *Historia de Los Incas* (*History of the Incas*), was published in 1572; once the first draft was written it was reputedly checked by indigenous readers to ensure its authenticity (though, of course, the author was far from an independent commentator on the subject). In the book, Sarmiento de Gamboa wrote:

> The natives of this land affirm that in the beginning, and before this world was created, there was a being called Viracocha. He created a dark world without sun, moon or stars. Owing to this creation he was named Viracocha Pachayachachi, which means 'Creator of all things'... And when he had created the world he formed a race of giants of disproportioned greatness painted and sculptured, to see whether it would be well to make real men of that size. He then created men in his likeness as they are now; and they lived in darkness.

Viracocha ordered the people to live together in peace and worship him, according to Sarmiento de Gamboa. But, inevitably, they fell into sin. Angered, Viracocha cursed them: some were turned into stone; others were swallowed up by the earth or the sea. Then came a great flood: 'They say that it rained for 60 days and nights, that it drowned all created things, and that there alone remained some vestiges of those who were turned into stones.'

No one escaped, instead, Sarmiento de Gamboa wrote:

> Viracocha began to create men afresh ... The flood being passed and the land dry, Viracocha determined to people it a second time, and, to make it more perfect, he decided upon creating luminaries to give it light. With this object he went, with his servants, to a great lake in the Collao, in which there is an island called Titicaca, the meaning being 'the rock of lead' ... Viracocha went to this island, and presently ordered that the sun, moon, and stars should come forth, and be set in the heavens to give light to the world ... the moon was created brighter than the sun, which made the sun jealous at the time when they rose into the sky. So the sun threw over the moon's face a handful of ashes, which gave it the shaded colour it now presents.

The Inca also believed the founders of their empire, Manco Cápac and Mama Ocllo, were created on Isla del Sol. Temples and shrines were built on the island and by the start of the 16th century thousands of pilgrims from across the Inca empire visited each year. How many of these beliefs were inherited or adopted from other societies is much debated. It seems likely the expansionist Inca sought to fuse their beliefs and myths with those of the Aymara speakers and the Tiwanaku culture around Lake Titicaca and beyond in an attempt to cement their rule.

***

On an overcast day, the lake a slate grey, I set off for Isla del Sol. The boat departed from Copacabana's dock at 8.30 a.m. with a multinational passenger list, mainly European and North American backpackers, though there were also a few career-breakers and thrifty retirees; wealthier travellers on package tours travelled on far grander vessels than our sputtering boat. The lake was ripple-free, but can get choppy; in the words of the British explorer Percy Harrison Fawcett, who crossed Titicaca in the early 1900s on a steamer, 'nowhere else is it possible for a traveller to suffer from sea-sickness and mountain-sickness at the same time'.

Two hours later we docked at Challapampa, the northernmost settlement on Isla del Sol, and were soon swarmed over by a crowd of waiting guides. We ducked our heads briefly into a small museum and then hiked briskly uphill for 20 minutes until we reached Kasapata, once a *tambo*, a way-station used by Inca pilgrims. All that remained some 500 years later were a set of stone doorways, a large carved block and a few piles of rubble. A further 20 minutes uphill was the focal point of the island and indeed much of the Inca world. Given its significance, the Santuario ('Shrine' or 'Sanctuary') was at first a little underwhelming: a cluster of ruined buildings, stone walls and passageways. The complex was set around a pink-grey-black sandstone outcrop with earth-brown streaks – Titikala, the sacred rock from which Viracocha brought forth the sun and the moon, and which gave the surrounding lake its name.

After nosing round La Chincana (The Labyrinth), a maze-like complex of interlinked, roofless rooms, with sturdy stone walls and impossibly low doorways, I continued along the Ruta Sagrada de la Eternidad del Sol (Sacred Route of the Eternal Sun). This 7-km path wound round the island, crossing hills covered with the stepped agricultural terraces found all across the central Andes. Dotted along the path were modern *tambos*, wooden huts with dusty bottles of Coke and Sprite and packets of biscuits on the counters.

At the edge of Yumani, the main settlement on Isla del Sol, I passed through a small white gate, paying a small entrance fee to an attendant wearing a pink cardigan. Perched on a headland at the south-eastern tip of the island, the village was a collection of rudimentary one and two-storey buildings with thatched or red-tiled roofs, several simple guesthouses and restaurants ('Organic vegetarian pizza – run by a gourmet chef' boasted one sign), and a couple of smarter 'ecolodges'.

The boat back to Copacabana was scheduled to depart at 3.30 p.m. from the dock below Yumani, a deadline that meant the hike from Challapampa was a brisk walk rather than a gentle stroll. I made it 15 minutes ahead of time, descending a precipitous set of stone steps through a series of terraced fields to a stony beach. The crops are watered by a series of man-made canals fed by the Fuente del Inca (Inca Fountain). If you drink from it, according to local legend, you will gain the ability to speak Quechua, Aymara, and Spanish fluently. I took a sip on the off-chance.

***

My visit to Copacabana coincided with the start of the carnival celebrations, which take place in the week before Lent. What I found initially looked more like a mass line dance. Troupes of men in cowboy outfits waltzed down the streets, clapping their hands and twisting in unison: each one wore shiny red trousers decorated with white stars, blue stripes and oversized, pulled-out pockets; red-white-and-blue tasselled jackets; feathery shoulder pads; and white Stetsons edged with silver tinsel.

Dancing beside them were women in billowing mauve-and-blue skirts, long pink shawls, and black bowler hats. Behind marched a 40-strong brass band complete with trumpets, trombones, drums, twanging guitars, and huge clanging cymbals, the musicians dressed in immaculate white suits, brown scarves, and fedoras. Bringing up the rear, a group of boys in jeans and yellow T-shirts vigorously shook maracas and flashed glances at the young women in the crowd. As the procession wound its way through the narrow streets, it picked up a collection of hangers-on: laughing children, gaggles of teenagers, the odd tourist, and, rather incongruously, a middle-aged gentleman in a sober grey suit. I tagged along at a suitable distance.

We ended up in Copacabana's Plaza 2 de Febrero – the main square, which takes its name from the 2 February date of the feast day of the local patron saint – and were soon joined by similarly attired processions from other parts of town. Eventually the din forced me to seek refuge in the cathedral that dominates the square. In doing so, it felt as if I had swapped Nashville for Andalusia. Built between 1589 and 1669 by Spanish members of the Order of Saint Augustine, the Basilica of Our Lady of Copacabana is a shimmering white beacon, decorated with Portuguese-style blue *azulejo* tiles, and capped by towers and domes. Inside the 'Moorish Cathedral', as it is sometimes known, protected within a glass chamber, is the reason the basilica was built in the first place: a simple wooden statue of an indigenous woman dressed in Inca-style robes flecked with silver and gold – the Virgin of Copacabana.

The arrival of Spanish conquistadors, colonialists, and religious orders in the Titicaca region heralded a wave of looting on a massive scale. Inca temples, shrines and other sites around the lake and on the islands were ransacked and often demolished, their stonework used to construct churches and other buildings. Although the Spanish appeared thorough in their looting, a legend subsequently emerged that some of the gold escaped their prying hands and was hidden in the lake. There were even rumours of a lost city, an Andean Atlantis named Wanaku. In the 1960s, French oceanographer Jacques Cousteau came with high hopes but found only pottery. Thirty years later, several boxes of gold and other artefacts were discovered just off Isla del Sol, and in 2000 an Italian team found the remains of a pre-Inca temple, crop terraces, a road and an 800-m wall on the lake floor. Since then, numerous caches of Tiwanaku relics have been discovered below the surface, including in 2019 one featuring gold medallions, turquoise pendants, and an exquisite lapis-lazuli puma figurine.

As well as the upheaval wrought by the Spanish, the region suffered a series of poor harvests and severe frosts in the 1570s and locals decided they needed some divine protection. Copacabana was rededicated to the Virgin of Candelaria, a popular representation of the Virgin Mary. A local man named Francisco Inca Yupanqui, reputedly a descendant of legendary Inca leader Atahualpa, fashioned an image of the Virgin. His first attempt was rejected as too crude, but after studying sculpture and woodcarving for several years, he later produced a more acceptable version adorned with gold and precious jewels. Sure enough, conditions improved, the statue was credited with a series of miracles, and the basilica was built to house her. Copacabana's reputation grew, and it swiftly became the most important Catholic pilgrimage site in this part of the Andes. An image of the virgin was later taken by Portuguese sailors to Rio de Janeiro, where it was installed in a chapel. This inspired residents to rename their beachfront neighbourhood, previously called Sacopenapã, in her honour.

The indigenous beliefs, however, never went away. Instead they mutated, merged with and even to some extent co-opted Christianity. A perfect example of this syncretism takes place most weekends in the Plaza 2 de Febrero: the blessing of the cars. A succession of brand-new vehicles, including taxis, buses, trucks and lorries, pull up outside the cathedral's gates, each one festooned with tinsel, steamers, rosettes, flowers, and confetti purchased from nearby stalls. The owners are there to ask for blessings from both the Virgin Mary and Pachamama. When I observed the ceremony, a priest dressed in white robes and a baseball cap emerged carrying a tin bucket of holy water. In a business-like fashion he approached the first vehicle and made the sign of the cross. After intoning a few blessings, he dipped what appeared to be a silver wand topped with a flower into the bucket and then flicked the holy water over the engine. A donation was made to church funds and the priest moved on to the next vehicle. The proud owners then splashed over their own benedictions of beer, sparkling wine or the local firewater, while others set off firecrackers. As the cars drove off the exhaust fumes mingled with the scent of flower blossom and alcohol.

Known as *ch'alla*, this type of ritual blessing is supposed to ensure the vehicle's safety – not an idle wish in a country with roads as treacherous as Bolivia's – and, in the case of a bus or taxi, its profitability. During the town's many fiestas, *ch'alla* is extended to toy cars and homes, wads of fake dollar bills, and other miniature items; local belief holds that within a year, they will be replaced by full-sized or genuine versions – a modern take on an ancient ritual.

Ch'alla may not be a traditional Christian practice, but in Bolivia the church has had to be pragmatic to maintain its spiritual authority. Throughout the country, 'pagan' ceremonies take place in churches and are often led by *yatiris*. Animal sacrifices are carried out, coca leaves chewed, offerings made, alcohol spilled on the earth. There is no contradiction in this for many Bolivians: it is simply the way things are done.

***

Certain ideas echo particularly loudly throughout Bolivian history and one of them is the search for lost cities and hidden riches. In his book *Royal Commentaries of the Incas*, Cuzco-born Spanish-Inca historian Garcilaso de la Vega writes about a major Inca military expedition into the Amazon in the 15th century. Apparently basing his account on oral testimony, much of it obtained from his maternal relatives, who were members of the Inca royal family, de la Vega describes the expedition's arrival 'two hundred leagues' east of Cuzco in a 'province called Musu', which is thought to be the Llanos de Moxos.

There they found a 'great many warlike people' who, while 'delighted to be ... friends and confederates' with the Inca, refused to submit to their rule. The Musu allowed some of the newcomers to settle in their lands, and sent ambassadors to Cuzco. As Richard Gott wrote in

Land Without Evil: 'This extraordinary tale suggests that, in the Mojos, the Incas felt that they were faced with a comparable civilization ... This tale was one of the origins of the tales of El Dorado.'

For centuries, this fantastical notion of an Amazonian El Dorado, a city of gold hidden in the rainforest and sometimes referred to as Paititi, attracted countless conquistadors, explorers, and adventurers. None succeeded, many lost their lives and, until archaeologists began to excavate the earthworks of the Llanos de Moxos, the notion that a complex ancient society could have existed in the Bolivian Amazon was widely dismissed.

But while the Spanish never discovered their lost city of gold, they did find a mountain of silver.

CHAPTER 2
The mountain that eats men

Silver, colonialism, and globalisation: Potosí

Deep inside Cerro Rico (Rich Hill), I attempted to ignore the chalky, yellowish-white dust that covered my face, hands, and overalls. 'Be careful – it's arsenic. Very dangerous,' my guide Antonio warned me, dusty streaks lining his face like war paint. It was, I guessed, at least a 45-minute scramble back to the surface. We'd long passed the point at which two travellers, overwhelmed by claustrophobia, had turned back. I wished I'd joined them. A bitter ball of mushy coca leaves had numbed my mouth to such an extent that I only remembered it was there when it became dislodged from my left cheek and rolled back to block my throat.

The rhythmic metallic thwack of pickaxes and persistent hum of pneumatic drills reverberated throughout the Candelaria mine and made my head ache. Despite the scarf wrapped tightly across my face, a rank, caustic odour invaded my nostrils. Steel trolleys rattled along narrow rails and the rocky floor gently shuddered from a distant blast. 'Explosions are the music of the mines,' said Antonio, offering a thin smile. I swung my headlamp around to illuminate a group of miners. One lit a cigarette and placed it carefully in front of a demonic-looking statue with horns, bulging eyes, evil grin, black boots, and a prominent erection: El Tío, 'The Uncle', lord of the underground, gets angry if he doesn't receive regular gifts.

The arrival of Christianity drove many of Bolivia's indigenous beliefs underground – literally in the case of El Tío – but didn't vanquish them entirely. Instead they mutated and fused with the invading religion. The miners of Cerro Rico saw El Tío not so much as an enemy but a fellow worker, albeit a short-tempered one who, if neglected, could unleash devastation. 'That's why we always have to remember him,' said one miner, his boots slick with the blood of a sacrificial llama. The offerings bind the men together, forging a sense of solidarity and a belief that they will be protected, despite plenty of evidence to the contrary. Watching the ritual was compelling but felt like an intrusion. My heart rate accelerated and every breath was an effort. Despite being simultaneously several thousand metres above sea level and several hundred metres below ground, I felt as if I was drowning.

Conditions in Candelaria, one of hundreds of mines in Cerro Rico, look as if they had changed little in 500 years. Miners hack away at the ceaseless rock with pickaxes and force dynamite into crevices. Skinny youths, some barely into their teens, pump in fresh air by hand. Cartloads of tin, zinc, lead and – rarely these days – silver are heaved out. Shifts can last 10 hours or more in temperatures that often soar well above 40°C; sometimes miners work for 24 hours straight. Cave-ins, explosions, electrocutions, and cyanide, mercury and carbon monoxide poisoning are common occurrences.

This is no land for old men. Few long-term miners live much beyond the age of 45. Silicosis, known here as 'mal de mina', ravages their lungs. But despite the risks there is no shortage of labour: miners can earn double the minimum wage and roughly half of the population of Potosí, the city that sits in the shadow of Cerro Rico, depends directly or indirectly on the mines for their livelihoods.

Earlier in the day we visited a market to buy presents for the miners: bags of coca leaves, chewed to provide energy and stave off hunger; thin white sticks of dynamite resembling church candles; packets of cheap cigarettes; and 96-per-cent-proof alcohol in plastic bottles with slogans like 'good taste' written misleadingly on the labels. A tiny sip of the liquor was enough to set my mouth and throat ablaze. It felt as if I'd swallowed a firework but the miners – after first offering a shot to El Tío – gulped it down without complaint. 'God reigns outside but the devil is in charge in the mines,' said Antonio, who spent 15 years as a miner before becoming a guide for thrill-seeking travellers.

There was a sense of heady euphoria when, a few hours after entering Candelaria, we re-emerged blinking into the sunlight. Back at my guesthouse I jumped straight into the shower, scrubbing at my skin under the low-pressure sprinkle. Still feeling dirty, I collapsed onto the bed and a woozy sensation came over me. I was violently sick.

***

In the 16th and 17th centuries, countless European explorers, adventurers and conquistadors died in Latin America searching for El Dorado, the fabled lost city of gold. They never found it and El Dorado remained that most appealing of myths – tantalisingly out of reach, but not quite implausible enough to completely dismiss. Yet travellers who make their way across Bolivia's *altiplano* today discover something equally astonishing – and tragic: Potosí, the city of silver.

Looming above Potosí is Cerro Rico, home to the biggest silver seams ever discovered. For 300 years Latin America produced around 80 per cent of the world's silver, and Potosí, the biggest single source, was synonymous with fabulous, barely imaginable wealth. According to legend, so much silver – an estimated 70,000 tonnes during the colonial period – was extracted from Cerro Rico that you could have used it to build a bridge from Potosí to Madrid, some 9,250 km away. Two such bridges, it is also said, could have been constructed from the bones of those who died mining the precious metal.

***

Nowhere has played a greater role in shaping modern Bolivia than Potosí. Its legendary mines are an anchor, chaining the country to the past, and simultaneously a source of both shame and pride. Potosí remains an emotive symbol of centuries of colonialism, foreign exploitation of natural resources, and the subjugation of indigenous people.

A decade after clambering through the Candelaria mine, I returned to the city to explore the legacy of its turbulent history and find out how one of the wealthiest places on the planet became one of the most deprived parts of Bolivia. Potosí's current plight is particularly stark when you consider how far its influence spread beyond the Andes. Anthropologist and historian Jack Weatherford has described Potosí as 'the first city of capitalism'. In *Indian Givers: How the Indians of the Americas Transformed the World*, he wrote that the city is probably the world's 'most important monument to capitalism and the ensuing industrial revolution ... Potosí made the money that irrevocably changed the economic complexion of the world.' This view is echoed by Colombian academic, philosopher and author Oscar Guardiola-Rivera in *What if Latin America Ruled the World?*. Potosí, he wrote, was 'the place globalisation started in earnest'. Yet this striking impact on world history has largely been forgotten, at least outside of Bolivia.

I travelled southeast from La Paz, a spectacular 540-km journey, though one only really enjoyed in retrospect. The approach to Potosí, 4,090 m above sea level and the second highest city in the world after La Paz's neighbour El Alto, is by turns awe-inspiring and bleak. In the words of Edmond Temple, a young Irishman who visited the city in 1825, shortly after Bolivia gained its independence from the Spanish empire:

> The country was more barren ... than any through which I had yet travelled, but still the scene was new and interesting; the track led sometimes almost perpendicularly up and down high

rocky mountains, sometimes along their steep shelving sides, sometimes through a ravine or a valley, and sometimes over a plain of little verdure, though covered with flocks of llamas, the only animal that can find subsistence on this unfruitful and inhospitable soil.

I made the rookie error of turning up just a few minutes before my bus departed from the main terminal in La Paz. The only available seat was at the back of the vehicle. To reach it I had to scramble over a shifting mass of suitcases, bin bags, cardboard boxes, and pots and pans tied together with cord. The woman sitting in front of me was moving home and the packages constituted all her worldly possessions.

We set off promptly, though not before a couple more bags were added to the teetering pile, neatly boxing me in. Shortly after passing the *altiplano* city of Oruro, we ground to a halt in a small village in what was to become a painfully familiar stop-start cycle. Most of my fellow passengers – apart from a young Japanese backpacker, all were Bolivian – shuffled off to buy paper cones of popcorn and plastic cups filled with jelly and spirals of whipped cream.

Every bump in the dusty road jangled up our spines. On several occasions, the bus hit potholes so large I was jolted clean off the seat, my head crashing into the ceiling. When I dropped back down, the wobbling mountain of bags and boxes around me threatened to collapse and envelop me in an avalanche of household items. It was impossible to read, and the cacophony of groaning brakes, rattling windows and shrieking children meant it was also too noisy to listen to music. The only way to pass the time was to gaze out the cracked window.

This should have been a visual treat, given the landscape of snowy mountains, hills the colour of smoked paprika, and deep stony valleys. In practice, however, it was terrifying: there were few roadside barriers and the bus, though rarely breaking 30 km an hour, swung dangerously close to the edge with alarming regularity. Cars overtook us on blind corners, and we passed a deep gully sheltering the rusted carcass of a jeep that had overshot the road a few weeks before. Every few minutes the woman beside me crossed herself and mouthed a silent prayer.

From time to time a yell went up and the bus halted, seemingly in the middle of nowhere. A passenger got off, heaved a heavy pack onto their shoulders, and slowly started to walk. There was rarely any sign of life at these stops – no people, houses, or even a track – and it was unclear where they were heading. When the bus did pass through a settlement of modest single-storey homes, packs of scrawny dogs emerged to chase it. The ground was stony and barren, apart from mottled patches of grass, browning cacti, and clusters of solar panels on short poles that looked like metallic sunflowers. Occasionally I saw a herd of llamas, colourful tassels tied to their ears and around their necks.

The steppe drifted by, almost unbroken, a desert of dust and scant scrub beneath an ultramarine sky. While the soils of the *altiplano* hold few nutrients, they are rich in minerals like lithium, tin, tungsten, copper, and silver. As we drew closer to Potosí, mining settlements – corrugated iron roofs, pairs of rubber boots lined up outside tiny doors – and a narrow-gauge railway line came into view. In isolated Andean communities like these, violent rituals known as *tinkus* take place. Young men, and sometimes women, from rival villages meet for hand-to-hand combat, followed by feasting, drinking, music, dancing, and general raucousness. Part rites of passage, part fertility ceremonies, *tinkus* can be bloody affairs and sometimes escalate out of control. The police tend to keep their distance and deaths sometimes occur.

The road climbed steadily upwards towards the sky, which over the course of the afternoon had progressed from blue to grey to brown. Rather incongruously, the first sign of Potosí itself was a telecommunications tower that would have looked more at home in the Soviet Union circa 1970. After yet another bend in the road Cerro Rico appeared, a rusty red smudge of a mountain gashed with white and yellow wounds.

As I left the bus station and trudged to my hotel, the altitude slowly swamped me. Regardless of how fit you are at sea-level, tackling even the slightest inclination in Potosí leaves you breathless, your lungs seemingly shrunken and weighted down. And this is a mild reaction, the receptionist told me. Altitude sickness itself, she warned, was far worse.

***

In the late 15th century, according to legend, Inca ruler Huayna Capac received a message from above. The Inca, who at the time ruled much of what is now western Bolivia, were on the brink of mining in Cerro Rico, but a supernatural voice warned them to stop: the gods were saving the silver for others who would come from far away. Huayna Capac took the message seriously and declared the mountain – which he named 'Potojchi' (or 'Potocsi'), meaning 'burst', 'deafening noise' or 'thunder' in Quechua – to be sacrosanct.

Around 1545, so the tale goes, a local man named Diego Huallpa climbed Cerro Rico in search of a missing llama. Night fell, the temperature plunged and Huallpa lit a fire to keep warm. As it burned he spotted specks of silver on the ground. Word of the incident soon reached the Spanish colonial forces, who had arrived a decade earlier, overthrown the Inca empire, and did not share Huayna Capac's reticence. Despite the inaccessibility of the location, mines quickly sprung up, followed by a town. Over the next two decades Potosí became the richest source of silver the world has ever known.

Conquistador Pedro de Cieza de León visited Potosí in the mid 16th century, by which time the silver rush was well underway. He later wrote in his epic *Chronicles of Peru*:

> [The] wealth became so famous, that Indians [indigenous people] came from all parts to extract silver from the hill ... The climate is cold, and there [were] no inhabited places in the vicinity ... So many people came to work the mines that the place appeared a great city. It may with truth be asserted that in no part of the world could so rich a hill be found, and that no prince receives such profits and rents as this famous town of [silver]. From the year 1548 to 1551 the royal [share of the silver was] valued at more than three millions of ducats, which is more than the Spaniards got from [Inca leader] Atahualpa, and more than was found in the city of Cuzco.

Within 30 years of the discovery of the silver deposits, Potosí's population topped 120,000, and the city was soon producing two-thirds of the world's silver, transferring almost 3,000 tonnes a year to Spain. The mines were privately operated but their profits bankrolled the Spanish empire, which benefited from an array of taxes, notably the 20 per cent *quinto real* (royal fifth). Problems emerged once the easily processed, high-ore deposits close to the surface ran out. This prompted the start of shaft mining, which allowed miners to get deeper into the mountain. The veins they discovered were poorer in quality, which increased processing costs. Working conditions were appalling; countless miners lost their lives. Many others died of mercury poisoning in the silver foundries outside.

This resulted in an acute labour shortage. To tackle it, Viceroy Francisco de Toledo adopted a revised form of an Inca practice of forced labour service known as the *mita*. At a stroke, this provided more than 13,500 indigenous workers a year for the mines and depopulated the surrounding regions of working age men. Toledo ordered the construction of a network of aqueducts, reservoirs and dams to power the water wheels essential for the ore-processing plants, modernising the whole process and creating what was then the world's largest industrial complex. He also had the Spanish city centre re-laid on a rigid grid system, though the poorer 'Indian' – as the colonialists referred to the indigenous people of the Americas – quarters that housed the miners were left disordered and chaotic.

A prominent critic of the *mita* was General William 'Guillermo' Miller, one of the many Britons who fought alongside Simón Bolívar and José de San Martín to liberate South America from Spanish rule. The Kent-born soldier served with distinction during the wars of independence, despite contracting malaria and being wounded 22 times (after his death, an autopsy revealed two bullets had spent 40 years lodged in his liver). He was subsequently appointed Grand Marshall of Peru, but his criticism of the treatment of the indigenous people – resulting partly from his experiences in Potosí – led to him being stripped of his position. His views on the *mita* were expressed in a two-volume biography written by his brother John and published in 1828–29:

> The *mitayo*, or labourer in the mines, received nominally ... about two shillings a day, which was one half of the wages of the ordinary day-labourer in the fields. Out of this sum, two-thirds were supposed to be paid to him; but as this amount did not suffice to meet the expenses of his miserable diet and lodgings, which were furnished by the mine proprietor at a most extravagant rate, together with the eight dollars of tribute for which his master was responsible, he found himself, if he outlived the year, still indebted to his employer: in this case he was not allowed to discontinue from work until all arrears were paid.
>
> Thus each succeeding year found him more and more deeply involved, and this was another link added to the galling chain by which he was fettered to his destiny. It generally happened, however, that, before the expiration of the first year he was released by a welcome death ... worn out with fatigue, grief, and disease, the wretched *mitayo* in a few months yielded to his fate, and found a refuge in the grave.

The grave injustices of the *mita* boosted silver production and Potosí rode a century-long boom. By the 1610s the city's population topped 160,000 – far bigger than contemporary Madrid and comparable to London – and it was one of the richest places in the world. Potosí was home to some of Latin America's finest architecture and boasted scores of elegant churches, mansions, and theatres. At least one street was literally paved with silver. There were also innumerable gambling dens and brothels featuring, respectively, '800 professional gamblers and 120 famous prostitutes', according to Uruguayan author Eduardo Galeano.

'Silk and fabrics came from Granada, Flanders, and Calabria; hats from Paris and London; diamonds from Ceylon; precious stones from India ... carpets from Persia; perfumes from Arabia; porcelain from China,' he wrote in *Open Veins of Latin America*. During this period Potosí entered the popular lexicon. In *Don Quixote*, published in 1615, the eponymous knight remarks to his squire Sancho Panza: *'Eso vale un Potosí'* ('It's worth a Potosí' – aka a fortune). The legend on the city's coat of arms boasted: 'I am rich Potosí, treasure of the world, king of the mountains, envy of kings.'

But this wealth came at a horrific cost. Over the course of 300 years of Spanish colonialism, Potosí's silver contributed to a demographic collapse in the Andes, with huge numbers of indigenous Bolivians – and enslaved people from Africa trafficked over to fill labour shortages – losing their lives in the mines and processing plants. As a result Cerro Rico became known as 'the mountain that eats men'.

***

'We had not been in Potosí many hours before we realized that it was a most fascinating place ... By the time we had been here a week we were ready to agree with those who call it the most interesting city in South America,' wrote American academic and explorer Hiram Bingham in the 1910s.

More than a century on, Bingham's description remains accurate, despite Potosí's precipitous decline. At the start of the 19th century, it was still one of the biggest cities in South America, but silver production had long since peaked and the population was steadily shrinking. Tin mining provided a fillip in the 20th century, but when global prices for the commodity crashed in the mid-1980s, scores of state-owned mines were closed or sold off.

Emigration rates from the Potosí region were among the highest in the country, as thousands of unemployed miners and their families – who were overwhelmingly Quechua and Aymara – fled in search of work. Many ended up in El Alto; others headed north to the city of Cochabamba or to the sprawl of Santa Cruz in eastern Bolivia. In the process, Potosí drifted into obscurity, a lonely, isolated city, lost in the Andes. Today the population is little bigger than it was at the height of the silver boom more than 350 years ago.

Yet as its residents departed, travellers began to arrive. The depressed local economy meant the historic buildings in the city centre were relatively untroubled by modern developments and in 1987 it was named a UNESCO World Heritage Site. Potosí has coped with its decline by becoming a heritage destination and today tourists patrol its cobbled streets, snapping photos of the stately churches and faded mansions with red-tiled roofs and ornate balconies. More than 2,000 colonial-era buildings remain, and I found remnants of the city's heyday almost everywhere I looked. But when the cold nights draw in, the atmosphere turns decidedly melancholic, the historic structures seeming to symbolise Potosí's downfall.

A simple stone gateway, the Arco de Cobija, still marks the divide between ordered, distinctly Spanish-influenced centre and the more haphazard 'Indian' district, whose winding streets are lined with both crumbling 18th- and 19th-century buildings and less attractive modern homes. The miners have always lived in this and, in an attempt to cement the Catholic faith amongst indigenous Bolivians, the colonial authorities built 14 simple parish churches. Rich Spanish mine owners also paid for the construction – using the labour of enslaved people – of 34 far more opulent churches for the exclusive use of their own community. These were ostentatious displays of wealth, rather than expressions of piety: they all face east towards Cerro Rico, as if paying respects to the source of the city's riches.

Many of these churches have survived and are now among the most important architectural relics on the continent. Despite the efforts to ensure a sharp distinction between the *mitayos* and the colonial rulers, the Spanish churches betray a mischievous local influence. Set to work on their oppressors' places of worship, the craftsmen deliberately blurred the lines between indigenous and foreign beliefs, with Andean religious symbols like the sun and the moon inserted alongside, or blended with, traditional Christian iconography. The style became known as *mestizo*-baroque.

I visited Potosí's neoclassical cathedral, reopened a few months earlier after an eight-year renovation process. The interior was a wedding cake of chunky white pillars, pink marble, stained glass, and gilt edging, and the smell of paint was still fresh in the air. I was soon joined by Defredo, a middle-aged man in an ill-fitting suit, who emerged from a recess, sidled up quietly and appointed himself my guide. His level of expertise was unclear, but what he may have lacked in knowledge, he made up for with enthusiasm, high-fiving me vigorously every few moments.

Periodically, Defredo also shared some intriguing pieces of information. He pointed out masonic symbols on the looming altarpiece, including a golden pyramid with a single all-seeing eye. 'This is the only church in Potosí with them,' he said. 'The three corners of the masonic pyramid match the three aspects of the Holy Trinity. There are many masons in Potosí, still. The independence leaders

Antonio José de Sucre, José de San Martín, Bernardo O'Higgins, Simón Bolívar, of course, were all masons.'

***

The most important building in Potosí is not a place of worship – at least not of religious worship. Covering an entire block in the city centre and bounded by forbidding metre-thick walls, unbroken apart for a few slit windows, the Casa Real de la Moneda looked like a fortress, but was actually the royal mint. So little sunlight penetrated the depths of the building the temperature inside was several degrees lower than outside. The mint took 24 years to build and was eventually completed in 1773 at the cost of more than a million pesos.

Today, it is a museum filled with artefacts from Potosí's heyday. My guide was Luis, who was more accomplished, if less enthusiastic, than Defredo. We walked through the vast halls and smelting rooms, which contained an array of colonial-era art and curiosities, including a sturdy 12-lock strongbox, several altarpieces and an array of brutal weaponry. Luis drew my attention to *La Virgen del Cerro* (*The Virgin of the Mountain*), one of the most significant pieces of art in Bolivia. It dates back to the 18th century, when it was painted by an unknown – presumably indigenous – artist. 'It is the perfect example of the *mestizo*-baroque style,' he said. 'The Virgin Mary, who represents both Pachamama and Cerro Rico, is in the centre of the painting. Above her are the Holy Trinity, as well as the sun and the moon. Below her are the Pope, an archbishop, knights and local dignitaries. The globe represents Potosí as the centre of the Earth.'

We moved on to a series of huge, heavy wooden mills. 'These were initially powered by mules who laboured for 10 hours a day,' said Luis. 'Each one only lasted three or four months. Local people and [enslaved] Africans, meanwhile, had to hammer out a thousand coins a day. So many died because of the conditions.' Among the hordes of coins on display was something I'd wanted to see ever since reading *Treasure Island* as a child: a *peso de ocho reales* (an eight-*real* peso), source of the piratical term 'pieces of eight'.

For centuries, these one-ounce silver 'Spanish dollars' could be spent virtually anywhere in the world; they were widely used in the British, Portuguese and Dutch empires, in France and much of what is now Germany, and remained legal tender in the United States as late as the 1850s. Historian William Bernstein described the coins as 'the Visa and the Mastercard and the American Express of the sixteenth through to the nineteenth centuries'. They also inspired the modern dollar symbol, which is a variant on the mark stamped on coins in the Casa Real de la Moneda – the letters P, T, S and I superimposed on each other.

The *peso de ocho reales* symbolises Potosí's seismic, but now neglected, impact on the world at large. Its silver was a crucial part of the so-called 'Columbian Exchange', the transfer of natural resources, people, animals, plants, goods, diseases and ideas between the 'New' and 'Old' worlds in the 15th and 16th centuries. Potosí helped to fuel the economic and political rise of Europe, kick-start global trade, and ultimately provoke financial crises across Asia and beyond. Globalisation is often thought of as a 20th-century phenomenon, but its modern iteration started here, in an isolated patch of the Bolivian *altiplano*, half a millennium ago.

For almost 250 years llama caravans carried silver ingots and 'pieces of eight' from the Casa Real de la Moneda across the Andes to the Pacific port of Callao in present-day Peru, a gruelling slog that lasted two months or more. This precious cargo was then shipped north to what are now Mexico, Panama, and Colombia. Some of the silver was then transported to Europe, but the vast majority of shipments travelled west to Asia. Once or twice a year, great galleons carrying thousands of tonnes of silver from Potosí (and, to a lesser extent, Mexico's mines) set sail from Acapulco. They generally took three to five months to cross the Pacific to the Spanish colony of Manila in the Philippines. Although the 'Manila galleons' were menaced by pirates and privateers like Sir Francis Drake, the route to the Philippines was quicker and easier than travelling via Spain.

In Manila, Spanish and Chinese merchants gathered to exchange silver for silk, spices, porcelain, lacquer, gold, ivory, tea and other luxury items – including, in due course, Catholic icons made in China for the Spanish and Latin American markets – from across Asia. This represented the first 'substantial, direct, and continuous trade between America and Asia … in history,' wrote academics Dennis Flynn and Arturo Giraldez in their paper *Born with a "Silver Spoon": The Origin of World Trade in 1571*.

This trade was driven by China's seemingly unquenchable thirst for silver. Centuries earlier the country launched the world's first paper currency but overprinting, widespread counterfeiting and hyperinflation meant the notes eventually fell out of favour. In the middle period of the Ming dynasty (1368-1644), the authorities turned instead to silver, using it to collect taxes and price goods. According to Charles C. Mann in *1493: Uncovering the New World Columbus Created*, this led to a 'voracious demand for the metal' as 'tens of millions of wealthy Chinese suddenly needed chunks of silver for such basic tasks as paying taxes or running a business'.

As a result, silver became more valuable in China than anywhere else on the planet. With its own silver reserves largely exhausted, the country was forced to open up its long-closed economy to foreign trade. Chinese merchants set up across Asia and silver, initially from Japan but then in far larger quantities from Potosí and Mexico, flooded in.

The silver trade propped up the Spanish empire, enabling it to wage costly wars against the Ottomans, England, France, the Netherlands and the Philippines. Much of the silver initially shipped to Europe subsequently made its way to Asia, greatly enriching Portuguese, Dutch and, to a lesser extent, English middlemen in the process and setting off a trading bonanza across the continent. As former British Museum director Neil MacGregor wrote in *A History of the World in 100 Objects*: 'Across Europe, Spanish-American treasure inaugurated an age of silver ... In the economic history of the world, nothing on this colossal scale, or with such grave consequences, had ever happened before.'

Meanwhile, the silver trade fuelled the growth of the Chinese economy and, wrote Mann, helped to pay 'for huge military projects, including much of the Great Wall of China'. But as the 17th century progressed so much silver flooded onto the global market that its value began to plunge. This caused economic and political turmoil across Asia and Europe. Chinese buying power dropped dramatically, inflation spiralled out of control, the Ming dynasty collapsed and the country took centuries to fully recover. Spain was similarly beset by crisis. Despite the great riches extracted from Potosí and its other Latin American colonies, its economy remained on shaky ground, suffering a series of bankruptcies, thanks in large part to its costly military endeavours. 'Spain's economy turned to ash, followed by the economies of a dozen other states ... Ruin was followed by riot and revolution,' wrote Mann.

Spain's European rivals, notably England and France, swiftly took advantage of the situation. Commodities like sugar, gold, cotton, tobacco and coffee became increasingly important but the worldwide interdependent networks created by the silver trade endure to this day. As Flynn and Giraldez argued, silver 'reverberated across all continents and gave birth to world trade.' Silver from Potosí and across Latin America heralded the dawn of globalisation, centuries before the word first entered the dictionary.

'Potosí was the building block of the modern world but now it's lost in time," said Luis, as he led me out into the Casa Real de la Moneda's entranceway. Above us was one of the emblems of the city, El Mascarón. At first glance, it looked like a plaster mask of the Roman god Bacchus, complete with a garland of grapes and a rather unsettling expression on its face. Like everything in Potosí, this 19th-century creation was open to interpretation. Some claimed it was llama herder Diego Huallpa, others that it was a caricature of the director of the mint. A few argued it was built to cover up the Spanish royal coat of arms after Bolivia claimed its independence. El Mascarón is appropriately asymmetrical: one side smiles, the other grimaces. 'I think it symbolises the rich and the poor, the Spanish and the indigenous people,' said Luis.

**

For a glimpse into the lives of Potosí's former silver elite, I took a taxi to Bolivia's oldest hacienda. In the lobby of Hacienda Cayara, as a hummingbird buzzed overhead, owner Luis Arturo regaled me with the exploits of a North American film-maker, who was using the grounds as the set for a raunchy take on Robert Louis Stevenson's short story *Olalla*. 'The heroine bit the village priest and was then chained naked to a cross, whipped and burned at the stake,' he said, gesturing towards the 500-year-old stone chapel. 'It was quite a scene.'

Some 20 km west of Potosí and around 500 m lower, the Cayara valley is another world: warmer, calmer, less oxygen starved. The road from the city descends through mountainous badlands before veering off past a brutalist tin-processing plant, crossing a perilously narrow, barrier-less bridge and entering a bucolic, agricultural land. Green mountains enclose the valley and a river runs through the centre, flanked by neat fields, herds of cattle and solitary, mournful donkeys. Quiet hamlets line the cobbled road, along which farmers drive sheep, the shepherds wielding long staffs.

Located at the far end of the valley, Hacienda Cayara is now a hotel and museum, as well as a working farm, dairy, family home and occasional film set. Its neat, ochre-red buildings with roofs of terracotta tiles are clustered around a collection of patios featuring fountains and cacti. My room for the night had high ceilings, wooden beams and dangerous-looking electric heaters that burned like the sun. Birdsong was the only sound in the tall cypress, pine and willow trees outside.

I met up again with Luis Arturo in his reception after dinner. Clad in a sleeveless red puffa jacket, he was a garrulous host, telling me about his Scottish-French heritage, work for Unicef, and the history of Cayara. 'This is the oldest hacienda in South America, built in 1557,' he said, stoking the fire and directing my attention to the Venetian mirrors, ceiling fresco, and paintings of Spanish kings and illustrious relatives covering the walls.

'The title was signed over by King Felipe of Spain, and the first owner was one of Francisco Pizarro's conquistadors, a man named Juan de Pendones. His share of Inca treasure would be worth around $50 million in today's money. Viceroy Francisco de Toledo stayed here and sent his troops across Bolivia and Argentina. Independence leader Antonio José de Sucre stayed here in March 1825 before taking Potosí from Spanish troops. It's only been owned by three families in 500 years; my family bought it in 1905. Walk through this house and you walk through Bolivian and South American history.'

The library was a particular point of pride, home to some 6,000 books, including a French-Spanish dictionary dating from 1731, the complete works of Voltaire, volumes of *National Geographic*, and a first edition of *The History of England* by Hume and Smollett. Upstairs the cavernous dining room was a treasure trove of objects from the colonial and early independence eras: a 500-year-old suit of armour worn by Juan de Pendones himself; an English musket made in 1750; mining lamps and shovels; a 19th-century Bolivian presidential guard's uniform; bullets from the gun of a Spitfire; and a conquistador's sword with the following inscription on its hilt: 'Don't take me out without reason. Don't put me back without honour.'

***

Given the lack of alternative sources of employment in the region, Potosí's surviving mines continue to attract workers to toil on their near-exhausted seams. But Cerro Rico, the 'mountain that eats men', is itself being eaten away. Nearly 500 years of mining have turned its interior into something resembling Swiss cheese. There are more than 600 mines and 100 km of tunnels and shafts, commonly known as 'rat holes'. Many are crumbling and accidents are common, killing scores of miners every year.

In 2011, a large sinkhole appeared on the summit of the 4,782 m conical peak, and smaller ones puncture its slopes. Stabilisation efforts – essentially pouring in tonnes of rock and cement – have had a limited impact, and geologists have warned a catastrophic collapse could be imminent. In an attempt to protect the summit, mining has officially been banned above 4,400 m, but work continues regardless. Cerro Rico's problems have been exacerbated by foolish backpackers and unscrupulous guides tossing around lit sticks of dynamite after their tours, an activity that is now also banned. In 2014, UNESCO placed Potosí and Cerro Rico on its World Heritage Sites in Danger list, stating 'continued and uncontrolled mining operations ... risk degrading the site'.

Around 15,000 people still work in Potosí's mines on tin, lead, zinc and – now extremely meagre – silver seams, and their wages continue to support the city as a whole. (They include children as young as 11 or 12: Unicef estimates hundreds of thousands of Bolivians aged between five and 17 do some form of economic activity; several thousand are believed to work in mines.) Miners, few of whom have health insurance or pensions, are generally employed by private bodies misleadingly called 'cooperatives'.

In his book *The Mountain That Eats Men*, Ander Izagirre argued many cooperatives are 'vehicles for fraud and exploitation' in which large numbers of workers 'have no right to participate in decisions or to share in the profits'.

***

Potosí's silver dominated Bolivian life for hundreds of years but as the 20th century approached two other natural resources came to the fore. As I found on the next stage of my travels, tin and rubber also generated great fortunes – and caused immense suffering.

CHAPTER 3
Tin kings and rubber barons

*Tin, rubber, and tycoons: Oruro,
Cochabamba, and Trinidad*

In the late 19th century the international price of silver plunged, curtailing the industry in Bolivia and the power of the silver-mining elite, who had dominated the political arena for many years. During the same period, global demand for tin began to soar. Largely ignored up to this point in Bolivia, the metal was soon the country's major export, creating a new, staggeringly wealthy class of magnate in the process. No one benefited more from this tin boom than Simón Iturri Patiño, who became one of the richest men on Earth.

Born in 1860 to parents of mixed Spanish and Quechua heritage, Patiño came from a humble background, though accounts of his early life and career are contested. According to one version of events, he was working as a lowly store clerk in a mining supply shop in the city of Oruro, 310 km northwest of Potosí, when a prospector offered him the deed to a plot of mountainous land as payment for a bill. Patiño accepted, but his bosses thought it was a bum deal and fired the young clerk. Reputedly, Patiño was forced to pay off the prospector's bill himself and was left holding the deed.

The land turned out to contain La Salvadora (The Saviour), one of the richest seams of tin in the world. Patiño moved quickly and expanded ruthlessly, buying out domestic competitors, purchasing foundries across the globe, and setting up his own bank. By the 1930s, his foundries were processing more than 60 per cent of the world's tin. His success earned him the nicknames the 'King of Tin' and the 'Rockefeller of the Andes'. In his book *Outliers*, author Malcolm Gladwell estimated that Patiño's wealth at its peak was equivalent to around $8.2 billion in today's money, and ranked him 26th on the list of the richest people of all time, ahead of the likes of Carlos Slim, Bill Gates and Warren Buffett.

***

From Potosí I caught a bus across the interminably flat and featureless *altiplano*. Stretching almost 1,000 km – roughly the distance between

London and Munich – from Bolivia and Peru to northern Chile and Argentina at an average altitude of 3,700 m, the plateau is one of the least hospitable places on the continent, a semi-desert, frigid, largely treeless and starved of rain. My destination was Oruro, the epicentre of Bolivia's tin boom and birthplace of Patiño's empire. Along the highway we passed huge public works programmes. Concrete skeletons of bridges connected empty patches of countryside. Water pipes big enough for a person to walk through without stooping lay in great holes in the earth. A forest of 'Men at Work' signs were planted in areas without any men present, working or otherwise.

Intermittently, the bus stopped at sparsely populated villages, jumbles of concrete shacks and disproportionate numbers of mechanic shops. Between these settlements were a few half-built, apparently unoccupied, homes, as well as a pair of isolated cemeteries. The region felt as if it had been suddenly abandoned because of some natural disaster.

Eventually the bus reached a roundabout with a monumental miner's helmet in its centre to signify that we had reached Oruro. My expectations were fairly low. 'Oruro is pretty bleak,' a British friend who lives in Bolivia had warned me. 'The people there are like Mancunians – they think it is the greatest place in the world, regardless of the reality. It does have the best carnival in Bolivia but you've missed this year's one. You can't imagine how different it is during carnival – as soon as it finishes, they start planning the next one. But the rest of the year, it's just bleak.'

My guesthouse faced the Plaza del Folklore, where the carnival processions had ended a few months earlier. The only signs of life in the square were a stray dog and an afternoon drunk with an empty liquor bottle and his head in his hands. High above, on a hill overlooking the city, stood a white statue of the Virgén del Socavón, patron saint of miners (*socavón* means 'cavern' or 'tunnel'). She cradled an infant and peered down at the city through the overcast sky. Carnival felt a long way away.

***

Situated at an altitude of 3,709 m, Oruro was once one of the most important cities in Bolivia, and indeed South America as a whole. The grey mountains nearby were filled with sizeable silver seams and even larger tin deposits. From the 19th century, Oruro was transformed into a cosmopolitan boom town, aided by its key position on the country's railway network, and gained the nickname 'the Chicago of Bolivia'. Mining barons like Patiño constructed brash, opulent mansions as testaments to their wealth. A few still exist. Amid the sports shops, cyber cafés, fried chicken joints, and shabby looking solicitors' offices just north of the central plaza is a large neoclassical mansion built for Patiño in the early 20th century. The industrialist spent a small fortune on the home, but never lived there.

Today, it is part of the city's technical university, which runs a small museum. When I visited I watched students hurry under dusty Venetian crystal chandeliers, past peeling gold-leaf cherubs, and over the once ornate, but now scuffed tiled floors. Among the jumble of exhibits were children's toys, a large mechanical organ, a sturdy safe, and countless portraits of Patiño, who looked neatly groomed, well-fed and extremely self-satisfied. My favourite part of the museum was the smoking room, where murals on the ceiling depicted angels clutching chunky cigars.

During Oruro's heyday, foreigners flocked to the city, including a number of Britons. 'You can still see the influence of the British,' my friend had explained. 'People still sit down for high tea, brass bands play at carnival and the *salteñas* are a bit like Cornish pasties.' According to local legend, they also created the *chuflay*, a potent mix of *singani*, a type of Bolivian brandy, and lemonade, which became one of the national drinks. The motley British contingent was made up of mining and railway engineers, businessmen, and adventurers. Lionel Portman, author of *Three Asses in Bolivia*, characterises the arrogant, strike-it-rich attitude of these interlopers. Fiercely patriotic, anti-German, contemptuous of 'the Latin' and an unashamed colonialist, Portman considered it a dereliction of duty for Britain not to take 'early and, where necessary, forcible possession' of any resources, wealth and parts of the world that might be of use, particularly in Latin America.

On his visit to Oruro in the 1910s, he pompously aimed to put this right – or at the very least secure some profitable business opportunities for himself. 'The lawyers, doctors, tradesmen, "travellers", clerks, officials and gentlemen of independent means, you will hardly find one among them who has not an interest of some kind in some mining property,' he wrote. 'Everyone hopes some day to bring off a big coup. And everyone talks, as is only to be expected, of other people's mining business ... There is always a boom coming or a slump feared.'

This heady period in Oruro did not last. Its mines helped Bolivia become one of the world's biggest tin producers. But when prices collapsed in the 1980s, thousands lost their jobs and the city entered a downward spiral from which it has never really recovered, although a number of mines in the surrounding area continue to operate. Much like Potosí, it now has the melancholy air of a place that knows its heyday is behind it and is unsure how best to move on.

Except, that is, for one a week a year, when Oruro rouses itself and stages one of the continent's most riotous carnivals. A moveable feast celebrated in late February or early March at the start of Lent, the Oruro Carnival's highlight is the Diablada, the dance of the devils. A lengthy, snaking procession of dancers in devilish masks and clanging brass bands trail behind Lucifer and Archangel Michael. The costumes are outlandish: 'The devils wear pink tights, red-and-white boots decorated with dragons and serpents, velvet capes sewn with silver thread, coins and bit of mirror,' wrote Christopher Isherwood in *The Condor and The Cows*. Despite the thin Christian veneer, the festivities have indigenous origins, with Lucifer representing the Andean god of the underworld.

During carnival week, Archangel Michael and the forces of good eventually triumph over the Devil and his band of evil-doers. For the rest of the year, though, the outcome in Oruro is not so clear cut.

***

After the cold, grey, faintly desolate weather in Oruro, it was a relief to descend some 1,200 m to Cochabamba, whose pleasantly warm year-round climate has earned it the title 'City of Eternal Spring'. Patiño was born in a village just south of the city, which lies in the centre of Bolivia, midway between the Andean highlands to the west and the searing lowlands that stretch out towards Brazil in the east. The southern edge of the Amazon, meanwhile, is just a three-hour drive to the north.

Surrounded by the fertile Cochabamba Valley, Bolivia's main agricultural region, the city has a friendly, modern, commercial outlook and a strong local identity. Most of the city's 850,000-plus population speak Quechua as a first language. This is largely a legacy of the Inca, who brought Quechua-speaking farmers to work the land 500–600 years ago. The name 'Cochabamba' comes from an intermingling of the Quechua words for 'lake' – the area's once abundant swampy lagoons have now largely disappeared – and 'plain'. After the arrival of the Spanish colonialists, who founded the modern city in 1571, the region was dominated by large haciendas that produced grain for Potosí, then riding its silver boom, and subsequently the rest of the country.

I travelled to Cochabamba to visit another of Patiño's former homes, the Palacio de Portales, which is open to the public. From my sprawling, eerily deserted hotel in the outlying Tiquipaya suburb I caught a taxi into the city centre, the 15-minute ride taking me past expensive homes with private gardens, high security walls and CCTV cameras. There were implausible numbers of mechanics and tyre shops. On the pavement, shaded by a rudimentary awning fashioned from an old bed sheet, a tailor worked furiously on an aged, hand-operated sewing machine. On the opposite side of the road a four-piece brass band played on the flatbed of a stationary pick-up truck. At a roundabout, we crawled behind a funeral procession: a line of mourners carrying wreaths and bunches of flowers followed the car as it slowly circled.

As the suburbs gave way to the city proper, it became clear that this part of Cochabamba – at least on the surface – was a wealthier, more comfortable place than either Oruro or Potosí, with smarter cars and smoother roads. On the edge of the city centre, gated apartment blocks and townhouses sat next to grassy parks filled with playing children. There was a tennis centre and a swimming pool showroom with empty blue moulds of varying sizes propped up against a wall. The change in geography was also clear: lush gardens, tall palm trees, and lines of bright pink flowers planted along the central reservations. It felt a little like northern Chile or southern Brazil.

But there were still patches of desperation. Homeless people were a more visible presence on the streets here. An elderly woman lay beneath a flyover, cradling a tearful boy who couldn't have been more than three or four; it wasn't clear what had happened to his parents. Later in the day, as I walked round the central Plaza Colón, with its non-functioning fountain, shoe-shiners, and ice cream sellers, a squad of heavily-armed police officers roared up. An array of firecrackers went off in the distance and then, much closer, what sounded like a gunshot. My heart raced as I joined the crowds running for safety down Avenida Ballivián, a glitzy strip of bars and clubs. That night, a waiter told me the police had clashed with 500 students, who were protesting about misspent funds. Twenty-two people were arrested, he said, and many more injured. 'Well, the police always describe them as "injuries",' he added.

At least I had been forewarned. My taxi driver, an agitated man in his early 20s, warned me repeatedly about the dangers of Cochabamba: 'Watch out because there are lots of thieves here. Thieves used to wear old clothes like these' – he gestured at a hole in his T-shirt – 'but now they wear smart clothes. Those are the ones you have to watch out for now.' When he dropped me off in Recoleta, one of Cochabamba's smartest neighbourhoods, he waggled his finger at me: 'Keep a hand on your wallet.'

***

Recoleta is a place of manicured lawns, perimeter fencing, 4x4s, security guards, overpriced restaurants, US-style sports bars with names like 'Hooligans', and supermarkets stocked with imported goods – I discovered Cadbury's chocolate, Marmite-flavoured crisps and even jars of Shippam's crab paste. In the heart of the neighbourhood is the Palacio de Portales, an ostentatious mansion – custard coloured with white trim – and botanical garden built for Patiño in the early 20th century. Today, it is home to the Patiño family's educational and cultural centre, and maintained by a small army of gardeners, security guards, cleaners, and handymen.

After paying my entry fee I strolled along gravel paths shaded by trees: soaring palms, slender ginkgos and cypresses, catalpas with large, heart-shaped leaves, and sharp-thorned acacias. Jasmine and pine scented the air. Lily ponds filled with plump goldfish were guarded by faux Greco-Roman statuary. A plaster-cast St Bernard's dog stood protectively over a fallen child. Nearby was an open-air theatre. Despite the surface perfection, flaws soon emerged: the paint was starting to flake off the benches; one of the ponds was dry; and strips of bark peeled off the eucalyptus tree in brittle curls and littered the floor, like a giant's nail clippings.

Inside the mansion I tagged along as a reverential guide showed round a group of tourists, mostly middle-class Bolivian women and bored secondary school students. The building, completed in 1922, was an indulgent melange of French, Italian, British, and Spanish influences: wood panelled walls, huge mirrors, stained-glass windows, marble fireplaces, Louis XV-style furniture, and scores of Venetian crystal chandeliers. Religious frescos were displayed alongside paintings of zodiac signs. The games room was designed in style of the Alhambra in Granada; its centrepiece a gilt-edged billiard table. There were also a few signs of the early 20th century; the rooms all had a prominently displayed telephone. Everywhere you looked – on the walls, crockery, artwork – were the King of Tin's initials: 'SIP' and 'SP'.

As with his mansion in Oruro, Patiño never actually lived in the Palacio de Portales, despite the great expense that went into building it. In 1912, he moved with his family to Europe, where they set about ingratiating themselves with the continent's aristocracy. Twelve years later the magnate suffered a heart attack and doctors advised him not to return to the high altitudes of Bolivia. In 1939, he left Europe for New York, before settling in Argentina in order to be closer to his homeland.

At the time of Patiño's death on 20 April 1947 his companies controlled around 35 per cent of the world's tin supplies. But the Rockefeller of the Andes and fellow tin barons Moritz (or Mauricio) Hochschild and Carlos Víctor Aramayo sowed the seeds of their own downfall through the repression of the thousands of workers – who were overwhelmingly of indigenous and *mestizo* descent – they employed.

When miners went on strike for better pay and conditions, they were often met with violence. One of the most notorious incidents was the 1942 Catavi massacre, in which hundreds of miners – some estimates suggest as many as 400 – at a Patiño-owned plant were killed by government troops following a five-day strike. The violence helped to give rise to the Federación Sindical de Trabajadores Mineros de Bolivia, a radical mineworkers' union that played a key role in the 1952 National Revolution, which ushered in wide-ranging reforms. Five years after his death, Patiño's mines were nationalised.

Today, a short walk from the King of Tin's former mansion in Oruro, is a statue of a miner holding a rifle aloft and raising his face proudly to the sky.

***

As Patiño built up his tin empire in the *altiplano*, similarly remorseless figures were carving out fortunes from Amazonian rubber. For an insight into this brutal period of Bolivian history, I headed back to the Llanos de Moxos and the city of Trinidad, which is indelibly linked with the country's most notorious rubber baron, Nicolás Suárez Callaú.

I was met at Trinidad airport by Lyliam, a curly haired woman who hobbled through the crowded baggage claim, swiped my backpack off the carousel and hustled me into her car. Lyliam, it quickly became apparent, was a force of nature. In the 10-minute drive to the centre of Trinidad, she unleashed a steady stream of consciousness, breaking off only to answer her mobile phone, which rang frequently. By the time we reached my hotel, I'd received a thorough run-down on the local political scene, the nuances of her extended family, and the reason she was limping (a motorcycle accident 15 years earlier). Lyliam allowed me 20 minutes – I managed to negotiate up from 10 – to freshen up before heading out for lunch.

La Santísima Trinidad (The Most Holy Trinity) was founded in 1686 by a pioneering Spanish Jesuit, Father Cipriano Barace. Thousands of indigenous people living in the surrounding area – a patchwork of cultural groups often referred to collectively as Moxeños (or Mojeños) – were corralled into Trinidad and other Jesuit mission towns and pressured into converting to Catholicism. The city lasted for almost a century before flooding and disease prompted a 14-km relocation to its current site.

The Jesuits were kicked out of the Spanish-controlled regions of South America in 1767 after growing too rich, powerful, and independent-minded for the liking of the colonial authorities. Afterwards many Moxeños were forced into conditions of virtual slavery by plantation owners from the city of Santa Cruz, 500 km south of Trinidad. Some of those who remained in the region went on to fight in the wars of independence and briefly formed an indigenous-run government in the city – a distant precursor to Evo Morales' administration some two centuries later – before being obliterated by royalist soldiers. Throughout this period, the semi-wild cattle brought to the region by the Jesuits thrived. Later they were cross-bred with hardy Brazilian zebus, and today cattle-ranching forms a dominant plank of the economy in Trinidad and the wider Beni region, which encompasses the eastern part of the Bolivian Amazon.

Inevitably enough, lunch was a steak. We drove a few kilometres out of the city to an open-air waterside restaurant, picking up Lyliam's 20-something daughter Geraldine en route. Over a lunch of *bife de chorizos* the size and thickness of bricks, Geraldine told me about her portfolio career, which included running a shop, digital design work, and helping out with her mother's travel agency. I asked about the family ranch, 100 km northwest of Trinidad. Spread over 45 sq km, La Victoria was once part of a much larger property founded by Lyliam's grandfather. 'We have around 1,500 cows but lost hundreds during the 2015 floods,' she said, between bites. 'We also have lots of wildlife, even jaguars. You can come and be a cowboy for a few days.' Lyliam alternated between talking about the ranch, conferring with her broker on the phone, and attempting to buy shares in Tesla and JCPenney on her laptop. Were these good companies to invest in? she asked me repeatedly. I told her I didn't know but gently suggested it was probably best to be cautious.

The restaurant sat on the banks of a large reservoir called Laguna Suárez, a popular spot for swimming and water skiing, despite its sizeable populations of piranhas and caimans. 'This used to be owned by Nicolás Suárez,' said Lyliam, making an extravagant sweeping gesture with her arms. 'The richest man in the Beni.'

***

The Amazon was largely ignored by successive mining-focused, Pacific-orientated Bolivian governments until the late 19th century, when the political elite was finally forced to take an interest. During the disastrous War of the Pacific (1879-1884) the country lost its entire mineral- and copper-rich coastline to Chile. The conflict was provoked by a tax hike on the Chilean and British exporters in the region. In some respects, Bolivia has never really recovered. Losing direct access to the sea crystallised the country's isolation from the outside world, stunted its economic development, and deeply affected the national psyche, the absent coastline becoming something of a phantom limb.

During this period, rapidly industrialising nations in Europe and North America developed an unquenchable desire for rubber – and the only source of rubber at the time was the Amazon. A boom was soon underway and a steady stream of fortune-hunters flocked to the region, eager to take advantage. The problem for the Bolivian government was that its section of the Amazon was especially isolated and inaccessible, hemmed in by mountains, the arid Gran Chaco plains and the vast Pantanal wetlands. As a result, it was difficult to transport out rubber and bring in workers. No large cities similar to Manaus in Brazil or Iquitos in Peru developed, and the government's influence over the territory remained limited at best. This vacuum was ruthlessly exploited by a caste of rubber barons who controlled huge swathes of land – the size of small countries in some cases – largely free of outside interference.

Voluntary labour was in short supply, so the barons relied on coercion. The population of Trinidad plunged as Moxeños were taken to work on plantations known as *barracas*. Indigenous peoples from across the Beni and the lowlands south of the Amazon, as well as impoverished Bolivians from across the country, followed in their wake, tempted by cash advances that plunged them immediately into debt. They were essentially enslaved, kept in check by violence and abuse. As Frederic Vallvé wrote in his paper *The impact of the rubber boom on the indigenous peoples of the Bolivian lowlands (1850–1920)*, the barons 'tied peons to the *barraca* by forcing them to purchase supplies on credit at inflated prices' and used 'private armies' to maintain control.

During the Amazonian rubber boom, which started in the late 1870s, the wealthiest and most powerful Bolivian baron was the impressively mustachioed Nicolás Suárez. Together with his family – collectively known as Casa Suárez or Suárez Hermanos & Co – he controlled most aspects of the life in the Bolivian Amazon, as well as in huge tracts of modern-day Peru and Brazil. The youngest of eight siblings, Suárez was born in 1851 in Portachuelo, a small town north of Santa Cruz, and brought up on a cattle ranch near Trinidad. His family had trading and money-lending interests, which grew steadily as the 19th century progressed.

Suárez initially worked with his brothers buying and selling goods such as animal skins and the quinine-rich bark of the cinchona tree. But in 1882 he established his first rubber-trading estate at a site named Cachuela Esperanza (Rapids of Hope), which overlooked a treacherous set of cataracts on the Beni river known as Hell's Cauldron, around 400 km north of Trinidad. Suárez had almost drowned here previously after his boat capsized, but knew a valuable location when he saw one.

A few hours' sail beyond the rapids is the confluence of the Beni and Mamoré rivers. Together they form the Madeira River, which stretches for almost 1,500 km and is the biggest tributary of the Amazon. From this strategic position, Suárez effectively controlled the key route between the rubber plantations of Bolivia and Brazil. This allowed him to monopolise transportation services and charge high tariffs on imports: a bottle of beer in a neighbouring settlement was 40 times more expensive than one in a London pub, according to a contemporary account.

Cachuela Esperanza became the headquarters of Suárez Hermanos & Co's rapidly expanding empire, which according to some estimates spanned around 70,000 sq km – three and a half times the size of Wales – and had around 10,000 workers at its height. There were grand brick-and-timber mansions for the family and their European senior staff and a hotel made of Canadian pine, as well as workshops, offices, a church, a jail, a theatre and cinema, tennis courts, and a British-built train to transport cargo. Cachuela Esperanza also had one of the continent's most modern hospitals – it was staffed with Swiss and German doctors, had Bolivia's first X-ray machine, and attracted patients from far and wide.

From here Suárez Hermanos & Co quickly came to dominate the Bolivian rubber trade, controlling 'all aspects of the supply chain', as Kathryn Lehman noted in a 2014 article for *The Appendix* magazine. As well as financial interests in mines, railways, and real estate around the world, the family – like Simón Iturri Patiño – moved into banking and made loans to the Bolivian government, which helped to cement a growing political influence. By the start of the 20th century the family was one of the richest in the Amazon. They had an office at 12 Fenchurch Street in the City of London – Suárez's eldest brother Francisco was for a time Bolivia's consul-general in the UK, a position he used to forge profitable business and political connections – and owned expensive properties in Hampstead.

In the 1910s, US journalist Charles Johnson Post travelled through Suárez territory and was shocked by the brutal feudal system he encountered. The rubber tappers, he wrote in *Across the Andes*, are 'in effect, in a state of slavery … The debt system prevails … [He] never gets free.' Violence was used to maintain the status quo. In one *barraca*, Post recorded 'stocks, with the rows of leg-holes meeting in a pair of great mahogany beams. A pile of chain-and-bar leg-irons … and a twisted bull-hide whip'. The *patrones* who ran the plantations were in little better condition, he added, describing 'a bare-footed, cotton-dressed over-lord who was scarcely distinguishable from his own debt-slaves. And he, in his turn, was in almost hopeless debt to the

commission-houses, who hold him by their yearly advances in trade.'
At the top of the pile, in debt to no one, was Casa Suárez.

***

The indigenous peoples of the Amazon paid the greatest price for the
profits of Casa Suárez and their counterparts. In 1886, a messianic
shaman in Trinidad named Andrés Guayocho led a non-violent
revolt, urging his fellow Moxeños to leave the city and establish new
communities where they could be free of prejudice, persecution, and
exploitation. In response, Suárez and other members of Trinidad's
rubber elite formed a so-called 'war committee'. The revolt was
violently put down, the rebellious Moxeños killed or captured, and
Guayocho whipped to death. In 1909, members of the indigenous
Caripuna community ambushed and killed Suárez's brother Gregorio.
A contemporary report of the incident said Gregorio's head was severed
and stuck on top of a spear, before the Caripuna drank his cognac.
In retaliation, wrote J. Valerie Fifer in an essay for the *Journal of Latin
American Studies*, Suárez led a band of men to track down the Caripuna
camp. When they found it, they 'annihilated every man within it'.
According to Vallvé, Suárez virtually wiped out the Caripuna people,
while the rubber boom as a whole redrew the 'ethnic map' of the
Amazon. Many indigenous groups, he wrote, 'disappeared or became
nearly extinct'.

Suárez's reign eventually came to an end. In 1902, he lost a huge
tranche of his empire when Brazil annexed the valuable northern
region of Acre. Although nominally Bolivian territory, Acre at that
time was three months' hard travel from La Paz. Suárez raised a
private army to fight a separatist revolt in the region but to no avail.
Twenty-three years after its coastline was removed following the
War of the Pacific, Bolivia lost a section of the Amazon almost as
big as Britain.

Suárez and the other Amazonian rubber barons later faced
competition from the more productive British-run plantations in
Sri Lanka, Malaysia, and sub-Saharan Africa. Between 1910 and
1915 the price of rubber plunged by around 80 per cent. The death
blow was finally delivered by the development of synthetic rubber
in the 1930s.

Suárez attempted to diversify his business. 'He moved into cattle
ranching and Brazil nuts – we harvest so many of them they should
be called "Bolivia nuts",' said my guide Lyliam. But it was not enough
to stem the decline. Unlike his contemporaries, and indeed much of
his own family, Suárez at least survived into old age, dividing his time
between Hampstead and Bolivia – 'I feel closer to England [than La Paz]',

he once said. He died at home in Cachuela Esperanza in 1940 at the age of 89. Twelve years later, revolution swept through Bolivia and the new government confiscated what remained of the Casa Suárez fortune. In 1961, the company – which was once worth as much as £10 million – was wound up with assets totalling just £1,500.

Cachuela Esperanza became a Bolivian naval base, before falling into disrepair. Ecotourism ventures were mooted as a potential saviour for the town, but failed to get off the ground. The population dwindled to 200 inhabitants and the once-grand buildings were swallowed up by the jungle. 'I went a few years ago, and it was amazing, like a museum' said Lyliam. 'But most of it has now burned down. Some slash-and-burn got out of hand. Terrible. Only the church survived.' Suárez's tomb also remains standing. It describes him as a 'heroic patriot and eminent industrial progressive'. On the rapids that helped make his fortune, meanwhile, there are plans for a massive hydro-electric dam.

Despite the horrors of his reign Suárez has managed to retain something of a romantic image as a frontiersman and foresighted businessman in the Beni. During my stay in Trinidad, I often heard the phrase 'in the time of Suárez'. It was used in the same way the British talk about the Second World War, a defining, almost mythical period whose impact continues to be felt many decades on. 'The family owned everything round here,' said Lyliam. 'Were they popular? Well, they did some terrible things but people didn't have much choice. Today, their descendants are still proud to have the Suárez name."

***

We drove back into Trinidad from Laguna Suárez. On the edge of the city I saw growing informal settlements, home to predominantly Quechua and Aymara-speaking migrants who had arrived over the last 15 years, often from mining areas in the Andes, in search of work. 'Life is easy here,' said Lyliam dismissively. 'It is easy to hunt for your food and do nothing.' Geraldine pointed out a row of garages and shops selling building supplies. 'Some of these businesses are just fronts to launder money from selling drugs,' she claimed. 'That's why all the things they sell are so cheap – they don't need to make a profit on them. You can get anything here, marijuana, cocaine, pills, whatever.'

I had the evening to myself, so set off to explore Trinidad. Home to about 100,000 people and built on the familiar Spanish colonial grid system, the city was a mix of ugly concrete blocks, 18th and 19th-century one-storey buildings topped with terracotta-tile roofs, and modern glass constructions housing banks, mobile phone shops and pharmacies. Deep, open sewers separated the road from the pavement; they appear to function as stinking, sludge-filled insect incubators. The pavements themselves were shaded by overhanging roofs to provide protection from sun and rain. Everyone in the city appeared to own a motorbike and be driving them at the same time. Just off the main square, I spotted a faded 'Suárez Hermanos' sign on the side of a building that had been repurposed as a school. In the playground a group of children who ranged wildly in height contested a furious game of basketball in the sticky heat.

***

On my final morning, Lyliam picked me up at my hotel and drove me back to Loma Suárez, from where I had caught a boat to the Chuchini nature reserve earlier in my trip. The small town took its name from one of the Llanos de Moxos' ancient earthworks, a man-made hill originally called Loma Monovi and later Loma Ayacucho. It was subsequently bought by the Suárez family. At the base of the *loma*, they built a grand mansion with whitewashed walls, red-tiled roof, elegant verandas, and a vague neoclassical air, before surrounding it with imported palm trees. Rómulo, one of Nicolás Suárez's brothers, was based here, Lyliam explained, and turned the area into a cattle-ranch, farm, factory, and administrative headquarters for the company, producing essential supplies for Cachuela Esperanza.

Today, the mansion and its grounds, which remain in immaculate condition, are part of a college owned by the Bolivian Navy, which has several bases in the Amazon and around Lake Titicaca, though no direct access to the sea. Outside the main entrance was the black-and-grey prow of the *Rodolfo Arauz*, a steamship once owned by the Suárez family, while nearby a group of fresh-faced cadets in a starched white uniforms were put through their paces by a perspiring middle-aged sergeant.

After the cadets were dismissed, I climbed up Loma Suárez, a bumpy, grassy mound, to Rómulo's mausoleum. It was a faded grey-white marble tower ringed by a wrought-iron fence and topped with a portrait of an elderly, heavily bearded man gazing stoically out across the Ibare River. Beneath him slumped a pair of mournful angels, unable to contain their grief. Nearby was a playground, empty except for a teenage boy, who sat on a bench pumping out reggaeton tracks from an '80s-style ghetto blaster.

***

The silver, tin, and rubber industries helped to shape modern Bolivia, and their legacies continue to loom large in the national psyche.

For the government of Evo Morales, they were a warning. A desire not to allow Bolivia to be exploited by the present-day equivalents of Simón Iturri Patiño and Nicolás Suárez Callaú – or their multinational counterparts – drove the administration's policies towards one of the most valuable resources of the 21st century.

For the next leg of my journey, I journeyed south to the far reaches of the *altiplano*, where the world's biggest salt flat is home to vast reserves of the element that powers the digital age: lithium.

CHAPTER 4
Flat white

*Lithium and salt: Salar de Uyuni and the
Reserva Nacional de Fauna Andina Eduardo Avaroa*

It wasn't clear when Henrique first fell asleep at the wheel. His hands remained locked in the 10-and-2 position and his light snores were muffled by the creaks of our battered Toyota Land Cruiser as it travelled across the Salar de Uyuni, the largest salt flat on Earth. My fellow passengers and I were bound up against the frigid cold, cocooned in alpaca-wool jumpers, scarves, shawls, socks, gloves and bobble hats, several layers of thermals, trekking jackets zipped up to our noses, and sunglasses to protect our sleepy eyes from the fierce glare. The temperature plunged to -10°C overnight and was slow to bounce back during the morning. Inside the Land Cruiser the windows were frosted and a sheen of ice had silenced the car stereo. Henrique's musical tastes were centred firmly on rock ballads from the 1980s, so this was no great loss.

There were no other vehicles in sight: the same view extended in every direction and only two colours were visible, the blinding white of the salt and the azure blue of the cloudless sky. I found it difficult to get my bearings and was not entirely sure we were actually moving. The vehicle felt as if it was caught in a bubble floating gently above the Salar. At around 8 a.m., a tiny green-grey smudge appeared in the top right corner of the windscreen and slowly grew into a craggy hill dotted with giant cacti. I glanced back through the rear window and was suddenly jolted from my fuzzy, dream-like state: the arcing tyre tracks revealed we had drifted drastically off course.

A jab in the ribs woke Henrique up with a start. He snorted, mumbled a half-hearted apology, and swung the steering wheel sharply to the left. It later emerged our driver had spent the previous night visiting a woman he described as his 'wife' in a nearby village, during which there was little time for sleep. It turned out Henrique had several 'wives' scattered across the region, his job as a tour guide providing a handy cover story to disguise his philandering. Ignoring our complaints, he continued with his nocturnal excursions for the rest of our four-day tour, returning each morning, just before dawn, in a post-coital stupor, with an empty bottle of Gato Negro wine in his hand.

The Salar – Spanish for 'salt flat' – is a remote and dangerous place, so despite our concerns, my group of backpackers had little choice but to stick with Henrique. Yet for the remainder of our trip we set up a rota, taking it in turns to keep him awake at the wheel and the rest of us alive, paying little attention to the otherworldly surroundings. I didn't know it at the time but this salt-encrusted landscape is part of the Lithium Triangle, an area that – according to US Geological Survey data from 2021 – contains around half of the world's reserves of a resource dubbed 'white petroleum' or 'white gold', a vital component of much of the 21st-century tech we take for granted.

***

A decade on from that first visit in 2004, I returned to the Salar de Uyuni for a closer look at the lithium industry and the wider challenges facing the region. My train, the *Expreso del Sur*, pulled into the isolated town of Uyuni, 315 km south of Oruro on the eastern edge of the salt flat, at 11.20 p.m., an hour behind schedule. I climbed out of the carriage into the bitter night air and collected my rucksack from a pile the conductor had unceremoniously dumped on the platform. The wind lashed dust into my eyes as I stumbled out of the station and down a long, deserted avenue, where flickering street lights barely pierced the gloom. Dividing the road in two was a series of modernist statues of miners and soldiers, which loomed menacingly out of the darkness, alongside a collection of vintage train carriages and engines. When I found my guesthouse, a few blocks away, the lights were off and it took five minutes of persistent knocking before the owner unbolted the door and let me in.

If anything, Uyuni appeared even more desolate in the daylight. In the morning I woke to the plaintive bleating of a lone sheep, yet when I drew the curtains all I could see was a building site. As I wondered where the animal could possibly be, a plane roared alarmingly low overhead, rattling my room as it came into land at Uyuni's airstrip. Situated 3,668 m above sea level, the town is ferociously cold and encircled by steppe and salt flats that steadily encroach through gritty, near-constant gusts of wind. 'Uyuni' in Aymara loosely translates as 'place with a cemetery', a title that felt grimly appropriate. The town was a muddle of unevenly paved streets lined with simple homes and felt largely devoid of life. Beyond heavily-laden jeeps and Land Cruisers ferrying tourists to and from the Salar de Uyuni, there was no traffic.

'[Uyuni] is just a small mining town set out in the middle of a flat, desolate plain, built of earth and mostly roofed with iron,' wrote

Lionel Portman in *Three Asses in Bolivia* in the 1910s, a description that remains broadly accurate more than a century on. 'What gives [Uyuni] so high a rank of beastliness in the eyes of all who know it is that during the winter the prevailing wind comes to it over a gigantic expanse of salt desert, whereon and wherewith the snow makes the best freezing mixture you can possibly imagine; and so the cold is such as can hardly be equalled in the temperate zone.'

Central Uyuni was at least busy. There were gatherings of boisterous school kids, backpackers in the regulation uniform of Gore-Tex jackets, sunglasses, and alpaca-wool bobble hats, and local women with pampered spaniels and golden retrievers. A security guard stood with folded arms outside the bank, a pistol poking out of a thigh-holder. Slabs of beef hung from hooks in an open-fronted butcher's shop, a thin trail of blood congealing on the street in front.

***

My guide Álvaro and driver Efrain arrived promptly at 9 a.m. to take me on a four-day journey across the far southwest of Bolivia, taking in the Salar and the isolated Reserva Nacional de Fauna Andina Eduardo Avaroa. (The reserve is named after a Bolivian hero of the 1879–84 War of the Pacific, in which the country lost its entire coastline to Chile, a lasting sore. Avaroa's last words, when surrounded by Chilean forces, were reportedly: 'Surrender? Your grandmother should surrender, you bastard.') Álvaro was a chatty 31-year-old, his eyes red from a broken night caring for his nine-month-old daughter. Originally from Cochabamba, he had spent the last five years leading tours of the Salar, but still struggled with the climate. 'You never get used to the cold,' he said, rubbing his gloved hands together vigorously. Efrain, younger and rather taciturn, had grown up in Uyuni. Crucially, given my experience with Henrique a decade before, he appeared well-rested and hangover free.

As we drove out of town, Álvaro provided me with a brief history lesson. Uyuni was now home to some 32,000 people, most of them reliant directly or indirectly on tourism, he said, but in its early 20th-century heyday the population was more than twice the size. Founded in 1889, the town was once a major transport hub. It sat on a railway line running from the Pacific port of Antofagasta – in the heart of a valuable nitrate-producing region and part of Bolivia until Chile claimed it during the War of the Pacific – to La Paz that carried nitrates, copper and other resources. 'Uyuni had been Bolivia's main gateway to the outside world ... its planners had envisaged a thriving cosmo-politan centre symbolizing progress, modernity and the country's hopes for a prosperous, industrial future,' wrote Michael Jacobs, whose grandfather worked as an engineer on the line in the 1910s, in *Ghost Train Through The Andes*.

Success, however, was fleeting. On the outskirts of town we stopped at the Cementerio de Trenes, a poignant reminder of Uyuni's decline. Amid a litter of broken glass, rusted beer cans and empty plastic bottles, the 'Train Cemetery' contained the remains of dozens of steam locomotives, wagons and carriages, many of them made in the UK. The lingering effects of the Great Depression combined with the invention of artificial fertilisers in the 1940s fatally damaged South America's nitrates industry. There was a sharp fall in demand, Uyuni and the railway became increasingly redundant. The once-vital trains were abandoned on the edge of town. Cannibalised for scrap, covered with graffiti and assaulted by the elements, they are slowly rusting away.

Uyuni only really started to recover from this body blow in the 1980s, as its namesake salt flat gradually developed into one of Bolivia's major tourist destinations, particularly with backpackers. Today, a truncated section of the railway line – running between Oruro in the north and Villazón on the Argentine border in the south, and calling at Uyuni en route – transports thousands of travellers every year (at least until the Covid-19 pandemic hit). Once they arrive in Uyuni there are scores of hotels, hostels, guesthouses, tour companies, restaurants, cafes, and bars to cater to their needs.

Over the last 15 years or so national and global interest has increasingly turned to what lies beneath the surface of the Salar. The salt flat contains an estimated 20-30 per cent of the world's lithium, a highly reactive element that helps to power the modern world. It is an essential component of the lightweight rechargeable lithium-ion batteries used in mobile phones, laptops, and electric cars, as well as to store energy produced by solar panels, wind turbines and other renewable sources. Lithium is also used in the thermonuclear process and to treat conditions such as bipolar disorder and depression.

There have been extraction projects in the neighbouring regions of northern Chile and northwest Argentina – the two other sides of the Lithium Triangle – since the 1980s. But it was only in the late 2000s, following the election of Evo Morales and with growing global awareness of the technological possibilities of the resource, that the government showed any real interest in its own deposits. Morales claimed Bolivia would never lose 'sovereignty' over the resource and must develop its own industry to both extract and process the metal in the country. Theoretically, the Salar's reserves – which are thought to be around 21 million tonnes and worth billions of dollars – could have

as seismic effect on the country in the 21st century as Potosí's silver
500 years ago.

In a much-quoted *New Yorker* article from 2010, author Lawrence
Wright speculated whether the global desire for lithium could earn
Bolivia the dubious title of 'the Saudi Arabia of the electric-car era'.
Since then demand for the metal has exploded, as increasing numbers
of countries announced plans to phase out petrol and diesel cars in
favour of hybrid and electric vehicles over the decades to come. To put
that in context, a single Tesla Model S uses 63 kg of lithium in its
battery alone, according to research by Goldman Sachs.

***

Spanning more than 10,500 sq km and flanked by mountains and
volcanoes, the Salar de Uyuni is a hallucinatory landscape. The salt
flat is so big – almost the size of Jamaica – it can be seen from space.
When astronaut Neil Armstrong gazed back at the Earth in July 1969
he assumed this vast white expanse was an ice field or a giant glacier.
My first sight of the Salar was a thick white band between the dusty
brown soil and the cyan sky. As we drove towards it the band gradually
became thicker until there was only white and blue ahead of us.
It was the dry season, which runs roughly from May until November.
During this period evaporation forms a network of pentagons and
hexagons, each one roughly 50 cm to 1 m in diameter, on the
surface of the Salar; from a distance they reminded me of fish scales.
By contrast, in the wet season, flooding transforms it into a giant
mirror (and renders much of it off limits to visitors).

The salt crust is 10 m deep in places and the Salar as a whole
is so flat you can see the curvature of the Earth, something NASA
takes advantage of to calibrate its satellites. Photographers use the
apparently endless horizon to play around with perspective and create
optical illusions – for example, a regular-sized person in the foreground
of the photo holding a seemingly miniaturised person (who is actually
standing way in the background) in the palm of their hand. There are
no roads, just faint tyre tracks and wave-like patterns caused by the
gusting winds. The monotony is mesmerising.

On the shoreline of the Salar, Efrain pulled into the village of
Colchani, a mix of ramshackle single-storey buildings and ruins; it
was hard to distinguish one from the other. Pigs drank from puddles,
stray dogs roamed about, and crude blocks of salt crystals were piled
up by the side of the road. The few people visible were engaged in
arduous tasks: a group of labourers hauled bags of concrete out of
a truck; an ancient woman, bent double and holding an upturned
plastic bottle behind her as if it were a tail, stumbled along a path;

a gang of boys took turns to thump a partially deflated football against a wall. Although now on the backpacker circuit – there were numerous stalls laden with alpaca-wool clothes and trinkets fashioned from salt – Colchani's focus remained on a local industry that long predates lithium and tourism: salt.

In the past salt was transported on llama caravans and traded with communities hundreds of kilometres away for coca leaves, grain, wool, water and other items. Salt gatherers known as *saleros* are still a common sight in and around the Salar, as are the waist-high pyramids of dried salt they produce. Wearing wide-brimmed hats and balaclavas to protect them from the sun, they hack away at the salt with heavy pickaxes. It is back-breaking labour for little reward, as I discovered when I visited one of Colchani's small-scale salt factories. The owner Don Juan, a burly, gregarious man, told me production here was still done by hand and that the salt was mixed with iodine, something landlocked Bolivians often lack in their diets. His factory can produce as much as 5,000 kg a day, yet the price of salt during the week I visited was only $0.04 per kilo. Salt production, it was clear, was not a profitable business.

The work of the *saleros* is an important part of the Salar's history and present; a short journey northwest gave me a glimpse of the industry likely to shape its future. Efrain drove across the bleached landscape until a neat grid of rectangular pools came into view. They were the size and shape of tennis courts and half-filled with a pale turquoise liquid. A jumble of overlaid tyre tracks led off into the distance. We got out of the vehicle and Álvaro pointed down: 'Look at the lithium. It is so light that it floats on the water.'

***

Swirling beneath the Salar is a sea of brine rich in minerals and metals, including magnesium, potassium and, most notably, lithium. To extract it, miners wearing considerably more modern protective gear than the *saleros* drill through the crust of the salt flat and pump the liquid up to the surface. The brine is then moved through a series of evaporation pools, some of which are as large as six football pitches. Over a period of 12-24 months, the water evaporates, impurities are removed, and the resulting mixture is taken to a nearby plant to be refined and purified. This produces lithium carbonate, a dry, white salt that is then shovelled into sacks by workers wearing full-face masks, hard hats, jumpsuits, and thick rubber gloves that stretch up to their elbows.

As the Bolivian government has discovered, lithium mining is expensive and technically complex, particularly in the extreme conditions of the

Salar de Uyuni. The evaporation process takes longer here because the salt flat is colder and much wetter (though rainfall has reduced in recent years) than many other lithium-rich areas such as Chile's Salar de Atacama, which is located in the world's driest non-polar desert. The brine in the Salar de Uyuni is also higher in impurities, particularly magnesium, which further pushes up costs. Moreover, the region's isolation, generally poor infrastructure, and lack of direct access to Pacific ports make transportation much more challenging and expensive.

Then there is the environmental impact. Lithium has a vital role to play in the global transition to a low-carbon economy – something that is particularly pertinent for Bolivia as the country has already been badly hit by the climate crisis. Although demand for the silvery-white metal slowed in 2020 because of the pandemic, it is forecast to increase significantly over the coming years. Yet although the Bolivian authorities say lithium extraction will only take place on small sections of the Salar, this could still have serious negative impacts on the salt flat as a whole and the wider region. As well as producing huge amounts of waste materials, the process is highly water intensive. An estimated 500,000 gallons are required to produce a tonne of lithium carbonate and there are fears local communities will lose out as rivers and aquifers are diverted. Recent devastating droughts in the *altiplano* have only heightened these fears.

There are also concerns about air pollution, soil and water contamination, and the impact of large-scale infrastructure development, including new roads, power lines, and processing plants. Friends of the Earth has warned that the global lithium industry can have 'significant environmental and social impacts', including 'water pollution and depletion', soil damage, 'air contamination', and the release of toxic chemicals that 'harm communities, ecosystems and food production'.

***

After a night at one of the region's 'salt hotels' – the roof, walls, beds, tables, chairs, and even the wonky pool table were made from the substance – Álvaro took me out onto the Salar. My feet crunched across the surface as if walking over compacted ice. We were almost 3,700 m above sea level, the sun beamed down like a spotlight and the whole scene was dazzlingly white – it was easily the brightest place I've ever been. Protected by 50-factor sun cream and sunglasses, we broke through the crust and reached into the milky brine below. Out of it I fished gem-like crystals, each one made up of a collection of perfectly smooth cubes of salt.

We drove on to Isla Incahuasi (Incahuasi means 'House of the Inca' in Quechua), the largest of several 'islands' on the Salar. A rocky promontory emerging out of the salt flat, Incahuasi is the peak of an ancient volcano. Once a rest stop and trading post for indigenous communities from across the southwest of Bolivia, the island is studded with large cacti, which are khaki green and cream and grow out of the volcanic earth at a rate of a centimetre a year. The tallest extant cactus was over 9 m in height, making it approximately 900 years old. A 1,200-year-old cactus once stood here, explained Don Alfredo, the island's elderly caretaker, but was toppled by a storm in 2007. He had been the sole permanent resident of Isla Incahuasi for more than 35 years, with only a menagerie of llamas, rabbit-like rodents known as vizcachas, finches and – during the summer – giant hummingbirds for company.

Over a packed lunch of fried chicken and quinoa soup, a staple meal on Salar tours, Álvaro talked about the salt flat's mythical origins. According to one of the legends, the Salar was the result of a torrid love triangle. When a mountain goddess, Yana Pollera, gave birth, two male volcanoes named Tunupa and Q'osqo fought a violent paternity battle. Yana Pollera sent the baby away to the west for safety, but grew increasingly concerned: how would her child survive without her? In a desperate attempt to provide her baby with nourishment she flooded the plain between them with a torrent of breast milk, into which she cried salty tears.

Scientists provide a less evocative explanation. The Salar was once the deepest part of a group of ancient, salt-water mega-lakes that covered much of the *altiplano*. Approximately 10,000–12,000 years ago, the last of these lakes evaporated for good, leaving behind a bed of salt. The fossilised algae on many of the rocks on Isla Incahuasi were a reminder of the region's origins. I followed a trail to the summit of the island and gazed west at a straight line that ran across the distant mountainside, roughly 70 m above the surface of the Salar. This band marks the shoreline of one of the ancient lakes, Álvaro explained, while to the north was a range of snowy peaks, including Tunupa, lonely and now extinct.

Later we left the Salar and followed a muddy, undulating path to a set of caves cut into the side of an imposing ridge. Walls of loose stones protected the entrances, forming low arched doorways and porthole-shaped windows. One of the caves contained the mummified remains of people who are believed to have been members of Aymara royal families who fled south to escape Inca invaders around 600 years ago. Most of the region's cave shrines had been looted but this one was largely intact. Inside a mummified puma hung disconcertingly above the entrance and three full skeletons, including a mother cradling a baby, lay on the floor. The skulls had been intentionally deformed, giving them a distended extra-terrestrial appearance. 'There are three theories about why they did this to themselves,' said Álvaro. 'One: to make themselves stand out as religious and royal leaders. Two: so that they were, literally, closer to the gods – the heads pointing up into the sky. Three: that they were aliens.' The tomb was still used for religious ceremonies, remnants of which were scattered across the ground: crisp coca leaves, miniature banknotes, coins, coloured streamers, and empty beer bottles. One of the skulls had a cigarette inserted between its chipped front teeth.

***

The next morning we drove south towards the Reserva Nacional de Fauna Andina Eduardo Avaroa, which is only accessible on guided tours in sturdy 4x4s. Bordering Chile and Argentina, this remote protected area spans 7,150 sq km and is home to numerous rare and threatened species, including Andean, James's, and Chilean flamingoes, pumas, and vicuñas, which are wild relatives of llamas and alpacas. As we gained in altitude, swapping the salt for tracts of sticky mud, the temperature dropped and the wind picked up. Snow materialised on the hillsides ahead and grey clouds massed in the sky. A stricken tractor lay on its side in an ice-flecked stream and above it circled an Andean condor, whose 3-m-plus wingspan makes it the world's largest bird of prey.

On the outskirts of San Juan del Rosario, a small town with a simple church, cemetery, windswept football pitch, and unadorned concrete homes whose corrugated iron roofs were held in place by heavy rocks piled on top, we came across the two main forms of employment in the region beyond salt production and tourism. A team of local women, spanning every age between teenager and pensioner, tended fields of quinoa, which is known locally as the 'golden grain' and is one of the few crops hardy enough to endure the sub-zero temperatures, periodic droughts and salt-rich soils. Harvest time was fast approaching and the stems of the plants provided the area's dull earth tones with a welcome flash of colour, ranging from green-yellow to pink and purple. Nearby three men attempted to herd two dozen independent-minded llamas, a source of wool, meat, and transportation, along a stony path. Bright tassels were fastened to the ears of the camelids to signify ownership and mark religious festivals and other celebrations.

There is also another less wholesome business in this part of the world. Over the last few decades, said Álvaro, smugglers have replaced the salt traders who once traversed the deep south. Around a quarter of foreign cars in Bolivia are thought to have been smuggled in across the region from neighbouring countries, predominantly Chile, with marijuana and cocaine travelling in the opposite direction. The isolated Bolivia-Chile border posts are easy to avoid and though many smugglers die after getting stranded or lost, the trade remains lucrative. 'That's why you see so many Mercedes, BMW and Lexus cars in Uyuni,' said Álvaro.

South of San Juan del Rosario, we crossed the Salar de Chiguana. At 415 sq km, this salt flat is only a fraction of the size of the Salar de Uyuni, but still considerably bigger than a country such as Malta. In the distance, the conical Ollagüe volcano straddled the Bolivia-Chile border, a wisp of smoke corkscrewing out of its 5,865 m summit. Dark clouds soon enveloped it, then the surrounding mountains, and finally us. The Toyota Land Cruiser rattled across the railway line that once ran all the way to Chile's Pacific coast and onto a sterile ancient lava field pockmarked with chunks of black volcanic rock. Near the base of Ollagüe a rusted bulldozer marked the entrance to an abandoned sulphur mine, a reminder that mineral extraction is not a new phenomenon in this region. Above it a yellow-brown tear of sulphur trickled down the slope.

We stopped at the Valle de Rocas, a breathless valley 4,500 m above sea level that takes its name from its collection of surreal, wind-blasted rock formations. The ashy earth was covered with spiky-haired shrubs resembling the hair of troll dolls. Scattered between them were bright-green llareta plants, which looked like brain coral covered in moss and can live for thousands of years. Willowy vicuñas and skittish rheas, large flightless birds distantly related to ostriches, eyed us warily. By the time we reached Laguna Cañapa, where James's flamingos waded through the sulphurous, semi-frozen water, the weather was deteriorating rapidly. Within 15 minutes, light snow flurries turned into a bombardment of hailstone the size of golf balls. A thick layer of them soon covered the ground.

Entering the reserve via an already treacherous 4,000-m pass was now impossible: the snow meant we could get stranded or worse; one group of tourists, it emerged, was already missing. So instead we joined a convoy of the remaining tourist jeeps and retraced our route. The 'white wind', as Efrain called it, whipped up the powder, reducing visibility to little more than a few metres. Midway up a particularly steep incline, the lead vehicle ground to a halt, its tyres wedged into a bank of snow, obliging us to dig it out. Several other vehicles soon required similar assistance. Progress was painstaking but eventually, as we descended, the weather brightened, the snow thinned and the sun re-emerged.

The convoy broke up and we headed along a paved road to Mallku Villamar. A ghostly figure, head covered by a brown shawl, guarded the road into the tiny hamlet. We paid him a few *bolivianos* to raise the barrier – a frayed length of rope – to allow us in. The road immediately plunged into a stream strewn with mini icebergs. Our lodge was a thin-walled construction in which the only source of warmth was a small stove emitting more smoke than heat. It quickly expired and I went to bed early, wearing all the clothes I possessed. Squeezed into a sleeping bag, I pulled over a silver-foil emergency blanket that crackled like autumn leaves whenever I made the slightest movement. At 2 a.m. I woke to discover the temperature inside the room had dropped to –21°C. The rest of the night passed agonisingly slowly until a few weak beams of light finally broke through the bed sheet that functioned as a makeshift curtain.

***

The next morning the weather had improved enough to allow us to visit the reserve's biggest lake. At an altitude of almost 4,300 m, the salmon-pink, ice-frosted Laguna Colorada was buffeted by winds so strong – perhaps 60 km an hour – I could lean into them and still remain upright. The temperature remained well below zero, but the sun gave off a piercing glare. The colony of James's and Chilean flamingos seemed oblivious to the harsh conditions, picking contentedly at the beta-carotene-rich algae that gave both the lake and the birds their distinctive coral hue. One nonchalantly took off and flew hard against the wind, an airborne salmon swimming upstream, before being swept back to the lake. 'They are strong birds, though,' said Álvaro. 'Sometimes the lake freezes overnight, trapping their legs in the ice. But they wait patiently for the ice to melt and get back to eating.'

As we left the weather started to deteriorate again. I gazed back at the mountain range we failed to cross the previous day, which was frosted like a Christmas cake. The grey desert around the lake quickly gave way to an alien terrain of ochre-red earth rippled with curls of snow. It felt like winter on Mars. The 'white wind' picked up again, obscuring our views. By the time it died down we were in another landscape, one increasingly lunar in appearance. The earth was ridged, and brown and grey dirt was thrown up as spiralling clouds.

We passed a borax mine with a row of huts and a football pitch scratched into the dirt, but no workers. On the ground were white, gravelly patches of the mineral – which is used in detergents and cosmetics – as well as green pools of its liquid form. As we descended a rocky dirt track, shards of ice crackling beneath the wheels, a careering jeep emerged suddenly from a dust storm, narrowly missing us.

Just beyond, near a spring, was a small shrine to two backpackers who died after their vehicle span into a chasm.

By the time we got back to Mallku Villamar and checked into another, much more comfortable lodge, a storm was rolling in. We spent the afternoon swapping stories. As usual, Álvaro had the best. Around 70 km west of Mallku Villamar, he told me, was the solitary hamlet of San Vicente. This was where Robert LeRoy Parker and Harry Alonzo Longabaugh, better known as Butch Cassidy and the Sundance Kid, finally got their comeuppance. On 3 November 1908, the duo intercepted a mining company payroll, stole $90,000 and fled with a band of miners and soldiers in hot pursuit. Three days later in San Vicente they were killed in a shoot-out; the police report suggested Butch shot his fatally wounded partner before turning the gun on himself. Perhaps inevitably, the account is contested. Some claim the pair escaped or that it was a case of mistaken identity. Over the following decades, history, legend, Hollywood and wishful thinking blended together.

As we talked endless waves of grit and hail hammered on the windows and the walls shook violently, as if on the verge of collapse.

***

On the drive back to Uyuni we passed San Cristóbal, one of the largest open-cast tin, silver, and zinc mines in the world. Marked by a great cloud of dust and jagged claw-marks on the mountainside, the complex accounts for roughly half of Bolivia's mining exports. It also reportedly sucks up around 10 per cent of the country's power supply, uses an estimated 50,000 litres of water a day, and generates – most significantly for its operator, the Sumitomo Corporation of Japan – some $14 million a week. When the mine opened in the 1990s, the original San Cristóbal town was moved 21 km to a new site. Its colonial-era church was dismantled, packed up and then carefully rebuilt stone by stone. The town now looked smarter than others in the region: fewer half-finished buildings, shops and restaurants that were actually open, pedestrians on the street, and smooth tarmacked roads. But the mine has also been the site of significant protests and strikes over pay and working conditions.

Around 60 km northwest of San Cristóbal, on the fringes of the Salar, is Llipi, a state-run pilot plant that has been producing relatively small amounts of lithium carbonate and carrying out related research projects since 2013. All the staff at the plant are Bolivian, though few are from the Uyuni region, Álvaro explained. Llipi was a key part of the Morales government's lithium industrialisation policy. In contrast with the country's silver, tin, and rubber industries, which enriched a tiny – and often foreign or overseas-based – elite, Morales asserted Bolivia would capitalise on its lithium in a way that actually benefited ordinary Bolivians. Rather than simply mining and exporting the raw material, Bolivia would develop its own manufacturing capacity, creating well-paid jobs, boosting skills and generating wealth for the country as a whole.

Achieving these objectives has proved incredibly difficult. After Llipi, a state-run lithium battery factory was set up in La Palca, north of the city of Sucre, but its output remains low. Progress lagged behind ambition and the government started to search for a foreign partner to help develop the industry. Eventually, in December 2018, a deal was signed with German firm ACI Systems to exploit the Salar's reserves. Under this joint venture, the state-owned company Yacimientos de Litio Bolivianos (YLB) and ACI Systems – which had limited experience in the lithium industry – would build a large lithium hydroxide plant and a factory to produce batteries for electric vehicles. For a reported 49 per cent stake in the venture, the German company would invest $1.3 billion.

In a bullish interview with *National Geographic* in early 2019, vice-president Álvaro García Linera asserted lithium would soon be 'the engine of our economy', whisking Bolivians 'out of poverty, guaranteeing their stability in the middle class, and training them in scientific and technological fields so that they become part of the intelligentsia in the global economy'. The ACI Systems deal was followed by a joint venture between YLB and a Chinese company to exploit lithium reserves on two other salt flats in the southwest of the country, Coipasa and Pastos Grandes. (By 2025, China will require 800,000 tonnes of lithium a year for its electric car industry, according to estimates.) Later in 2019 Morales held talks with Vladimir Putin over potential Russian involvement in Bolivia's lithium industry. In early October, La Palca launched the first 50-strong batch of Bolivian-made electric cars, which sold out in less than a week. Morales was photographed driving one of the dune buggy-like vehicles at the opening of a new lithium-focused education centre in Potosí.

Yet his plans were already crumbling. Arguments raged between an array of local and regional interest groups over the ACI Systems deal: would it actually benefit communities in and around the Salar de Uyuni? What about the wider region and, indeed, the country as a whole? How should the profits be shared? Was the government giving away too much to a foreign company? Would enough of the industrial process actually take place in Bolivia? There were protests, blockades, and even hunger strikes. The results of the 20 October 2019 election were contested: Morales' party, the Movimiento al Socialismo (MAS), was accused of electoral fraud and protests and riots broke out across the country. In early November, the government annulled the ACI Systems deal. Within a week, amid intensifying violence on the streets and political turmoil, Morales was ousted and replaced by a right-wing interim administration that stubbornly clung to power.

Claims, counter-claims, and conspiracy theories over the role lithium played in the downfall of Morales began to swirl. He claimed the US government was involved and was eager to get its hands on Bolivia's reserves. 'I'm absolutely convinced it's a coup against lithium,' the exiled former president told Agence France-Presse, though the reasons for his downfall appear more varied and complex. A prominent right-wing politician tweeted Elon Musk, co-founder of electric car manufacturer Tesla, and urged him to 'build a Gigafactory in the Salar de Uyuni' to produce lithium batteries. YLB went through three different managers in the space of two months. Amid an embittered political, social, and economic crisis, Bolivia then faced a public health emergency when the pandemic struck.

The future of the country's lithium industry and the Salar de Uyuni remains uncertain. But one way or another, change is coming to the region and its inhabitants.

***

From Uyuni I travelled north to La Paz to catch a flight to the Amazon, a region with a completely different climate, landscape, history, and culture. Yet its inhabitants face many of the same challenges as their counterparts in Bolivia's far south.

CHAPTER 5
Amazon primed

*Development projects, ecotourism, and the climate
crisis: Rurrenabaque, Parque Nacional Madidi,
and Lago Poopó*

The Yacuma River was the colour and consistency of over-stewed tea.
Perched on the prow of our motorboat, I peered into the cloudy water
and weighed up recent events. It was my first visit to the Bolivian
Amazon in 2004 and over the previous three days I'd taken a guided
tour through the rainforests of Parque Nacional Madidi, the most
biodiverse protected area on Earth, and across the waterways, swamps,
and seasonally flooded grasslands of the neighbouring Pampas
del Yacuma. That morning alone we'd seen scores of black caimans
sunning themselves on riverbanks or raising their prehistoric-looking
snouts and beady eyes a fraction above the surface of the water.
My guide, Andrés, had caught half a dozen piranhas, and then there
was the anaconda – 6 m long, coiled like a Cumberland sausage, body
as thick as my thigh. Tethered to a tree outside a hut, the snake was
subdued, vulnerable even. In those artificial circumstances it was easy
to be brave, tip-toe over and fleetingly touch its surprisingly firm, cool
skin. The thought of encountering one in the water, on the other hand,
filled me with terror.

Andrés gave me a gentle nudge. It was safe to swim in this part
of the river, he insisted. Are you coming in too? I asked but he
just smiled and remained seated. The water was perfectly still. Too
still, I thought suspiciously, as a giant red-tailed dragonfly – more
dragon than fly – buzzed around my head. I contemplated the embar-
rassment of returning to my seat, squeezing awkwardly past my fellow
backpackers, versus the prospect of being eaten alive. Pride overcame
reticence, just. As I entered the silty water, my toes brushed against
something slimy – a reed probably but in that instance I couldn't
be sure – and I almost jumped straight back into the boat. Then there
was a flash of movement in the thick pampas grass fringing the river
and a pod of five dolphins – locally known as *bufeos* – appeared.
The biggest was 2.5 m long with a mottled pink-and-grey body and
flat dorsal fin. Found across the Amazon region and consuming

everything from turtles to crabs, *bufeos* are grey-blue as youngsters but gradually change colour as they get older, with pink scar tissue – often resulting from fights – increasingly covering their bodies, particularly on the males.

The dolphins swam towards me, submerged, and for a few seconds all was calm. Two other travellers slipped into the water beside me and we instinctively clung together, half-anticipating a nip on the toes. Suddenly there was a splash behind me. I spun round to see a dolphin briefly pop above the surface. It then dived, swam beneath my feet and re-emerged behind me. I swung round to face it, but the dolphin reversed its manoeuvre and appeared behind me again. As I turned round for a third time, it twisted its torso and used its fluke to splash me in the face, an action that felt deliberately mischievous. Moments later the same dolphin reappeared in front of me, barely a half a metre away, and gazed at me curiously with its gimlet eyes. A staring contest lasted for 10 to 15 seconds. I blinked first. Once again, it ducked under the water and then resurfaced with a twig in its mouth. It waggled the twig briskly from side to side before released it in front of me, as if offering a present. With a final splash, the *bufeo* swam off.

***

During that first visit I had only a limited understanding of the environmental threats facing the Bolivian Amazon, but this soon began to change. Twelve months later, when I was back home in south London, I read about how the region had been hit by a historic drought and then wild fires that spread across 5,000 sq km. These were followed by several extreme floods; the one in 2014 was particularly devastating. Blamed on mass deforestation, unusually heavy rainfall and hydroelectric dams over the border in Brazil, it killed at least 60 people and displaced tens of thousands from their homes.

After coming to power in 2006, President Evo Morales was fond of evoking the sacredness of Pachamama in his rhetoric. In 2010, he hosted the World People's Conference on Climate Change, which brought together representatives of indigenous communities, civil society groups, environmental campaigners, and progressive social movements. Two years later, his government enshrined the Ley de Derechos de la Madre Tierra (Law of Mother Earth), which established a legally enforceable bill of rights for 'Mother Earth'. It recognised Bolivia's susceptibility to climate change, noting in particular the threat posed by 'mega-infrastructure and development projects' to ecosystems and communities. At global summits, Morales blamed capitalism for the climate crisis, called for more ambitious carbon reduction targets, and urged higher-income countries to pay reparations. He also co-sponsored a UN resolution to recognise the right to water and sanitation of all human beings, signed up to the 2015 Paris climate agreement, and warned of the dangers of a 'climate holocaust' if action was not taken. Within international environmental circles, Morales was fêted as a hero, but the green mask soon began to slip.

During his near 14 years in office, agribusiness and hydrocarbons became central to his extractivist economic policy, with serious consequences for areas such as the Amazon. Although continuing to pay lip-service to the Law of Mother Earth, Morales pushed ahead with gas and oil exploration – including in national parks and reserves – and championed a new highway through the Isiboro-Sécure Indigenous Territory and National Park (aka TIPNIS), a protected area in the south of the Amazon. These policies were promoted as essential tools of development, redistribution and poverty alleviation, but prompted mass marches and sustained protests, especially from indigenous communities.

Parque Nacional Madidi, which is home to thousands of different species, was also threatened by plans for one of South America's biggest hydroelectric schemes. I realised that if I wanted to return, I needed to do so as soon as possible.

***

My opportunity came in 2017. The journey started at El Alto airport, on the canyon rim above La Paz. After checking in, I sipped a *cortado* made from coffee beans grown in the Amazon and watched a pan-pipe band march through the terminal, simultaneously playing their instruments and wheeling their luggage. There was no one at the departure gate so I wandered down the tunnel until I found myself on the edge of the runway. A woman in an Amaszonas airline uniform waved away my proffered passport and showed me towards a 19-seater plane. No one checked whether I had a ticket or if my seat belt was fastened. A sign on the wall informed me that if an oxygen mask dropped from the ceiling I should attach it to the tap above the seat. The plane was only half full and I could see the pilot and co-pilot chatting away in the cockpit. It felt like travelling in the 1950s or '60s, before the era of terrorist threats and security checks.

Few flights transport you so rapidly between such sharply contrasting environments as the one from La Paz to the Amazonian town of Rurrenabaque. Although cloud obscured Mount Illimani, El Alto's crowded streets and the barren *altiplano* beyond them stretched out beneath us. The white-tipped Cordillera Real drew closer and the plane was soon parallel with its tallest peaks. Clouds swaddled us for several minutes and by the time we emerged the landscape below had transformed into a wilderness of snow and ice seemingly untouched by humans. After we crested this Andean range, the earth plunged thousands of metres in the form of the lush slopes of the Yungas valleys. Gradually the Amazon appeared, its meandering rivers cutting through a sea of emerald green, largely flat with only a few hilly spurs, the last gasps of the Andean foothills. After 33 minutes, slightly ahead of schedule, we made a bumpy landing at Rurrenabaque's tiny airstrip, a short stretch of tarmac petering out into a grassy track. The terminal was the size of a village hall, with mosquito netting for walls. The pilot smiled and shook my hand. You're lucky, he said, the runway was only paved in 2010. Before then it was really rough.

***

Backed by jungle-clad karst-like hills, Rurrenabaque sits on the banks of the placid, muddy Beni River, a major tributary of the Amazon. Some 260 km northeast of La Paz, it was founded in 1844 on the back of the growing trade in quinine – extracted from the bitter bark of the evergreen cinchona tree, which has been used by indigenous peoples for medicinal purposes for millennia – to treat malaria. But quinine was soon supplanted by a far more valuable commodity: rubber. British explorer Percy Harrison Fawcett visited Rurrenabaque in the early 1900s, a time when the Bolivian Amazon was 'more remote from La Paz than was London'. He was not impressed, dismissively describing the town in his book *Exploration Fawcett* as 'miserable' and complaining that most residents 'appeared to be suffering from one or other of the many diseases common in the interior, such as *beriberi*, *espundia* and malaria'. But everything is relative. After several months of intense hardship deep in the jungle, Fawcett revised his opinion of Rurrenabaque, declaring it a veritable 'metropolis'. (In 1925, he disappeared for good during a quixotic search for what he called the lost Amazonian city of 'Z', which had much in common with the myths of El Dorado and Paititi.)

The Amazonian rubber boom ended in the early 1910s and the industry went into rapid decline. Logging became the main form of employment in Rurrenabaque, but the town slumbered through much of the rest of the 20th century. Its awaking was inadvertently prompted by the exploits of a 22-year-old Israeli traveller named Yossi Ghinsberg, who set off into the surrounding rainforest with three companions in 1981. The group quarrelled, separated, and after a rafting accident, Ghinsberg found himself lost and alone. With no training and little food or equipment, he somehow managed to survive for three weeks. In the process, he reportedly fought off a jaguar, killed a venomous snake, and was nearly consumed by mosquitoes, leeches and flies.

He also suffered hallucinations, and almost drowned on multiple occasions. His body was cut to ribbons and his feet started to rot. But he held on and was finally rescued.

Ghinsberg went on to write a best-selling book about his experience entitled *Back from Tuichi* (it was republished as *Lost in the Jungle* and later turned into the film *Jungle* starring Daniel Radcliffe). The book became a traveller classic. Soon thousands of young Israelis began to flock to Rurrenabaque for their own rainforest adventures (albeit adventures that were – generally – well organised by local guides). In a further boost for the town, the government officially established Parque Nacional Madidi in 1995. Increasing numbers of backpackers from Europe, North America and beyond started to arrive and before long Rurrenabaque developed into a centre for ecotourism and a popular stop on the Gringo Trail.

***

At midday Rurrenabaque was languid to the point of hibernation. The stifling heat and humidity felt like a bear hug. A brown-and-white dog dozed in the middle of the pebbly, vehicle-free road, while a pair of free-roaming chickens pecked contentedly at some stray morsels. In the ten-minute walk from my hotel to the town centre I only passed three other people.

When I reached the centre, the sky darkened, providing momentary relief from the scorching sun, and then sent down a barrage of torrential rain. I sheltered under the thatched roof of a *moto-taxi* stand, where a pair of drivers offered me nodded welcomes before turning back to a TV rigged up on a narrow shelf. A teenage couple who had somehow squeezed both of their bodies into a single orange poncho rode by on a scooter. After 10 minutes the rain disappeared as quickly as it arrived, as if a celestial tap had been turned off. It left behind ankle-deep puddles, even though the roads were lined with deep, hazardously uncovered drains.

Few buildings in Rurrenabaque – known to residents as Rurre – were more than two storeys. Most had roofs of corrugated iron that radiated heat in the sun and thundered during the rain; a few were still thatched. The majority housed businesses aimed at tourists – travel agencies, hostels, bars, restaurants, souvenir shops – with signs in English, Spanish, and Hebrew. Hand-written adverts offering copies of *Lost in the Jungle* were taped to windows and around street lamps. As the afternoon wore on, the heat faded and the town slowly woke up. Locals roused themselves from siestas and travellers returned from rainforest excursions. Most headed to the riverside *costanera* for their evening stroll, to claim one of the prime benches for watching the sunset, or to simply enjoy a few moments peace while their children burned off some energy in the playground or with a football.

I joined them and soon found a tiny naval base flying three flags: the red, yellow and green Bolivian tricolour, the blue naval ensign, and the square, rainbow-coloured *wiphala*, which is used by indigenous people across the Andes and was given 'dual flag' status with the tricolour in the 2009 constitution. Tottering mounds of chunky green bananas and watermelons were piled up on the grassy banks. Stalls sold barbecued chicken and fish, bags of popcorn, fresh coconuts, pots of jelly and cream, and cups of shaved ice drenched with syrup. Flatbed barges carrying tractors and lorries chugged past, the sailors shouting *chica* (girl) and *rubia* (blondie) at any women they caught sight of. On the opposite bank was the smaller town of San Buenaventura, which according to Google Maps was connected to Rurrenabaque by a bridge. This was little more than an aspiration: the initial sections of a bridge had been built on both sides of the river, but a 400-m gap yawned between the two. I asked an old man who was out walking his dog when the bridge would be finished. 'It's been like that for ages,' he said, shaking his head. 'There's not enough money for the work.'

There was little action after dark. Bars with names like Funky Monkey and Moskito promised happy hours that lasted most of the night, cocktails with suggestive names, and raucous times all round, but drinkers were few and far between. To pass the time I sat down to read in the main square, Plaza 2 de Febrero, named for the date the town was founded, until a naval brass band took up residence nearby for a practice session. On the walk back to my hotel I passed a group of teenagers taking part in a ballroom dancing class on the street.

***

A decade after his escape from the jungle, Ghinsberg returned to visit the people who rescued him. The indigenous Quechua-Tacana community of San José de Uchupiamonas, nine hours upriver from Rurrenabaque, was 'struggling for survival'. Founded in 1616 by Franciscan missionaries and members of a Quechua-speaking group from the lowlands of eastern Bolivia, San José de Uchupiamonas is one of the largest settlements in Parque Nacional Madidi. (In total, around 3,700 people live in the park; the majority are indigenous to the region, though migration from other parts of the country is growing.) By the early 1990s, extreme poverty was entrenched in San José de Uchupiamonas, with residents lacking basic educational and medical facilities. 'They had no options for income other than slash-and-burn agriculture, hunting, or working as cheap labour for the loggers and miners, who are in a process of [overwhelming] the region,' wrote Ghinsberg. The government provided no help, and 40 families – roughly a third of the town's population at the time – had left in search of a better life.

The Josesanos knew they could only rely on themselves and developed plans for a collectively owned and run ecolodge, the first of its kind in this part of the Amazon. In 1992, they started to build a group of traditional huts on the shores of Chalalán lagoon, 25 km south of the town. They used sustainable materials and aimed to be as 'low impact' as possible. When the project ran short of money, Ghinsberg pledged to help. He contacted a US NGO, Conservation International, which provided technical assistance and helped the community secure a grant from the Inter-American Development Bank. In 1997, the Chalalán ecolodge opened its doors to the public.

Since then it has become a model of community-based ecotourism and conservation, receiving rave reviews and a string of international awards. Chalalán has created scores of local jobs, provided training and skills development, and generated funds to improve water supplies and build clinics and schools. Life in San José de Uchupiamonas improved so much that a number of the families who had left in the 1980s decided to return. Chalalán inspired neighbouring communities to set up their own lodges and travel companies, and strict guidelines to govern ecotourism in the Madidi region were also drawn up.

Although far from perfect, the situation in San José de Uchupiamonas was undeniably better than in many other areas of the Amazon. A United Nations assessment of Chalalán described it as a 'successful model of sustainable, responsible ecotourism' that 'has brought substantial conservation and development benefits to the region and the resident indigenous population'.

In a better world, that would be the end of the story. But Chalalán, San José de Uchupiamonas and other indigenous communities in the region now face an existential threat.

***

My guide for the trip to Chalalán was William, a wiry Josesano in his mid-20s who wore a green football top, aviator sunglasses, and a money belt. His second in command was Don Luis, a quiet, older man with bushy grey hair springing out from beneath a baseball cap. He directed me and a trio of French travellers onto a motorboat with aeroplane-style seats shaded by a turquoise awning, handed out lifejackets, and then balanced – sans lifejacket – on the prow of the boat. We set off on the five-hour journey upstream with William at the wheel. Initially, there were several other vessels on the chocolatey water but we soon left them behind and open water stretched out in front of us.

As we puttered along, William told me about Parque Nacional Madidi. Spanning around 19,000 sq km, it encompasses both Amazonian and Andean ecosystems, including rainforests, cloudforests, grasslands, and wetlands. The park is home to at least 1,028 species of bird – almost 10 per cent of the world's total – 265 species of mammals, 204 species of reptiles and amphibians, 1,544 species of butterflies, and more than 5,500 species of plants, many of them endemic. 'There are jaguars, anacondas, stingrays, birds of paradise, capybaras [the world's largest rodent], spectacled bears, macaws, many, many others,' he said. In 2018, following a two-and-a-half-year study, the Wildlife Conservation Society, a New York-based international NGO, declared Madidi 'the world's most biologically diverse protected area' having identified 124 species thought to be previously unknown to science, including the whiptail lizard and the spiny rat.

Gradually the river narrowed and steep, impenetrable cliffs rose up on either side. Trees sprung out of the fissured rock and tobacco-coloured clouds choked the cliff tops. After 45 minutes we reached the Bala gorge, the proposed site of a new hydroelectric mega-dam, said William, as he nimbly tiptoed around the edge of the boat to adjust a loose rope: 'If the dam is built this journey we're taking today will not be possible. It would end tourism in Rurrenabaque and Chalalán would close. There is lots of fighting and lots of protests from the community, but ...' He trailed off and looked away.

There have been discussions about damming the Bala gorge since the 1950s. The Morales government's plan involved constructing a pair of dams, one here and another in the nearby Chepete canyon, to generate thousands of megawatts of electricity, most of which would be exported to Brazil, Argentina, and Peru. Ministers claimed the $6–8 billion project would transform Bolivia into the 'energy heart of South America', affect only a tiny section of the park and create tens of thousands of jobs. Jointly the two dams would flood almost 800 sq km of rainforest, including large chunks of Madidi and the neighbouring Pilon Lajas Biosphere Reserve. Around 4,000 indigenous people – including the San José de Uchupiamonas community – in and around the park would be displaced from their homes and many more would have their lives and livelihoods disrupted or curtailed, according to some estimates. Detailed resettlement and compensation plans were noticeable by their absence.

Scientists have warned that inundating so much of the forest would irrecoverably damage Madidi and exacerbate the impact of the climate crisis on the region. A local NGO, the Coordinadora Para la Defensa de la

Amazonia (Coordinator for the Defence of the Amazon), said the dams would devastate the 'quality of the environment, habitats, diverse ways of life, the cultural patrimony of the Bolivian Amazon'. The message sent out in graffiti, posters, and banners around Rurrenabaque was even blunter: 'No to Bala Chepete. Dams equal death, debt and pain.'

Pablo Solón, formerly Bolivia's ambassador to the UN and now a human rights and environmental activist, is a prominent critic of the project. As well as its environmental impact, he challenged the economic case and called for an independent investigation. When Morales was in power, Solón and his colleagues were harassed and threatened with legal action. 'The El Chepete and El Bala hydroelectric dams are not profitable at current electricity prices according to the [the government's] own identification study,' he wrote in 2017. 'Sending me to prison will not make these mega-dams profitable.' Morales has since left office, but it remains to be seen whether his successors will take a more progressive or sustainable approach to the project.

The El Chepete-El Bala project is just one of a series of energy-related threats to the Bolivian Amazon. There are several other hydroelectric dams proposed or in place in the far north of the region, including at Cachuela Esperanza, the former headquarters of Nicolás Suárez's rubber empire. Oil and gas companies also have concessions to search for and exploit hydrocarbon reserves in Madidi, Pilón Lajas, and other supposedly protected areas across the country.

***

On the other side of the Bala gorge, the rocky cliffs flattened out and the hills beyond them slowly disappeared from view. We stopped briefly at the entrance to the park to show our entry tickets. It was a lonely place – brick hut, thatched shelter, wretched toilet. The riverbanks beyond were dense walls of green foliage, save for the odd tree with ghostly white trunks and branches, the latter providing perches for statuesque storks and woodpeckers. Dragonflies and butterflies zipped a few inches above the water. A solitary fisherman on a stony beach watched as we chugged past. Further on a pair of men in ripped shorts sluiced water and mud through a machine on the bank. Gold miners, said Don Luis, breaking an hour's silence.

Gold mining, dredging, and panning are growing problems across the Bolivian Amazon, including in and around Madidi and Pilón Lajas. The precious metal is currently the country's third biggest export (after natural gas and zinc), thanks largely to rising demand since the global financial crisis in 2007–08. Bolivia's gold rush has echoes of the rubber boom a century and a half earlier. Much of the activity in this region is illegal yet its remoteness, the limited numbers of rangers, and a lack of political will mean there is little enforcement. The miners on the beach were only small-time players, said William, but many operations are big businesses and often linked to organised crime, human trafficking, forced labour (including child labour), and sexual exploitation. The Global Initiative Against Transnational Organized Crime, a research organisation based in Geneva, estimates that some 45,000 people work in illegal gold mining in the Bolivian Amazon – including 13,500 children – and that 68 tonnes of gold worth $3 billion were smuggled out of the country between 2006 and 2016.

Large dredging vessels known as 'dragons' are an increasingly common sight, hoovering up silt from the river beds and sifting through it for gold. Many are operated by Chinese crews, further evidence of the superpower's rising interest in the Amazon and its resources. Gold mining and dredging cause huge environmental damage: swathes of rainforest have been cleared and the levels of mercury – which is used in the gold-extraction process – in the waterways are steadily rising, poisoning the indigenous communities, wildlife, and wider ecosystems.

After two hours we turned off the Beni River and onto the narrower Tuichi. Mud-banked cliffs topped with spindly trees stood on one side of the river, sandbanks ran along the other. William steered past a series of rapids and around several floating islands formed from trunks, branches, and clumps of earth, washed downstream until they snagged together and coalesced. At the front of the boat, Don Luis sat in silence, gesturing left or right so William could avoid debris and sandbars. He wielded a thin stick for testing the depth of the water and a thicker one to push the boat away from hazards. The hum of the engine, gentle rocking motion, hug of the lifejacket, cooling breeze, and warmth of the sun sent me off to sleep.

We stopped for lunch on a shingle beach. Don Luis handed out plastic boxes of fried chicken, slices of fried cassava, an *alfajor* biscuit filled with *dulce de leche*, and fruit. It was briefly enjoyable, before seemingly endless waves of biting ants and insects began to wash over me. I was slathered in 50-per-cent Deet repellent but it proved no more effective than in the Llanos de Moxos. My arms and neck were soon covered in itchy red welts, and it was a relief to get back on the boat, where the breeze kept the smaller critters away. After five hours on the river we arrived at a small wooden dock around 100 km southwest of Rurrenabaque. From here a 2-km track led through the jungle to Chalalán.

It was called the Jaguar Trail, but the only animal that made an appearance was a tapir, a dark grey, cow-sized creature with an elephantine snout. It took fright as we approached, issuing a high-pitched squeal and crashing through the undergrowth, leaving behind a trail of muddy hoof prints. The largest surviving land-based mammals in the Amazon, tapirs are often described as 'living fossils' because their bodies have barely changed since they first appeared in the Ecocene period (56–33.9 million years ago). Today, however, their numbers are falling because of poaching, trafficking, and habitat loss.

Many other species in Madidi are also at risk. Jaguars, the biggest cat in the Americas, have been particularly badly hit, said William, gently lowering my expectations of seeing one during my stay at Chalalán. Only around 4,000–7,000 of the animals survive in Bolivia and their numbers are declining, with the trafficking of their skins, teeth, and bones to China an increasing problem. Members of indigenous communities are the only people allowed to hunt for food and chop down trees for wood in Madidi, though these items cannot then be sold or traded, William continued. Yet the law is difficult to police and poachers and traffickers are rarely brought to justice. Logging, cattle ranching, and farming – particularly of sugar-cane – are also intensifying in and around the park, resulting in ever-increasing road building and rapid deforestation. To put the situation in context, Bolivia lost 32,000 sq km – an area larger than Belgium – of humid primary forest between 2002 and 2020, according to Global Forest Watch estimates.

Eventually the trail emerged into a clearing. A-frame huts raised on stilts with thatched roofs and hammocks on the verandas were shaded by trees so heavy with fruit the branches arched like bows. Periodically there was a thud as an overripe orange, lime or pomelo fell to the ground. Other branches drooped with large teardrop-shaped nests belonging to yellow-tailed crested oropendolas. Beyond a set of solar panels and a large satellite dish was another path leading down to a wooden deck facing a gorgeous lagoon. As we sank glasses of sugared lime juice, hoots, shrieks, rustling leaves, and monkey calls sounded from the surrounding forest.

After dinner we picked our way through the inky darkness to the deck, where William was waiting to take us out onto the lagoon in a wooden canoe. When the Josesanos were building Chalalán, he said, they realised a malign spirit was present at the site – a ghostly white man who paddled across the lagoon late at night. William then grinned at us and said not to worry: the villagers conducted various ceremonies and the apparition has not been seen since. We took it in turns to scan our torches along the shoreline, sometimes catching a caiman eye, which flashed red in the light. The reptiles had thin, gangly bodies and were about half a metre long. 'Just babies,' said William, 'they can grow to twice that size.'

Afterwards we switched off our torches and sat in silence, gazing up at the cloudless sky, countless stars on a perfectly black background. I'd never seen the Southern Cross so clearly. The only sounds were the gentle lapping of the water on the shore, croaking frogs and toads, high-pitched bat clicks, and the hum of cicadas.

***

Early the next morning we set off into the jungle. William, dressed in rolled-up jeans, sports sandals and socks, and with a small machete fastened to his money belt, led the way. Our destination was the Santa Rosa lagoon, 6 km to the east. A rough path had been cut through the undergrowth a few weeks earlier, but the jungle was already reclaiming it and William's machete was quickly required to hack away at the foliage and entwined branches clad with ferns and bromeliads. We scrabbled up and down undulating hills, encountered fresh jaguar and tapir tracks – made earlier that morning according to William – and tip-toed over 15-m-long trails of leaf-cutter ants. Parrots, toucans, macaws, red-breasted trogons, and spiky-crested, blue-faced hoatzins sounded their calls as we approached, like a chorus of car alarms.

William pointed out medicinal plants, cut the bark of one tree rigged with creepers to expose its poisonous white sap, and pointed out another that appeared to have been plucked from the pages of a Gabriel García Márquez novel. The cashapona, or walking palm, grows a succession of stilted roots that gradually move it across the forest floor in search of the sunniest spot and the richest soil. Some specimens have reportedly moved as much 20 m in a single year. The cashapona's branches were draped with shaggy epiphytes and alive with lizards, fire ants, and a fist-sized tarantula.

Shards of sunlight pierced the canopy, but there was no breeze and sweat matted my shirt and trousers. The smell of decomposing vegetation filled the air and the trail grew progressively worse. My hiking boots were almost sucked off my feet in one patch of gloopy mud. Elsewhere streams and small rivers blocked our route. Anxious to avoid sodden feet, we balanced precariously on fallen tree trunks to make our way across them. One river was so wide William was forced to quickly construct a rudimentary pontoon bridge. He sliced off strips of bark and wound them together into a rough twine. This was then used to tie a floating log to a tangle of tentacle-like roots that sprawled down the bank. As he skipped easily over to the other side of the river, the rest of us made considerably slower progress, inching across barefooted to give us more traction on the slippery wood and using branches as crude walking sticks.

The trail subsequently ascended a steep hill to a plateau that was the once the site of a coffee plantation. Interspersed between pomelo, mandarin, banana and lime trees, the coffee bushes were still fruiting. Nearby was a cluster of wooden huts: a couple of dorms with wooden bed frames and mosquito netting tacked to the open windows; and a processing room with a handful of gnarled coffee beans scattered across a drying rack. Curiously, given the remote location and meagre possessions inside – glass bottles, a khaki rucksack, a half-full tin of white paint – all the doors were padlocked. But if the locks were unnecessary, the presence of a guard – a taciturn, middle-aged man named Esteban – felt vaguely ridiculous. A three-and-a-half-hour hike from Chalalán, the nearest settlement, Esteban and his dog led a solitary existence. We exchanged pleasantries, but he seemed anxious in our company and dashed off to carry out some unspoken task at the first opportunity. Next to his thatched-roof hut was an overgrown airstrip, overlooking a cliff above a bend in the Tuichi and once used to transport workers in and coffee out.

We stopped for a lunch of catfish steaks, rice, plantain, corn, and super-sweet bananas. A similar carbohydrate-rich diet combined with cassava, small portions of wild game, and plenty of physical activity has given one indigenous community in the Madidi region the healthiest hearts in the world. In 2017, a study published in the *Lancet* revealed heart attacks and strokes were virtually unknown among the 16,000-strong Tsimané community, who hunt, fish and farm along the Maniqui River. Blood pressure, blood glucose, heart rates, and cholesterol levels were also remarkably low. 'Most of the Tsimané are able to live their entire life without developing any coronary atherosclerosis. This has never been seen in any prior research,' wrote Dr Gregory S. Thomas, co-author of the study.

After lunch we hiked down to the Santa Rosa lagoon. It was a glorious sight: a pristine pale blue-turquoise mirror whose edges were shaded by overhanging trees. A wooden jetty reached out into the water, the final section partially collapsed. Esteban paddled up with a bucket of freshly caught catfish. He greeted us politely, told us to make use of his rowing boat, and hurried away. We rowed out into the centre of the lagoon to fish for piranha. William showed us how to bait a line with strips of raw beef and cast it off, and within 30 seconds he had snagged his first piranha. He casually removed the hook from its fangs and tossed the fish, half alive, into the puddle of water that had accumulated in the bottom of the rowing boat. It was soon joined by 14 others, all caught by William; the rest of us were out of luck. As we paddled back to the jetty, the piranhas thrashed around in the shallows between my feet until they finally expired.

We spent longer on the lake than anticipated and when we got back to shore, William appeared anxious. He shovelled the piranhas into a plastic bag and set off back down the trail at a furious pace, eager to reach Chalalán before nightfall. As we trailed in his wake, a group of peccaries charged across our path, four tiny youngsters trailing in the wake of a pair of adults. Similar to wild boars, they left behind a pungent porcine scent that hung in the air. By this stage, we had drunk all of our water and were dehydrated. It was 4.30 p.m. but the temperature still hovered around 35°C. I've never been so thirsty, my throat was rasped and my tongue felt like sandpaper. Finally, we reached the grove of pomelo trees on the edge of the coffee plantation. Over the course of the day, I'd seen William use his machete to scrape away poisonous tree sap, slash through vines, and chop up raw meat. He briefly cleaned it one point: a perfunctory wipe on some damp leaves. But as he used it to peel the pomelos and slice them into chunks, I couldn't have cared less. I sucked up the tangy juice of five of the fruits, devoured the pink flesh, and gnawed on the skin. I could have done the same to five more.

Thirst proved a great motivator and we covered the final 5 km in an hour and 40 minutes, a record time William assured us. We reached the lodge muddy, sweaty, and sticky with pomelo juice. After guzzling jug after jug of water, I launched myself into the lagoon to cool off. As I swam, keeping an eye out for any caimans that might be in the vicinity, troupes of squirrel, capuchin, and howler monkeys crashed through the canopy, competing for the choicest leaves. For dinner we ate William's piranhas, peeling the tasty white flesh from the bones and piling up the oversized jaws into a gruesome cairn.

***

Overnight it rained solidly for 10 hours straight, turning Chalalán into a morass and submerging the trail back to the jetty. There were no rubber boots in my size, so I walked to the motorboat in my hiking shoes. I moved gingerly at first, but after plunging into calf-deep mud for the second time gave up and resigned myself to sodden feet for the rest of the day. When the boat set off, I felt a sharp pang of sadness with the realisation that I was unlikely to experience this kind of wilderness – at least in the Bolivian Amazon – again.

The Tuichi was a different beast after the rain: several metres higher, faster flowing, churning violently. We travelled with the current, skimming along at a great pace and sending up ballooning clouds of spray. Sections of the bank had collapsed under the weight of the run-off, plunging dozens of trees into the river. The trunks, some of them 20 m or more in length, whirled menacingly in the current.

But Don Luis, hunkered down at the front of the boat and drenched to the skin, navigated a slaloming route through them, calling out orders over the wind and fiercely gesturing left and right with his arms. We were back in Rurrenabaque in less than two and half hours.

At the dock William clasped my hands, thanked me profusely and promised to visit me in London. I was equally grateful and effusive in return. We smiled but sadly, both aware that our pledges were unlikely to be kept. In the grey drizzle, Rurrenabaque felt a bit bleak, especially away from the riverbank. Bare brick shacks with ill-fitted roofs conveyed a general sense of decay; the doctor's surgery was particularly ramshackle. Signs advertised ice cubes, paint, mechanics, and – bizarrely – a private 24-hour guarded car park. I'd only seen a handful of cars during my stay and found it hard to imagine that theft was a big problem in the middle of the jungle.

It was approaching peak season, but tourists were thin on the ground. Although it remains the Bolivian Amazon's traveller hub, by 2017 the town was far quieter than my first visit 13 years earlier. As a travel writer, I've grown familiar with tourism's relentless forward-march. In the two- to three-year gap between guidebook updates, 'hidden gems' become Gringo Trail favourites, family-run guesthouses turn into foreign-owned boutique hotels, Nescafe instant is replaced by Illy espresso. But in Rurrenabaque the process had not only stalled, it had gone into reverse. A local newspaper reported visitor numbers had halved in recent years, a great blow for such a tourist-oriented economy. It blamed three factors: destructive floods; a hike in Madidi's entry fee; and the introduction of visa restrictions for Israelis – who previously accounted for a third of all visitors to Rurrenabaque – and Americans. The unrest following the 2019 general elections and, more seriously, the enduring impact of Covid-19 on global travel means Rurrenabaque's tourism industry is unlikely to recover any time soon.

Alongside threats like hydroelectric dams, deforestation, gold mining, poaching, and road-building, this may seem a trivial issue or even a positive development – tourism can undoubtedly cause great damage. Yet people in places like Rurrenabaque and the wider Madidi region lack a sustainable alternative and receive little government support. When responsible, community-based ecotourism is done right, as at Chalalán, it can provide communities with jobs and financial incentives to conserve the environment: take it away and people are forced to find other ways to survive.

***

I left Rurrenabaque a few months before the annual *chaqueo*, the slashing and burning of forest and grassland to clear space for agriculture and grazing, which takes place towards the end of the dry season and fills the sky with acrid black smoke. People across the Amazon have used limited, small-scale forms of slash-and-burn agriculture for thousands of years. But over the last few decades loggers and cattle ranchers have used huge fires to clear massive tracts of the region for agribusiness. This is now taking place on an unprecedented scale and is having a devastating effect. As Greenpeace has warned: 'Deforestation and fires inhibit the capacity for tropical forests to absorb carbon dioxide from the atmosphere. The Amazon is a globally important carbon sink, but studies suggest that as fires accelerate and pump out thick plumes of carbon dioxide-laden smoke, the region could be at risk of transformation to a net carbon source, causing an acceleration in climate breakdown.'

In August 2019, the most intense fires in a decade broke out across the Amazon. International attention focused on Brazil, but the situation in Bolivia was equally grave. Thousands of fires raged over more than 53,000 sq km of the north and east of the country, destroying huge areas of rainforest, tropical dry forest, grassland and wetland, including in several national parks, reserves and UNESCO World Heritage Sites. At least six people died and thousands more were affected. Millions of animals, including jaguars, anteaters and other rare and endangered species, also perished. Amnesty International described the situation as an 'environmental and human rights crisis'.

The fires were widely blamed on large-scale agribusiness-driven *chaqueos* – which have increased significantly over the past decade – that got out of control in what was a particularly dry year. Morales and his government came in for fierce criticism, most notably from indigenous communities. Despite its environmentally friendly rhetoric, the administration's support for agribusiness had grown steadily. Expanding Bolivia's food production capacities was seen as a way of diversifying the economy away from a reliance on natural gas and zinc exports, and the government announced plans to triple the amount of farm land and accelerate beef exports to China. An association representing Bolivian ranchers compared the policies to a 'goose that lays golden eggs'. The predictable result was a great jump in the rate of deforestation in the Amazon and neighbouring regions. Just a month before the 2019 fires broke out, the government passed a controversial piece of legislation authorising 'controlled burns' over wider areas than previously permitted in order to clear land, primarily for soy farming and cattle ranching.

The fires eventually subsided in October after concerted local efforts, belated government action, and a bout of heavy rainfall.

But they had already done lasting damage to the environment, indigenous communities and the reputation of Morales. National political upheaval followed, but although the presidency has changed, the same problems persist. Conservation NGO Fundación Amigos de la Naturaleza warned 23,000 sq km of Bolivia's forests and vegetation – an area larger than Belize – were ravaged by fire in the first nine months of 2020.

***

There is also an environmental crisis on the *altiplano*. Located between the city of Oruro and the Salar de Uyuni at an altitude of 3,680 m, Lake Poopó was once the second largest body of water in the country after Titicaca. At its peak the lake spanned around 3,000 sq km, though its brackish water was rarely more than 3 m deep. When I took the train to Uyuni in early 2014, I gazed out at a seemingly endless expanse of greenish water. Tufts of reeds burst above the surface and tiny fishing skiffs were visible in the distance, as well as hundreds of ducks and flamingos, who took flight as the train approached. Around 200 bird, fish, animal and plant species were once found in and around Poopó and nearby Lake Uru Uru, which lies just to the north. Among them were pumas, vicuñas and as many as 120,000 James's, Andean, and Chilean flamingos. In 2002, the two lakes were jointly named as a wetland of global importance under the international Ramsar convention.

As the train continued south I saw tiny villages along the marshy lakeshore. They were made up of virtually windowless adobe buildings, often with thatched roofs, the clothes on the washing lines outside the only signs of life. Larger villages had water towers or a church, small herds of sheep, pigs in dry-stone corrals or a few llamas. There were also occasional farmsteads, one of which had a stationary nodding donkey, the scrub around its base matted black with oil. The Poopó region has been inhabited for thousands of years. Most villages are now predominantly Aymara (Evo Morales himself was born in one near the lake's west shore; near the village is a glitzy $7 million museum dedicated to the former president, who inaugurated it in 2017), but there are also small indigenous Urus communities. Considered one of the oldest cultures in South America, the Urus people have lived, fished and hunted in this region since approximately 2000–1500 BCE.

To my untrained eye Poopó appeared full of life. Yet by that point the lake was already shrinking and within 18 months of my journey was barely two per cent of its former size. The transformation was so rapid and dramatic I still find it hard to properly conceptualise – a lake that was once the size of Luxembourg now resembles a desert.

Poopó's evaporation was an ecological and social disaster: tens of thousands of birds and millions of fish died, thousands of people lost their livelihoods, and settlements along what was once the shoreline were turned into ghost towns as residents left to seek work elsewhere. The Bolivian and international media were filled with photos of dead fish, abandoned homes, and upturned boats lying on the dusty lake bed.

Poopó is fed predominantly by the Desaguadero River, which flows south from Titicaca. The lake has always oscillated in size and even dried up completely on occasion, including in 1994, after which it took several years to refill. This time, however, scientists fear the lake may never fully recover. The catastrophe was the result of several interlinked factors, not least the climate crisis. Over the last half a century, temperatures in this region have risen by more than 2°C, with 2015 and 2016 among the hottest years on record. This increased the rate of evaporation from the lake in what is already an extremely arid environment.

Droughts, often fuelled by the El Niño effect, have also grown in intensity across the *altiplano*: the 2016 drought was the worst in a quarter of a century and prompted the government to launch a state of emergency and announce water rationing in La Paz, amid a backdrop of widespread protests. Waterways such as the Desaguadero that feed into Poopó have been diverted for industry and agriculture, while rising soil erosion and desertification linked to the 'mono-cropping' of quinoa for export has resulted in extreme sedimentation in the lake. This has been compounded by hundreds of mines dumping their often toxic waste upstream, clogging up many of the lake's tributaries; the water that did find its way into Poopó was high in zinc, lead, arsenic, and other heavy metals.

The evaporation of Poopó is just one example of the climate crisis in the *altiplano*. Uru Uru has shrunk in recent years and there are fears for the future of Titicaca. Bolivia's glaciers have been similarly hard hit: a 2016 study found they have shrunk by more than 40 per cent, causing serious water shortages and heightening the risk of floods from melt water lakes. (Another, far more minor impact, was the collapse of Bolivia's only ski resort, when the Chacaltaya glacier disappeared in 2009.)

One of the many impacts of these climate crisis-charged events has been mass migration from rural areas to cities like La Paz and El Alto – and the impact of this on Bolivia's politics, economy, and national identity has been seismic.

CHAPTER 6
The future is behind us

Indigenous identities, migration, and urbanisation:
La Paz and El Alto

A lifeless figure with a noose looped around its neck dangled limply from a flickering lamppost. We sped by and I initially thought my exhausted mind was playing tricks on me. It was a foggy evening in La Paz in 2004, and I'd been on a bus from the lowlands for the last 15 hours. Wedged against a scuffed, steamed-up window, I peered through increasingly irritating contact lenses into the half-light, desperate for a distraction from the nagging headache that had accompanied me since reaching the *altiplano*. My neighbour, a short, stocky grandma, sucked loudly on a straw protruding from a clear plastic bag containing a cloudy drink made from dried peaches, the fruit motionless at the bottom like a dead fairground goldfish.

Further along the street I saw another effigy hanging from a lamppost and then, around the corner, two more. Their legs swayed gently in the breeze and the weak orange-white light gave the bloated faces an unearthly pallor. A slogan was spray-painted on the wall below: 'Thieves will be burned.' Locals ambled by unfazed.

***

A decade on from that first visit to La Paz, my early-morning flight touched down at El Alto's airport, 4,061.5 m above sea level. The lethargic immigration officials seemed a little surprised by the sudden appearance of a dozen foreign travellers. They conferred briefly before waving us through to the deserted arrivals hall. The cafés and souvenir shops were closed and the only sounds were plaintive yelps from a dog carrier, which circled slowly on a luggage carousel. Outside the terminal a pair of taxi drivers leaned idly on their cars, barely summoning the energy to conjure up an inflated fare for the arriving gringos.

This low-key arrival was scant preparation for the views that soon materialised before me. Few cities have as dramatic a location as La Paz, which is draped across a canyon high in the Andes. I stared down at a carpet of terracotta-coloured, Lego-block-style homes clinging precariously to the near-vertical slopes. Tower blocks poked out of the city centre like flowers stretching for the sun and the triple-peaked, snow-topped Illimani, the second highest mountain in Bolivia, loomed prominently in the background beneath an unblemished sky.

The approach to the city has long captured the imagination of travellers. In 1924, the first edition of the *South American Handbook* described it as 'one of the wonder-sights of the world', with 'peaks covered with perpetual snow' and canyon walls 'picturesque in colouring and formation'. But as my taxi wound its way down into the canyon, the altitude – roughly 3,650 m in the city centre – began to take its toll. La Paz is one of the world's highest cities and arriving here from lower elevations feels like ageing prematurely. The altitude is a powerful invisible force that made climbing the short flight of steps up to my guesthouse seem comparable to scaling Everest. As I sat on the bed in my room I became increasingly aware of the pressure on my lungs and struggled to catch my breath. My dull headache was soon pounding and I became sluggish, irritable and unable to focus. Nausea dulled my appetite but I had an unquenchable thirst. Sleep that night and the next proved elusive. Instead vivid, unsettling waking-dreams occupied my mind as I lay shivering beneath the woollen blankets.

To aid the acclimatisation process, locals advise first-time visitors to the city to 'eat little, drink little and sleep alone'. The most expensive hotels go so far as to provide guests with oxygen tanks; my guesthouse offered a pot of coca-leaf tea and a bowl of boiled coca sweets, which are also supposed to help. The former tasted like blitzed-up lawn clippings, the latter like grassy cough drops. My symptoms gradually eased over the next few days but never entirely disappeared. A strange sensation persisted throughout my stay in La Paz, as if I wasn't quite there.

***

I'd returned to the city to see how it was coping with some of the thorniest issues of the early 21st century: mass migration, urban-isation, and shifting identities. Bolivia is currently undergoing rapid change. According to statistics from the World Bank, some 2.6 million Bolivians – roughly a quarter of the country's population – migrated to cities between 2006 and 2011, and the rate has since increased. Around 70 per cent of Bolivians now live in urban areas, compared to 55 per cent in 1990. Hundreds of thousands of these internal migrants have flocked to the plateau above La Paz, interrupting the near isolation of a city that had sat alone in its canyon, surrounded by the inhospitable *altiplano*, for some 400 years.

La Ciudad de Nuestra Señora de la Paz (The City of Our Lady of Peace), to give the city its full title, was founded in 1548. A major seat of Spanish colonial power in the Andes, it prospered as a stopping place on the valuable trade routes between Buenos Aires and Lima, and the silver mines of the *altiplano* and the Pacific coast. Today, La Paz is regularly described as the world's highest capital city but this isn't quite right – although it is the country's political hub, Sucre, 700 km to the southeast, is the official capital. The majority of La Paz's approximately 955,000 residents have indigenous Aymara heritage, their language one of the few in South America to have survived the arrival of both the Quechua-speaking Inca and the Spanish-speaking conquistadors.

La Paz, wrote Pico Iyer in *The Man Within My Head*, is 'an ironist's delight with its defiance of all reason'. Here the poor look down on the rich. Literally. Working-class districts range across the canyon's precipitous slopes in tightly-knit clusters of brick-and-corrugated-iron homes in varying stages of completion. Below them are the middle classes in slightly smarter houses, and the neighbour-hoods grow more prosperous still the further you descend. Despite progress under the Morales government between 2006 and 2019, Bolivia remains profoundly unequal, with class, ethnic and racial structures that, in some respects, have changed depressingly little since the colonial period. The city's wealthiest residents congregate at the base of the canyon in the Zona Sur neighbourhood, overlooked on all sides, their escape routes blocked by regular strikes and protests.

Outsiders often unfairly depict La Paz as if it is stuck in some kind of vacuum, distant from the wider world, globalisation and modernity. But spend a bit of time here and you will quickly realise the future has firmly arrived in La Paz. In the early 20th century, railway lines were built across the *altiplano* to link La Paz with Lake Titicaca to the west and Chile's Pacific ports to the southwest. These were followed by an airstrip and an air force base. A fledgling settlement named El Alto (The Heights) developed on the canyon rim above the city to service these new transport links. It remained little more than a village until the 1952 National Revolution.

One of the key moments in Bolivian history, the revolution led to universal suffrage, land reforms that freed many workers from near-feudal conditions, nationalisation of the valuable tin mines, and increased industrialisation. Coupled with a major drought, these changes prompted great population movements and thousands of people, the vast majority of whom were from indigenous backgrounds, travelled across the *altiplano* to La Paz in search of work. Few could afford to live in the city itself, so instead settled in El Alto, whose population grew steadily, reaching 30,000 in the mid-1960s.

'The next wave of migration was linked to the construction boom of Hugo Banzer's dictatorial regime in the 1970s, fuelled by foreign debt and US aid,' wrote Sian Lazar in *El Alto, Rebel City*. By the mid-1970s El Alto's population topped 100,000, and migration rates to the conurbation accelerated in the next decade as the country plunged into a deep depression and extreme droughts decimated agricultural communities.

Throughout this period, the Bolivian government tended to view El Alto as little more than a satellite of La Paz, a loose collection of crime- and poverty-ridden 'shanty towns'. Some even described it as merely an 'appendix'. There was scant investment in infrastructure and city status was granted only reluctantly. Nevertheless, El Alto's population continued to grow vigorously, hitting 650,000 by the turn of the millennium, thanks in part to the impact of the climate crisis on already struggling rural communities. Along the way it developed a distinct Aymara identity and political consciousness, the influence of which has since rippled out across the country. Today, El Alto is the second biggest city in Bolivia with around 1.1 million residents, roughly 150,000 more than La Paz. The moon has outgrown the Earth.

***

On a sunny autumnal morning a few days after arriving in La Paz, I waited in Plaza San Pedro, my head still fuzzy from the altitude. Dogs in woollen jackets took turns to chase each other, commuters hurried to work, and huddles of schoolgirls in maroon knee-length socks chattered and joked. The only stationary figure in the area was on a plinth in the centre of the square: General Antonio José de Sucre y Alcalá, independence leader, close friend of 'El Libertador' Simón Bolívar (from whom the country takes its name), early Bolivian president and, for a few moments that morning, perch for a passing pigeon. For such an exalted figure the 'Great Marshal of Ayacucho' – a title he earned after leading his soldiers to a decisive victory over Spanish forces in what is now Peru – had a deeply depressing view: barely 20 m away was San Pedro, one of South America's most notorious prisons.

Alejandra arrived as I gazed up at the nearby Hotel Osira, wondering whether guests in the top-floor rooms could see into the prison yard. (The hotel's website attempted to provide a positive spin on the location, which it claimed was one of the hotel's 'principle features', as it is on a 'traditional square' close to numerous 'typical buildings'.

The prison itself was never mentioned.) A brisk, efficient university student in her early 20s, Alejandra divided her time between writing a thesis on sustainable tourism and guiding travellers around the region's less heralded attractions, in particular El Alto.

As we waited for a *trufi*, shared taxis that ply fixed routes, she told me about life in San Pedro prison. Violent and overcrowded, the hulking monolith was a semi-self-governing, highly stratified society. Inside were shops, restaurants, workshops and pool halls, as well as 'poor' and 'rich' neighbourhoods. Cocaine, reputedly the purest in Bolivia, was widely available. 'Prisoners "rent" their cells,' said Alejandra. 'Some pay thousands of dollars for a bathroom, living room, cable TV and even a hot tub. They're like rooms in a five-star hotel. A friend of a friend pays about $100 for a small cell with a bed and a desk. Many families pay five *bolivianos* [around 50p] a night to stay in the prison with their jailed husbands.'

The most luxurious cells are occupied by drug traffickers and corrupt politicians. By contrast, the poorest of the 2,400 inmates were essentially homeless, forced to sleep in corridors or in the yard and survive on basic rations. Scores die of exposure during the bitter winter months. Protests and riots are common, with the women and children who live with the prisoners popular targets for violence and abuse. Tellingly, however, some still deemed San Pedro preferable to the world outside.

Thick walls, sheet metal roofing, watchtowers, and a group of muscular guards gave it a forbidding look, but San Pedro was easier to leave than it appeared. 'Apparently, a few weeks ago a prisoner paid a guard $5,000 to let him throw a rope over the wall and climb out,' said Alejandra. 'He still hasn't been caught.' It was even easier to get into the jail, which had become a macabre tourist attraction. English-speaking inmates – generally drug smugglers or mules – offered tours, with the connivance of corrupt guards.

During my first visit to La Paz 10 years earlier, I attempted to take a San Pedro tour but an outbreak of unrest meant that security was briefly tightened up. In retrospect, I was very glad I didn't get in. Quite apart from being both illegal and unprotected, the tours were linked to a prison mutiny that resulted in the deaths of a number of inmates and their relatives. This grim touristic fascination with La Paz's prisons is nothing new. When Hiram Bingham, the American academic, senator and 'discoverer' of Machu Picchu, visited the city jail in the early 1900s he claimed he found a 'barbarous state of affairs'.

A *trufi* arrived for our journey up to El Alto, a place some people in La Paz view with little more affection than San Pedro. As we crawled up a precipitous hill, I spotted a figure dressed in a zebra costume gently supporting the arm of an elderly woman as she crossed the street. Further on another zebra danced a jig, waving enthusiastically for the traffic to stop and gesturing flamboyantly to waiting pedestrians. 'The city authorities get young people in zebra costumes to promote traffic safety and help people cross busy roads,' Alejandra explained. 'Others wear donkey costumes and hug you if you cross at the wrong time. People respect the zebras more than the police. A few weeks ago, an angry driver pushed over a zebra and was beaten up by some passers-by. We love our zebras.'

The *trufi* continued to wheeze uphill until we reached a forest of telecommunications towers that mark the edge of the pancake-flat expanse of El Alto. 'Welcome to the Aymara capital of the world,' said Alejandra as we disembarked. The streets were lined with mismatched bare-brick homes, their roofs sprouting knots of cables, antennae, satellite dishes, and metal rods for additional storeys, a symbol of optimism for the future. Several were linked by strings of colourful flags, the remnants of a recent fiesta. There were building sites everywhere I looked and the air thrummed with the sound of drills and saws. Alejandra guided me to a small market whose stalls were laden with fruit and vegetables, leathery strips of dried llama meat, mutton carcasses, and feathery chickens in cages. Vendors sold tasty deep-fried doughnut-like *buñuelos* doused in syrup, overflowing glasses of rose-red cinnamon sorbet, and *papas rellenas*, stuffed balls of mashed potato served in greaseproof paper with an array of salsas. Nearby, a group of men sat on plastic stools, slurping bowls of nourishing soup filled with tiny silver fish. Behind them stood an abandoned tower with a satellite dish at the top and a half-built revolving restaurant.

'El Alto is the youngest city in Bolivia. It is only around 35 years old, and the highest in the world at 4,150 m, even higher than Potosí,' said Alejandra as we nibbled chunks of quinoa chocolate and slices of sweet, brilliantly pink cactus fruit. 'Hundreds of thousands of people migrated to find better opportunities in La Paz, stopped off here as it was cheaper, and built their own homes. There was nothing really in El Alto, just the airport. Now there are over a million people here, more than in La Paz. Only Santa Cruz in the east is bigger. There are probably more people here – nobody trusts the census. Most people speak Aymara and identify themselves as such, though really in Bolivia we're all *mestizos*.'

She explained that many of the migrants came from *altiplano* mining towns, whose long decline accelerated in the 1980s thanks to the collapsing price of tin, hyperinflation, and a looming economic crisis. Others came from rural communities badly affected by droughts, floods, mudslides, crop failures, and sometimes all of these factors combined. Despite their shared heritage and the fact tens of thousands of *alteños* commute to La Paz every day for work, with similar numbers of *paceños* passing through El Alto, the two cities exist uneasily alongside each other. When I mentioned El Alto to the receptionist at my guesthouse in La Paz she shook her head vigorously: 'Why would you go there? It's dangerous. Many, many thieves.'

This appeared a common belief, though not one necessarily rooted in reality. The only reason most *paceños* spend time in El Alto is to catch a flight or shop at the sprawling Feria 16 de Julio, one of the largest markets in South America, where everything from food, clothes and household goods to electronics, cars and farming equipment are for sale (alongside a fair share of illicit items). Stung by *paceño* denigration, many *alteños*, in turn, dismiss La Paz as *'la hoyada'* (the hole). A famous billboard stands above one of the city's busiest intersections: 'El Alto is not part of Bolivia's problem. It is part of Bolivia's solution.'

'There are still racist views of El Alto: that it is dirty, chaotic, a shanty town,' said Alejandra. 'People still have this idea, especially in the Zona Sur [area of La Paz], amongst so-called "high society". Because of the 16 de Julio market, *paceños* come here now. But they won't eat anything, still say it's dangerous, and wouldn't dare come at night. They'd rather pretend it wasn't there.'

But as it expands upwards and outwards at great pace, El Alto is now impossible to ignore. After decades of neglecting the city, the government belatedly decided to act. In 2014, shortly after my visit with Alejandra, the world's highest and longest urban cable-car system opened, linking El Alto and La Paz. The $234-million Mi Teleférico (My Cable Car) echoed a scheme in the Colombian city of Medellín that connects deprived outlying neighbourhoods with the city centre and is credited with reducing crime and promoting social inclusion. It is dramatically quicker than travelling via the cities' painfully congested roads: many commutes that take an hour or more by bus or *trufi* are reduced to around 10 minutes on Mi Teleférico, whose 10 lines are used by hundreds of thousands of people every day, even though fares are a little higher than other forms of public transport.

The project also had huge symbolic value. For Morales it was seen as a demonstration of his left-wing government's adroit handling of the economy, and also showcased the country's innovation and techno-logical prowess. As with Bolivia's telecommunications satellite – launched in 2013 to expand access to internet and mobile phone services to millions of people, and celebrated on countless billboards across the country during my visit – Mi Teleférico was an elegant rebuttal to outsiders who have attempted to paint the country as backward, poverty stricken, and trapped by the past. The project was perhaps even more significant for the residents of El Alto. It recognised the city's permanence and economic importance and challenged a process of othering that has painted *alteños* as somehow fundamentally different from their *paceño* neighbours.

***

El Alto has always been a vibrant political force. In 2003, a year after narrowly edging out Morales in the presidential elections, the neoliberal Gonzalo Sánchez de Lozada (commonly known as 'Goni') was forced to resign and flee Bolivia after mass demonstrations broke out over the fate of the country's vast natural gas reserves. The politically engaged residents of El Alto played a key role in the 'Gas War', their protests essentially cutting off La Paz from the rest of Bolivia and laying the groundwork for the rise of Morales to the presidency following the 2005 elections. 'Ever since politicians have been scared of El Alto,' said Alejandra.

These protests echoed an indigenous uprising against Spanish colonial rule led by Aymara revolutionary Túpac Katari (Brilliant Serpent) and his wife Bartolina Sisa two centuries earlier. From the edge of the canyon rim, an area now occupied by El Alto, their 40,000-strong army laid siege to La Paz for 184 days in 1781. Finally, Sisa and then Katari were captured, killed and dismembered. Katari's last words were reputedly: 'I die as one, but will return as millions.' In some respects, he was right. The story of Katari and Sisa continues to inspire radical indigenous (and particularly Aymara-based) movements, while blockading La Paz remains a popular form of political protest. Moreover, El Alto's population is predicted to top 2.5 million by 2050.

Today, the city remains a cauldron of political activism. It was a stronghold of Morales, who oversaw significant economic growth and poverty reduction during his time in office, and the site of significant upheaval in the wake of the disputed 2019 election, after which he was temporarily forced into exile. But despite its links with the former president's nominally socialist political movement, the city is also a thriving hub of capitalism. Alongside the Feria 16 de Julio and myriad other activities that straddle or flagrantly cross the line of legality, there are thousands of factories, warehouses, and workshops. By some measures, El Alto is now the second biggest manufacturing and industrial centre in Bolivia. Poverty and unemployment rates are high but widespread participation in the informal economy means they do not tell the whole story. 'El Alto is simultaneously the most revolutionary city, perhaps in all of Latin America, at the same time as it's the most neoliberal city, the most individualistic city in all of Latin America,' Professor Benjamin H. Kohl of Temple University, Philadelphia, told the *New York Times*.

When I visited El Alto was calm and relaxed, its streets far quieter and cleaner than many in La Paz. Chaos and criminality were notable by their absence, something remarked upon by local graffiti artists. On the walls I saw the same scrawled message again and again: '*Mi ciudad está cambiando*' ('My city is changing'). But this neighbourhood, Ciudad Satélite (Satellite City) was one of the more prosperous areas, Alejandra reminded me, as we approached a disused water tank. Other parts of El Alto – as I later discovered – were rather more turbulent.

The water tank now houses a museum and cultural space, the Museo de Artes Antonio Paredes Candia, which takes its name from a much-loved author and enthusiastic art collector. Staff at the ticket desk looked surprised to see us – foreign visitors are apparently a rare species in these parts. Inside there were more than 500 pieces of contemporary art, thousands of books, architectural artefacts, and an evocative collection of black-and-white photos of El Alto from the mid-20th century, when the city was little more than empty land and a rudimentary airstrip. But the highlight for me was the superlative top-floor view of El Alto's growing number of *cholets*.

A compound of the words '*cholo*', a pejorative term used by the Spanish to refer to indigenous Bolivians, and 'chalet', these buildings represent a new and inventive form of architecture that is distinctly Aymara and *alteño*. They emerged in the early 2000s, the brainchild of former bricklayer Freddy Mamani Silvestre, who later became an engineer and architect and has since been compared to Gaudí, Oscar Niemeyer and even Michelangelo. He has created dozens of flamboyant, vividly coloured, layer-cake *cholets* that blend traditional and modern elements and have spawned countless imitators.

It may have been the altitude – a disorientating light-headedness had enveloped me in El Alto – but the reflective glass, elaborate façades, swooping arches, domes and pillars, constellations of lights, and rainbow shades of the buildings made my eyes swim. The buildings were unlike anything I'd seen before and it was easy to see why they have been dubbed 'spaceships'. Amid the dusty streets and dull grey- and terracotta-coloured homes, these playful confections appeared to have arrived from another planet. Which, in financial terms at least, they had: some of the *cholets* designed by Mamani are worth $2 million or more. This architectural style has been dubbed 'new Andean', 'indigenous postmodern', even 'psychedelic baroque', but Alejandra had a better description: 'Some people call it "firecracker architecture" because it explodes in front of your eyes.'

***

A few years later, in 2017, I returned for a closer look at the *cholets* with another guide, Jorge. We met at my guesthouse in downtown La Paz before taking the *teleferico* up to El Alto, soaring over densely packed working-class neighbourhoods. In the distance was the Estadio Hernando Siles, one of the highest football stadiums on Earth; the Bolivian national team has a predictably formidable home record and had beaten Argentina a few months earlier. We got off at El Alto's Ciudad Satélite *teleferico* station, which was modern, efficient and scrupulously clean. Students took advantage of the free wifi and stray dogs, adopted by the staff and kitted out with warm coats, lay contently in the main hall. We caught a taxi to the Santiago I district, which is known for its expensive *cholets*. As we drove Jorge, curly haired and intense, spoke about Andean cosmography and the concept of *ayni*, which highlights the importance of reciprocity, balance, solidarity, and inter-connectedness. 'It emphasises the links between everyone and nature,' he said. 'People should work together and make sure no one goes without.'

We were dropped off at an elaborate red, blue, and grey *cholet* designed to resemble the *Transformers* character Optimus Prime; another of the architect's creations is based on the Marvel superhero Iron Man. These buildings, Jorge explained, allow wealthy Aymara residents to assert their status and heritage: we have money, we are proud of our identity and we – and El Alto – are here to stay, they appear to say. 'There have always been rich Aymara, but before Evo [Morales], they were timid. They didn't want to draw attention to themselves,' said Silvestre in one interview. 'Now they say: "This is where the successful Aymara live".'

Beyond their symbolic value, the buildings are profitable businesses; Jorge described them as 'tools' for their owners. Most of the *cholets* have a similar layout: the ground floor have stores or a shopping arcade; the floors above host event spaces to be hired out for the lavish religious celebrations, weddings and birthdays that form a key aspect of Aymara culture; further up there are apartments for rent; and at the very top of the building is a 'chalet', typically a duplex home for the *cholet*'s owner and their family. The fanciest *cholets* boast swimming pools or indoor five-a-side football pitches, while towers, spires and even Russian-style onion-domes are used to decorate the roofs.

Jorge showed me round a five-storey *cholet* owned by one of his contacts. The kaleidoscopic exterior combined peach, burnt orange, maroon, lime green and chrome decorations to dazzling effect. More mundanely the shops on the ground floor sold mobile phone accessories, party costumes, and DIY goods. Inside the entrance, the hallway was functional, even austere, with plenty of bare concrete and every scrap of space utilised for storage, mainly of empty beer crates. By contrast the cavernous party halls on the second and third floors were a riot of colour and ornamentation. The high ceilings had galaxies of tiny white lights and huge multi-tiered chandeliers. There were long marble bars, curvaceous balconies and pastel-shaded pillars, as well as flashing panels and cloud-shaped mirrors. The walls were decorated with murals and reliefs of traditional Andean symbols and Tiwanaku iconography: condors, *chakanas* – which have four equal-length stepped sides and are also known as 'Inca' or 'Andean' crosses – pyramids, agricultural terraces, and the sun, moon and stars. Many of the designs and colour-schemes were inspired by traditional Aymara textiles and ceramics, said Jorge. The gleaming tiles were patterned with swirls, checks, and chevrons. The room felt like a technicolour dream or a fairground ride, gaudy but glorious.

This *cholet* could cater for 600 people but some have the capacity for a thousand or more. Parties can last several days and feature live music, copious amounts of food and booze, and outfits costing hundreds or even thousands of dollars, Jorge continued: 'In Aymara culture, people dress simply, live humble lives, but spend a lot of money on fiestas.' Although synonymous with El Alto, *cholets* are now springing up across Bolivia – I saw versions as far away as the Amazonian city of Trinidad – as well as in areas of Peru, Brazil, and Argentina with sizeable Bolivian communities. In the 2018 documentary *Cholet*, Mamani spoke powerfully about aiming to restore Aymara 'values', 'identity' and 'culture' through his work. 'Famous architects go to study abroad and they come back indoctrinated with an ideology from the west ... We need to get closer to the clients, to the users, to our society and people ... This is what I am doing,' he added.

***

We rode the *teleferico* back down to La Paz to look around an area known as the Mercado de Hechicería or Mercado de las Brujas (Witches' Market), whose colourful stores have become an essential stop on most tourist itineraries. Yet as Jorge explained *'bruja'* ('witch' in Spanish) is a pejorative term and another example of the othering of indigenous Bolivians. 'When the Spanish came they called these women "witches",' he said. 'But that is not what they are. They are *chifleras*.' Loosely combining the roles of healer, therapist, and mystic, *chifleras* play an important role for Aymara, Quechua and other indigenous people across the *altiplano*. They collect, sell and prepare items for use in traditional medicinal treatments, rituals and ceremonies, as well as offering guidance and advice. The othering of these women continues today in much of the travel writing about La Paz (including, to my shame, in guidebooks I've worked on in the past).

We stopped at one of the stores and Jorge introduced me to the owner, Lucia. Dressed in a blue-and-white checked dress, brown shawl, and tiny, delicately placed bowler hat, she was in her early 20s and looked bored. To enter her minuscule store, which was barely bigger than a cupboard, I had to duck under a bunch of shrivelled llama foetuses hanging from the door frame (Jorge later told me that only miscarried or stillborn foetuses were used in rituals and that live animals were never killed for this purpose). Lucia's mobile rang to the tune of Shakira's 'Hips Don't Lie' and she broke away from painting her finger nails purple to tap out a flurry of WhatsApp messages.

The low-ceilinged room was jam-packed. One wall was lined with aphrodisiacs with lurid photos of amorous couples and names like 'Come to me, come to me', 'Love Honey' and 'Erectol'. Perfumes promised to improve your mood or attract a partner, while plastic tubs contained potions for prostrate problems, hair loss, asthma, and various other ailments. Plastic bags enclosed honeycombs, coca leaves, chia seeds, and powder made from the root of the maca plant, which grows in the high Andes, as well as 'extracts' from creatures as diverse as snails and sharks. Shelves on the opposite wall were covered with incense sticks, soapstone figurines, phallic-shaped candles, clumps of feathers, and strings of beads. There were also wads of tiny dollar bills, and miniature cars, houses, mobile phones and other items. A menagerie of dead armadillos, birds, turtles, starfish and frogs, dehydrated and brittle, sat beneath the llama foetuses.

With a little encouragement, Lucia was drawn away from her phone and began to talk. 'People ask me to prepare *mesas blancas*, offerings, to burn on the last Friday of the month to bring good luck,' she said. Lucia then pointed at a crowd of stone figurines and talismans: 'Those go on the *mesas*. Each one represents something different. The owls mean education; the entwined couple, love; the puma, safety; the condor, travel.' She paused, before adding: 'Now you should buy some condors, to bring good luck on your journey.'

Although the market is increasingly touristy, most of the shoppers were *paceños*. I eavesdropped on a young, smartly dressed couple as they approached another *chiflera*, who was busy knitting a shawl. A llama foetus was purchased and shoved unceremoniously into a cloth bag, its dilated eyes peeking out of the top. Jorge explained the foetuses are used in many different rituals. 'Sometimes they are buried under the foundations of buildings as an apology to Pachamama for digging into her and to bring prosperity,' he said. 'Sometimes they are burned for luck before a long journey.'

Jorge also spoke about the Kallawaya, members of an indigenous community based in a remote valley north of La Paz. For centuries they have worked as healers, herbalists, doctors and religious figures across the Andes; some made it as far as Panama, more than 3,000 km north of Bolivia. The Kallawaya have an extensive knowledge of plants and herbs dating back centuries; they are thought to have been the first to have used the bark of the cinchona tree, the source of quinine, to treat malaria. UNESCO has described the medical knowledge of the Kallawaya as 'extraordinary' and their 980-species 'botanical pharma-copoeia ... as one of the richest in the world.'

***

The Mercado de Hechicería bisects the thigh-achingly steep Calle Sagárnaga, traditionally the centre of the Aymara district of La Paz and now the city's backpacker heartland. Founded as a so-called 'Indian parish' during the colonial era, the area retains a strong indigenous character. Although sometimes dismissed today as 'Gringo Alley', the street has always had a transient nature. In the 17th century, it provided rest and sustenance for travellers moving between the Pacific coast and the silver mines of Potosí, some 420 km southeast of La Paz. Now it caters for a steady stream of panting foreign visitors, who hike up and down the smooth cobblestones, dodging lumbering, multico-loured buses patched together from spare parts, the drivers crunching through the gears to make it up the sharp incline.

After visiting the market, I said goodbye to Jorge and trudged uphill, pausing every few minutes to catch my breath. Young and elderly locals – many with children fastened to their backs in papooses – streamed past at an impressive pace. Women in tight black shawls and waistcoats guarded baskets of doughy pastries. Shop fronts overflowed with llama- and alpaca-wool products – bobble hats, socks, ponchos, shoulder bags, and water-bottle holders. Travel agencies advertised trips to the Salar de Uyuni, flights to the Amazon, cycle tours down 'the most dangerous road in the world', and guided ascents of Mount Illimani.

A few streets to the west, I reached the Mercado Buenos Aires, an open-air market that stretched over 30 blocks. This was a no-go area after dark, I'd been warned at the hotel, and none too safe during the day. But I was eager to find out more about La Paz's Aymara heritage. Also known as Huyustus, the market had a rough-around-the-edges charm, aided by the fact that I saw only a couple of other travellers in the area, both of whom looked rather lost. The stalls sold just about anything you might want and much more you wouldn't. There were stacks of guavas, avocados, custard apples with green, dragon-like scales, and tropical fruits such as the *lúcuma*, whose dry, orange flesh tasted vaguely of butterscotch. I ran my hands through sacks of black, pebbly *chuños*, potatoes freeze-dried in an ancient process that involves repeated exposure to sunshine and frost. Other stalls had white goods smuggled in from Chile and Peru, fake designer clothes, and mining outfits, boots and equipment. Women sold *salteñas* and *tucumanes*, pastries stuffed with meat or vegetables, pots of thick, bubbling stew, hunks of roasted meat, and plastic bottles of 100-per-cent-proof alcohol.

Beyond the market, along Avenida Buenos Aires, devilish masks with protruding eyes, bulbous noses, wild tufts of hair and leering grins stared out from shop windows. Huyustus is the spiritual heart of the raucous Fiesta del Gran Poder (Festival of Great Power), which started life as a small-scale affair among migrant market workers, but has grown into a city-wide celebration involving locals of all classes and ethnicities. A mix of Catholic and Aymara beliefs and rituals, the fiesta features masked and costumed dancers, parading brass bands, and vast amounts of alcohol.

On nearby Calle Max Paredes, shops sold the high-waisted pleated skirts known as *polleras* and bowler hats that have become the trademark of the *chola paceña* (or *cholita*, as they are commonly known). This was once a derogatory term for Aymara women who had moved to the city from the countryside. In La Paz they faced racism, discrimination, and restrictions on where they could go and what forms of public transport they could use. But over the last couple of decades *chola paceña* has been reclaimed as a badge of pride by indigenous women born and brought up in the city. In recent years, they have found success in areas of society previously denied to them, from academia to politics. Meanwhile, *cholita* wrestling shows, which have a similar mix of soap opera, pantomime violence and physical prowess as WWE in the USA and *lucha libre* in Mexico, have become popular forms of entertainment.

Cholitas typically wear their hair long and plaited, earrings and brooches, petticoats, and shawls known as *mantas*, as well as *polleras* and carefully balanced bowler hats. The origin of the latter, popular since the 1920s, is the subject of much debate. According to one story, a British trader imported a cache of the hats but failed to interest local men in them. Instead, his son suggested adding coloured ribbons and tassels and marketing them to women. Married women originally wore the hats angled to the right, single women to the left. (This signalling has since died out: today married and single women alike tend to wear their bowler hats dead straight.)

'Tourists think *cholitas* are poor, but that's not true,' said a young woman working in one of the shops. 'Some of us are but others can spend more than $5,000 or $10,000 on clothes and jewellery. They are investments. It is important for us to show we have money too, that we can dress nicely, that we are proud. Even if you can't afford to buy new clothes or jewellery, we'll rent them for Gran Poder.' These outfits are as potent a symbol of indigenous pride – and wealth – as the *cholets* of El Alto.

A short walk downhill took me to Calle Illampu, where a few genuine items bobbed in an ocean of counterfeit brand-name hiking and snow boots, insulated sleeping bags, Gore-Tex jackets, ski gear, crampons, and all manner of backpacks, from miniature day sacks to 80-litre monsters for mountain ascents. The presence of counterfeit Quechua gear provided a certain pleasing irony: a French sportswear company that branded itself with the name of an indigenous Andean people – the largest ethnic group in Bolivia, just ahead of the Aymara – had in turn been knocked-off in the Andes.

***

On my final day in La Paz Jorge suggested I visit the clock in Plaza Murillo, which lies in the heart of the Casco Viejo, the Old Town. It was a 40-minute walk from my guesthouse but despite the labyrinthine warren of streets, it is difficult to get lost in La Paz: head downhill for long enough and you always hit Avenida Mariscal Santa Cruz, the city's main artery. Also known as the Prado, the tree-lined avenue is a lonely stretch of green in a largely grey city centre. Couples walked hand in hand, university students smoked on benches, and school children streamed out of the Dumbo ice cream parlour clasping over-burdened cones. Crouching women sold batteries, padlocks, inky newspapers, self-help books and copies of *Harry Potter*.

Amid the cacophony of car horns and choking exhaust fumes, you could almost miss the sand-coloured *mestizo*-baroque façade of the Iglesia de San Francisco, which sits at the junction with Calle Sagárnaga. Originally built in 1549, the church was restored in the 1700s after being damaged by heavy snowfall and has since survived arson and insurrection. Above the entrance is a statue of St Francis, arms aloft in adoration, or perhaps despair at the onslaught of the afternoon rush hour beneath him. The church square is a popular spot for political protests, a regular occurrence in La Paz. But when I visited there was only a faded banner and a few torn posters. Supplicants huddled outside or ate from food carts. Shoeshines known as *lustrabotas* touted for business, wearing balaclavas because of the stigma that some people attach to their job. A group of *paceños* queued at a voter-registration desk; one man had a sink unit tucked under his arm, as if he had just popped away from a kitchen installation.

I hiked up to the old colonial-era district, passing a new Mormon church and several offices of state, before stumbling into a demonstration. Outside the municipal council a group of women banged sticks on Coke bottles, wielded saucepans and demanded restitution. They menaced three heavily-armed police offices, bulky in body armour and armed with assault rifles; one wore a chunky necklace of grenades.

***

I continued on towards Plaza Murillo, crossing constantly between sun and shade, perspiring one moment, shivering the next, trapped in a seemingly endless cycle of removing and adding layers of clothing. After passing an internet café with a hand-written sign warning 'pornographic pages are banned' and a joint that claimed to be 'La Paz's first absinthe bar', I found the square, which is flanked by the presidential palace, parliament, and cathedral. All was quiet but Plaza Murillo has a bloody history. In 1946, 79 years after the British ambassador was supposedly paraded naked around the square, President Gualberto Villaroel met an even worse fate. Inspired by reports of the death of Mussolini, protesters lynched Villareal, who combined reformist and fascist tendencies. Today he is known as *'el presidente colgado'* (the hanged president).

At the apex of the mustard-and-white parliament was the clock Jorge had mentioned. As I approached it through a crowd of *lustrabotas*, pigeon feeders and elderly couples, I noticed something strange and slightly unsettling on the clock face: the numbers were reversed and the hands ran anti-clockwise. It was like *Alice in Wonderland* – time was literally running backwards.

I later tracked down an interview with Bolivia's then foreign minister, David Choquehuanca, who described it as a 'clock of the south'. '[We're] trying to recover our identity,' he said. 'In keeping with [this] ... our clocks should turn to the left ... Who said clocks always have to run the same way? Why do we always have to be obedient?' Some said the clock was a symbol of decolonisation, others saw it as a political stunt, yet it also reflected a fundamentally different conception of reality. To outsiders, Bolivia can sometimes feel like a place where western conceptions of time and space do not apply. Ancient beliefs and practices not only exist alongside modernity but interact and even shape it. The past here is not another country.

For speakers of the Aymara language, this sense is even more pronounced: the past is in front of them, the future behind. In a 2006 paper, Rafael E. Núñez and Eve Sweetser of the University of California wrote: 'In Aymara, the basic word for "front" (*nayra*, "eye/front/sight") is also a basic expression meaning "past", and the basic word for "back" (*qhipa*, "back/behind") is a basic expression for "future".' This is not merely a linguistic quirk, Núñez and Sweetser argue, but something that indicates an understanding of time and space profoundly different from every other studied culture. Aymara speakers know what happened in the past – they can see it in front of them. The future, however, is not known – it is behind them, hidden from view.

***

In the evening I caught a bus bound for the eastern lowlands, another area where new settlements, revolutionary movements, and invigorated identities have helped to shape modern Bolivia. On the outskirts of El Alto I received a jolt from the past. Another effigy dangled from a lamppost beside a building site. He was bent double by the wind, as if suffering from a terrible stomach ache. We drove on and I spotted several more: doughy figures, with fat fingers poking out of woollen gloves, and awkwardly angled feet. Some of the heads were bowed down, as if out of shame; others faced forwards, their faces impassive but unsettling. Most were dressed in brown or grey trousers and jackets or hooded sweatshirts. Some wore trainers; one had a pair of football boots. There were so many of them I lost count.

When I first visited Bolivia, the effigies I saw typically represented corrupt politicians; now they generally stood for common criminals or miscreants: murderers, thieves, even drunks. It felt like progress of sorts. Most had signs attached to them or messages scrawled on their torsos. 'Antisocial gangsters are banned,' read one. 'Criminals will be killed – obey the junta,' another warned. The effigies were not idle expressions of discontent. Lack of faith in the authorities mean some people take the law into their own hands. The effigies were often accompanied by the slogan '*los vecinos*', which literally translates as 'the neighbours' but in this context suggests something akin to 'lynch mob'. When thieves are caught they are sometimes stripped, beaten, and in extreme cases even killed. The police are often unwilling to intervene.

As we left El Alto, I spotted a final effigy. It was dressed in an orange jumpsuit, an outfit commonly worn by Bolivian miners but also disturbingly reminiscent of a Guantánamo Bay detainee.

CHAPTER 7
Mission control

The Jesuit legacy in the eastern lowlands:
Santa Cruz de la Sierra and Chiquitos

We made it to the edge of central Santa Cruz de la Sierra before the fast-encroaching flood waters forced me and my fellow passengers to abandon the bus. A violent storm had raged for hours. Sheets of rain lashed against the windows, lightning flashed overhead, and thunder rattled through the frame of the seat and up my spine. Overflowing drains gushed muddy torrents across the roads and into ground-floor shops and homes. The bus driver was forced to plough a circuitous route, the water lapping at the hub caps. Many roads were impassable and eventually we ran out of options and halted 500 m short of the Terminal Bi-Modal, the city's main bus and train station.

I grabbed my backpack and sheltered in a shop doorway in the vain hope the downpour would abate. After half an hour of unceasing rain, I gave in and set off on the 30-minute walk to my hotel, which was located just off Plaza 24 de Setiembre, Santa Cruz's main square. Although soaked within seconds, I made steady progress along a raised hump of earth that ran down the central reservation and kept me just above the water line. I'd almost reached the end of it when a lorry surged past, sending out a barrage of metre-high waves. As the tide engulfed me up to my chest and almost knocked me off my feet, the cliché 'a flood of Biblical proportions' sprang to mind. This at least felt appropriate, given that I'd travelled to Santa Cruz to find out about the legacy of a utopian Catholic order.

Eventually I reached the hotel and checked in, leaving behind a trail of wet footprints in the lobby. By the evening the rain had stopped, the heat picked up and the flood waters began to subside, exposing a carpet of detritus: plastic bottles, fast food cartons, sodden balls of newspapers, a broken umbrella, and a child's shoe. The streets were virtually deserted, apart from an elderly homeless man, bare-chested, carefully wringing out his jumper.

***

Arriving in Santa Cruz from the *altiplano* feels like landing in another country, even when you don't have to contend with an epic tropical storm. Located around 600 km east of La Paz, the city is the biggest and wealthiest in Bolivia, with a distinct regional identity and strong independent streak. It sits in the (generally) hot and humid eastern lowlands, a fast-developing region that has seen increasing droughts, wildfires, and floods in recent years. The last of the Andean foothills lie in the west, while in the east, bordering Brazil, is Bolivia's chunk of the Pantanal, the world's largest tropical wetlands. Northeast of Santa Cruz are the grasslands and tropical dry forests of the Chiquitos region. Further north is the Amazon and the inaccessible Parque Nacional Noel Kempff Mercado, a UNESCO World Heritage Site whose pristine Huanchaca plateau was reputedly one of the inspirations behind Arthur Conan Doyle's *The Lost World*. (More than 60 sq km of the park were engulfed by fires in 2020, according to Bolivian conservation NGO Fundación Amigos de la Naturaleza.)

In the southern part of the eastern lowlands stretching down into Argentina and Paraguay, is the Chaco, an arid, largely uninhabited wilderness. Between 1932 and 1935, a large swathe of this territory was the site of a catastrophic war between Bolivia and Paraguay, both poor, landlocked and smarting from the loss of territory to more powerful neighbours (Paraguay's land mass essentially halved as a result of its defeat to Brazil and Argentina in the 1864–70 War of the Triple Alliance). The war was fuelled by a desire to control the Paraguay River, a vital route to the Atlantic for both countries, and speculation, later proved to be unfounded, that the region held rich oil reserves. As Pablo Neruda suggested in his poem 'Standard Oil Co.', the agitations of competing foreign oil companies – which 'buy countries, seas, police, country councils, distant regions' – also played a role in the conflict.

La Guerra de la Sed (The War of the Thirst) was the most devastating conflict in South America in the 20th century: approximately 65,000 Bolivians and 36,000 Paraguayans were killed, 2 and 3 per cent of their respective populations. To put those figures in context, the UK lost less than 1 per cent of its population during the Second World War; France lost less than 1.5 per cent. Ultimately, Paraguay emerged victorious and gained most of the disputed territory, though Bolivia was given a corridor to, and a port on, the Paraguay River. Given the scale of the casualties it is perhaps more accurate to say that neither side 'won', Paraguay simply lost more slowly.

Today, Santa Cruz is expanding rapidly. Its centre remains a neat grid of predominantly colonial and independence-era architecture, mostly whitewashed buildings with overhanging red-tiled roofs providing shade for pedestrians on the pavements below. But head out in any direction and you discover a city that would not look out of place in the United States, with sprawling suburbs, buzzer-entry tower blocks and mammoth shopping malls that span several blocks. Santa Cruz was markedly more modern, prosperous, and consumerist than anywhere else I visited in Bolivia, even though many here live in poverty, particularly recent migrants from the *altiplano*. There were plenty of international chains, including Starbucks, Hard Rock Cafe, KFC and Argentine ice cream parlour Freddo. Imported cars, business suits, iPhones and flashy trainers were ubiquitous sights. Brazilian, US, Japanese, and Chinese voices were commonly heard. Newspaper adverts promised leafy neighbourhoods with gated apartments and private security. Thriving restaurants sold expensive sushi and sashimi, thin-crust pizzas, craft beer, and barbecued *pacamutus*, giant shish-style kebabs.

The foundations of Santa Cruz's prosperity were laid more than 300 years ago, when groups of European Jesuits arrived in the eastern lowlands and founded a series of mission towns they hoped would develop into utopian societies.

***

Early the next morning, which was dry but overcast, I set out in search of the legacy of the Jesuits. My guide Walter was a portly, middle-aged *cruceño* – as residents of the city are known – smartly dressed in a salmon-pink polo shirt with a white collar. He took an obvious pride in his pristine Toyota, which was kitted out with two mini TV screens, a fridge stocked with bottles of mineral water, a rubbish bin, and a glove box filled with boiled sweets. Like many people I'd met in Santa Cruz, he had relatives working overseas, including a sister who was married to a firefighter in London.

As we left the centre and passed through the outlying *anillos* – the concentric ring roads that divide up Santa Cruz – the city's agribusiness and hydrocarbon focus became increasingly apparent. Dozens of farm supply stores, hardware shops, and builders' merchants lined the multi-lane highway. Forecourts were packed with rows of gleaming tractors, harvesters, loaders, trailers, diggers, and other farming machinery, alongside car showrooms and massive hypermarkets. Construction work had started on a new highway, and there were cranes, scaffolding, and building sites on virtually every block. Billboards showcased manicured golf courses, upmarket housing developments, and leisure resorts like Güembé Biocentro, whose attractions included several swimming pools, an orchid park and a butterfly dome.

Eventually we left the city behind and drove on to the town of Cotoca. Every December thousands of *cruceños* make a pilgrimage here to pay their respects to the patron saint of the department of Santa Cruz, the Virgin of Cotoca, whose image was reputedly discovered in the centre of a tree trunk. 'So many people walk here from Santa Cruz, a distance of 30 km or so, that the authorities have to close off the highway,' said Walter, as he pulled into the main square. I spotted a pair of sloths slumbering in the branches of a palm tree and wound down my window. A pungent odour reminiscent of damp, stale laundry left too long in the washing machine invaded the car. One of the sloths, a bundle of shaggy black fur and claws that curled back on themselves, lethargically shifted position, sending down a shower of twigs and leaves onto the benches below. 'Sometimes they even shit on your head,' Walter warned, his face wrinkled in disgust.

Just beyond Cotoca we came to a halt at a toll booth. The car was immediately surrounded by a crowd of hawkers touting their wares: wheelbarrows of *cuñapés*, balls of yucca dough filled with chewy cheese that fell midway between a biscuit and a cake; baskets of ripe mandarins; piping-hot coffee; family-sized bags of peanuts and packets of chocolate biscuits; boxes of tissues and mini first aid kits. Walter drove on through the tortilla-flat plains, passing soy plantations – a mainstay of Santa Cruz's agribusiness sector – cattle fields and processing plants. After two and a half hours a low range of green hills appeared in the distance. At the entrance to the town of San Ramón, near a turn-off for the Amazon region, was a monument dedicated to three former Bolivian presidents born in the area – Germán Busch Becerra (1937–39), José Miguel de Velasco Franco (1828, 1829, 1839–41 and 1848) and Hugo Banzer (1971–78 and 1997–2001).

As we drove on the terrain grew greener and more fertile, with thickets of shaggy green trees and pockets of shocking-pink flowers. Walter explained we had entered the Chiquitano dry forest, which forms a transition zone between the Amazon and the thorny scrub of the Chaco. (In 2019, a couple of years after my visit, this biodiverse region, already under pressure from cattle-ranching, industrial agriculture, hydrocarbon extraction, infrastructure projects, and commercial logging, was ravaged by wildfires. The following year the forest was hit again: according to research by the Monitoring the Andean Amazon Project, more than 2,600 sq km of it were consumed by blazes in 2020.) Four hours after departing Santa Cruz we arrived in San Javier, home of the oldest Jesuit church in the Chiquitos region.

***

Until the mid-16th century, the eastern lowlands were blanketed with forests, savannah and swamps, and home to dozens of linguistically and culturally diverse indigenous communities. Thanks to the region's isolation, they had managed to escape much of the violence meted out by the conquistadors elsewhere in Latin America. But given their location between the valuable silver mines of the Andes and burgeoning Spanish towns in what are now Paraguay, Argentina, and Uruguay, the eastern lowlands eventually proved too strategically important to ignore. In 1561, a conquistador named Ñuflo de Chavez established the frontier settlement of Santa Cruz, 200 km east of the site of its modern-day successor. Raiding parties were sent out into the surrounding region, which became known as Chiquitos, a reference to the small doors on the traditional homes of its inhabitants.

Despite fierce resistance, huge numbers of indigenous people were enslaved and forced to labour on settler farms. Slavery soon became a business in its own right for the settlers and many enslaved people from the region were sold to sugar plantation owners in Brazil or mine operators in the Andes. But the security of the Spanish colonialists in Santa Cruz remained precarious. They failed to fully subdue the indigenous communities, despite launching a string of costly and brutal military expeditions. Another threat came in the form of the Portuguese colonialists in neighbouring Brazil, who also laid claim to the region. In the 1680s, as a final resort, the authorities in Santa Cruz turned to the Jesuits, who were seen as an inexpensive means of securing lasting control over the eastern lowlands and their inhabitants.

Founded in 1540 by St Ignatius of Loyola in response to the Reformation, the Jesuits soon expanded overseas. Priests from the order landed in Brazil in the 1560s and set about converting as many locals as they could. Encouraged by generous tax breaks from the colonial authorities, they quickly spread throughout the central part of South America, a disputed zone for much of this period. Their strategy was simple: missionaries were dispatched to remote areas and charged with persuading or forcing indigenous people to settle in newly formed mission towns. These settlements became known as *reducciones* as their indigenous residents were given the dubious pleasure of being 'reduced' to 'European civilisation', as well as converted to Christianity.

The Jesuits slowly gained a foothold in Chiquitos and between 1696 and 1760 established 10 missions in the region, as well as others in the Bolivian Amazon (including Trinidad). These towns were self-sufficient, largely independent of the Spanish authorities, and highly profitable. Some indigenous people came to them of their own volition, understandably desiring a more peaceful existence after enduring decades of Spanish military assaults and raids; many others, though, were brought by force little different to that deployed by the Spanish and Portuguese enslavers. 'This was no namby-pamby, turn-the-other-cheek Christianity,' wrote Richard Gott in *Land Without Evil*. 'This was the church militant.' Inside the missions, he argued, the Jesuits deployed a mix of brainwashing and inducements and 'forced the Indians to enjoy their new freedoms'.

The Jesuits drew inspiration from the idealised societies depicted in humanist works such as Thomas More's *Utopia* and Philip Sidney's *Arcadia*. There were strict guidelines on the location, layout and architecture of their missions. Large areas of land were cleared for agriculture and ranching, and European farming techniques, livestock, and crops were introduced. Some indigenous social structures and customs were maintained and many *caciques* (chiefs) were co-opted, used to disseminate Jesuit teachings and reinforce their authority. The priests provided religious instruction in indigenous languages, one of which, Chiquitano, was subsequently adopted as a *lingua franca* across the missions, spurring the development of a new collective identity. They also taught the latest construction, arts and craft techniques, creating a skilled class of indigenous artists and artisans.

There were usually only a couple of priests in each of the missions at any one time, which obliged them to take on a wide variety of roles, as a 1744 letter from Swiss Jesuit Father Martin Schmid, quoted in *Cultural Worlds of the Jesuits in Colonial Latin America*, indicates. The priests, he wrote, were 'councillors and judges, doctors and surgeons ... builders, carpenters and cabinetmakers ... blacksmiths, locksmiths, tailors, cobblers, millers, bakers, cooks, shepherds, gardeners, painters ... and whatever else is required.'

Music played an important role in the proselytising process. The inhabitants of the missions were taught to play imported instruments such as organs, violins, cellos, harps and trumpets, and later started to make their own versions. Choirs and orchestras were set up and soon rivalled the finest on the continent. Over time a distinctive form of music known as 'Bolivian baroque' or 'missional baroque' emerged. It was highly praised by the French naturalist and explorer Alcide d'Orbigny, who visited the region in the 1820s. '[In] all of America I had heard nothing better,' he wrote in *Journey into South America*.

***

Today, six of the Chiquitos missions survive. The oldest, San Javier, dates back to 1691. As we drove into the centre the dusty roads were lined with beautifully maintained but modest 18th- and

19th-century buildings, most of them a single storey in height; more modern constructions were few and far between. One-room stores sold ice cream, groceries, and children's clothes. The centre of the town was laid-out in the classic Jesuit fashion. There was a large, leafy rectangular plaza ringed with wooden lampposts. Its focal point was a twisted wooden cross, a sharp contrast with the military and political figures more commonly found in Bolivia's plazas. Around three of its sides were terraces of identical buildings that were once home to the *caciques* and their families. They had cream walls with blood-red bands along the base, moss-speckled tiled roofs overhanging the pavement to create an open gallery, and patches of grass and palm trees out in front. Several parallel streets were lined with smaller versions of these homes.

On the fourth side of the square, in prime position, was a wood-and-adobe church. Even for a non-believer, it was an impressive sight. Completed in 1752 under the guidance of Schmid and – like everything in the Jesuit missions – thanks to the skill and labour of the indigenous residents, the church was easily the biggest and most formidable building in town. It blended Germanic architecture with local influences such as the huge indigenous Guaraní 'long huts', some of which could accommodate a thousand people or more. The squat A-frame roof was tiled and supported by thick wooden posts, while the facade, a pale stony grey colour, was covered with faded mustard decorations such as cornices, reliefs, coving, and geometric motifs. A portico provided a suitable sense of grandeur and a wide cobblestone entranceway stretched out in front. Above a set of imposing doors that would not have looked out of place on a castle was an inscription in Latin from *Genesis*: *'Domus Dei Et Porta Coeli'* ('House of God and Gateway to Heaven').

The church was the centrepiece of a much larger complex, which included schools, workshops, recital rooms, and living quarters for the priests and visitors, as well as cloistered courtyards and patios with closely-cropped lawns and a free-standing bell tower. Originally there would also have been vegetable gardens and orchards, plus separate cemeteries for male and female residents. 'The church was restored in the 1980s and 90s but around three-quarters of the church is original,' said Walter, as we watched an evangelical group attempt to hang a banner above the entrance. Their efforts were undone by an inopportune gust of wind and the banner fluttered over the road and landed in the square, coming to rest like a giant butterfly. The cavernous interior of the church was less ostentatious than others I had seen in Bolivia. Exposed wooden beams, plain tiles, and a few simple murals and psalms on the wall. Today, there are pews but Walter told me that in the time of the Jesuits worshippers were obliged to kneel or sit on the tiled floor during services. It was supremely peaceful, except for the faint hum of a motorbike idling outside, and incredibly clean, save for a lone mauve flip-flop in the courtyard, and an empty Coke bottle that had been lobbed onto the roof of one of the outbuildings.

An hour drive north-east of San Javier took us to another of the Jesuit missions. Although it had a similar feel and layout to its neighbour, Concepción was larger, more developed and home to an army barracks. As we stopped for lunch in the main square, a company of light-footed soldiers jogged past, the only residents out on the street at this time of day. Walter and I ate a lunch of vegetable soup, chicken *milanesa* and *flan casero*, a local version of crème caramel, in a shady garden. We were watched over by a pair of tame green parrots, who paused periodically to screech 'hola' and peck at a plastic bowl filled with cold pasta.

Concepción's church was finished a few years after its counterpart in San Javier and the work was also overseen by Schmid. At first glance, it looked like a giant, well-maintained barn, but a closer inspection revealed a high level of detail and craftsmanship. Its roof was raised up by 121 wooden poles, each one twisted like a candy cane, while an adjacent open-sided bell tower at the front was accessed via a spiral staircase. The gold-leaf-covered interior was more opulent than the church in San Javier and felt almost garish by comparison – it was impressive as a display of wealth if not of religious piety. Walter looked at me and rubbed his fingers and thumb together, a reminder that beyond the idealistic rhetoric the Jesuit missions were also extremely profitable enterprises. (This has given rise to all manner of myths of hidden Jesuit wealth – notably of gold and silver mines – which proved particularly popular in the early 20th century and still circulate today.) Several of the wood-carving and painting workshops set up by the Jesuits remain in use and a rhythmic tapping sound drifted in through the open doors.

I spotted a note tacked up on the wall near the entrance of the church: 'Here you come to talk to God – turn off your phone.' Minutes later I heard a familiar ring tone and saw a teenage girl in a class at the far end of the church scrambling about in her rucksack. On the top of the retablo was the Jesuit symbol: a sun encircling the initials 'IHS' – an abbreviation of 'Jesus' in Greek and representative of the Latin phrase 'Jesus, saviour of man', Walter informed me – topped with a cross and set above three nails. Alongside classical biblical imagery, the walls were covered with a series of modern murals. One set placed the Easter story in a contemporary local context: a forlorn

Christ was shown in the fast-disappearing forests of Chiquitos beside a pair of rifle-toting hunters carrying the carcass of a dead jaguar on a pole, a gang of loggers cutting down tree after tree with their chainsaws, and an angry mob gathering in Concepción's main square. These messages about the threat of environmental destruction had an added resonance, given the devastating wildfires that have swept the region in recent years.

***

As the 1700s wore on tensions grew between South America's colonial rulers and the increasingly powerful and independently minded Jesuits. The order was accused of supporting indigenous rebellions, participating in a conspiracy to kill the Portuguese king, and fomenting riots in Madrid. In 1767, the Spanish expelled Jesuits from their territories, following similar moves by their Portuguese and French counterparts. The 10 missions in Chiquitos, which by this point had a collective population of more than 24,000 indigenous people, came under the control of the colonial authorities.

Some historians have described the missions as 'utopian societies' or even 'socialist theocracies'. In theory land was commonly owned, the indigenous inhabitants were free men and women, and the priests strove to create a harmonious paradise on Earth. Yet they were simply another form of colonialism, even if the Jesuits managed to be somewhat less brutal than Santa Cruz's Spanish settlers. In the missions the Chiquitanos were treated like children. Despite being granted a semblance of autonomy – through indigenous councils, for example – the Jesuits retained true control. The missions were also fertile breeding grounds for European diseases, and epidemics amongst the indigenous residents were common and disastrous.

Nevertheless, the quality of life for the majority of Chiquitanos undoubtedly declined sharply after the expulsion of the Jesuits. The valuable ranches of the mission towns were seized and thousands of indigenous people forced to labour on them in atrocious conditions little different to slavery. Meanwhile, the churches and many other Jesuit buildings fell into disrepair, though their remoteness helped to spare them the destruction that befell their counterparts over the following centuries. The mission towns 'returned to scrub and swamp' and the Chiquitanos 'were soon worse off than they had ever been before,' wrote Gott. In the 19th century they were 'exterminated by the successor regimes to the Spanish crown'.

By the 1920s, the Chiquitos region was seemingly in terminal decline, according to one visiting British author. 'Every reader of fiction is familiar with the man who is dying because he has nothing to live for … That, briefly, is the way of Eastern Bolivia,' wrote Julian Duguid in his book *Green Hell*.

In many respects, Bolivia essentially remained a feudal country until the mid-20th century, with predominantly indigenous workers labouring in mines or on ranches owned, by and large, by Bolivians of European descent. But the disastrous Chaco War proved to be one of the catalysts for change. It created what became known as the 'Chaco Generation', whose largely middle-class members were increasingly critical of the corrupt, incompetent military-political elite and open to radical ideas.

This fed into the growing movements of indigenous *campesinos* and miners that drove forward the 1952 National Revolution. In the years that followed, President Víctor Paz Estenssoro instituted sweeping land reforms and broke up many of the biggest estates, nationalised the mining industry, extended the vote, improved welfare provision, and provided greater legal recognition of indigenous rights and languages in the new constitution. This provoked a backlash. By 1964 the army was involved and a coup forced Paz Estenssoro out of office and into exile. 'I am taking you either to the airport or the cemetery. Which do you choose?' he was reportedly asked by his replacement, General Alfredo Ovando.

Hugo Banzer, Concepción's most famous son, was involved in the coup and subsequently appointed minister for education and culture by Ovando. A graduate of the notorious US School of the Americas, he rose to the rank of colonel in the Bolivian army. After taking part in another military uprising against a left-leaning government, he became dictator himself in 1971. Banzer in turn survived a series of attempted coups and ruled with an iron fist. His regime is estimated to have arrested around 15,000 people and been responsible for hundreds of politically motivated killings. Banzer – who had links to drug traffickers and Nazi war criminals – was eventually ousted and briefly forced into exile in Argentina. He was later elected president in 1997, when under pressure from the US, he belatedly joined the 'war on drugs'. Ill health forced him to step down in 2001 but he remained unrepentant to the end.

Banzer's childhood home, on Concepción's main square diagonally opposite the church, is now a museum, though the exhibits skirted over the many dubious aspects of his life. Instead there was a hotchpotch of religious icons, including innumerable statues of Christ, scale models of the Chiquitos churches, and baroque music scores, as well as a wooden bust and several portraits of Banzer in military regalia. Pride of place was given to his Order of the Condor of the Andes medal. Other recipients of the award, among Bolivia's highest honours, include former emperor of Ethiopia Haile Selassie I, notorious Paraguayan dictator Alfredo Stroessner, the ex-Yugoslav leader Josip Tito, and the Duke of Edinburgh.

***

I spent the night at a small hotel a short walk from the museum, while Walter went to stay with a friend outside town. In my room I spotted the bloodied remains of a mosquito on the wall above the bed. Several rather more vigorous mosquitoes soon appeared. After being pursued remorselessly for 15 minutes, I gave up and headed out for an early dinner. I ate to an eclectic soundtrack of the Red Hot Chilli Peppers, 90s trance, Rod Stewart, and furiously tolling church bells. The next morning, a Sunday, I found a spot at the back of the church for mass. As the congregation rose in song I thought back to a letter from Schmid to one of his superiors in Europe. 'I have a happy and even rejoicing life, for I sing... and dance,' he wrote, before adding: 'But you would ask, what do your superiors say about this kind of music? I answer: "If I am a missionary, it is because I sing, I dance and play music".'

In recent decades the mission towns in Chiquitos have undergone something of a revival. During the 1970s, an ambitious restoration project was launched to bring six of the church complexes – including those in San Javier and Concepción – back to their former glory. In 1990, they were collectively declared a UNESCO World Heritage Site, a significant boost for local tourism. During the restoration process thousands of pages of original musical scores – many written by anonymous indigenous composers – were discovered, which sparked renewed interest in Bolivian baroque. The Chiquitos musical scene began to revive and the region now plays host to the bi-annual International Festival of American Renaissance and Baroque Music, which draws thousands of concert-goers from across Bolivia and around the world.

***

Beyond their enduring religious, cultural and musical influence, the Jesuits also paved the way for the modern Santa Cruz economy by opening up the region to large-scale agriculture, cattle ranching, and timber extraction. At the start of the 20th century, the eastern lowlands remained sparsely populated. But the agrarian reforms that followed the revolution of 1952, the construction of a railway line east to the Brazilian border, improved road connections with central and western Bolivia, and the growth of the region's agricultural industry sparked significant migration from other rural areas, mainly the *altiplano*.

The population of the city of Santa Cruz jumped from around 40,000 in the early 1950s to more than 1.9 million today, a growth super-charged by the development of the region's gas and oil industries in the 1970s and the continued expansion of the agribusiness sector, as well as the coup that installed an eastern lowlands man – the afore-mentioned Banzer – in the presidential palace. Since then there have been further boosts, including the discovery of new gas reserves, the construction of a pipeline to transport gas to Brazil, and soaring global demand for soy beans.

The eastern lowlands have also seen significant immigration from overseas, and as Walter drove me back to Santa Cruz I noticed road signs to towns named La Bélgica, Mercedes, Warnes and Okinawa. The latter was founded in the 1950s by a group of settlers from the eponymous island in southern Japan. Some were displaced by the construction of a large US military base after the Second World War; others were fleeing poverty and seeking a better life. They were welcomed by a Bolivian government that was eager to develop the eastern lowlands and offered each family their own plot of land.

The early years in the community were tough: water was in short supply, the weather was stifling hot, and illness and disease claimed the lives of roughly half of the original 272 settlers. Of the approximately 3,300 Okinawans who ultimately emigrated to the eastern lowlands, around two-thirds later moved on to Peru or Brazil or returned home to Japan. Yet many of those who stayed in the new settlement of Okinawa eventually flourished, using loans from the Japanese government to expand their holdings into large and profitable farms.

It was a similar story in the smaller town of San Juan de Yapacaní, which lies 120 km to the west and was established by migrants from mainland Japan during the same period. The Japanese and Okinawan languages are still widely spoken in both places, though many members of the younger generations have moved on to Santa Cruz or further afield, Walter explained. In total, around 14,000 Bolivians are estimated to have Japanese heritage.

Later we stopped briefly in the town of Cuatro Cañadas, whose streets were thronged with market stalls and farmers. Many were Mennonites, the men in navy blue dungarees, white or sky blue shirts, work boots, and navy caps or straw hats, the women in long dresses, their hair covered by black handkerchiefs. Founded in the Netherlands in the 16th century by a radical protestant, Menno Simons, the group spent centuries moving from country to country in search of religious freedom. Tens of thousands travelled to Paraguay at the start of the 20th century, with a group of them heading over to the eastern lowlands in the 1950s, attracted by the privacy granted by the region's remoteness and the relatively low cost of land.

Today, there are an estimated 50,000 Mennonites in the eastern lowlands. Most reside in a small rural communities often referred to as 'colonies', speaking Plattdeutsch (Low German), living austerely and following a strict moral code that includes pacifism, community based agriculture (Mennonites here are big soy producers), conservative dress and customs, and a rejection of many of the trappings of modern life – at the most extreme end of the scale this includes avoiding the use of electricity, computers and cars. Women's lives are profoundly circumscribed, to say the least: most leave school before their teens, they are rarely allowed to venture further than their own settlements on their own, and very few marry outside the faith. (Not all Mennonites live these lives – back in Santa Cruz, I met a friendly young couple who told me they had a home in the suburbs and made regular trips to their favourite pizzeria.) On the edge of Cuarto Cañadas I saw a horse-drawn buggy driven by a ruddy-faced man, accompanied by two teenage girls with flaxen hair and floral dresses. Walter leaned over, lowering his voice: 'Some people did some very bad things.' He refused to elaborate. 'I don't want to say the words.'

I later looked up the story to which he obliquely referred. In 2011, seven men from the ultra-conservative Mennonite village of Manitoba, 150 km northeast of Santa Cruz and with a population of 2,000, were convicted of raping more than a hundred women and girls. They sprayed a chemical used to anaesthetise cows through bedroom windows at night to sedate whole families before carrying out their assaults. 'Out of shame, many of the women no longer attend church, the colony's only real social space; the younger among them say they fear they are "stained" and will never be able to marry,' *Time* magazine reported.

Back in Santa Cruz, we made a detour through Barrio Equipetrol, one of the city's brashest nightlife districts and as stark a contrast with the traditional world of the Mennonites imaginable. Walter, who had slowly warmed to me over the course of our trip, pointed out lavish apartment blocks and hotels built with the proceeds of the cocaine industry, which gave the Santa Cruz economy a shot of adrenaline in the 1970s and 80s. 'I'm worried for my son,' he said. 'He's 16, a dangerous age. There are lots of drugs everywhere. It's a problem all over Bolivia, particularly Santa Cruz. The kids see these *narcocruisers* – those flashy tank-like cars, black windows, loud music – and they want them. And they don't care what they have to do to get one.'

***

Santa Cruz – and, indeed, eastern Bolivia as a whole – has always had a distinct identity and there have long been calls for greater autonomy or even independence. The demands of Santa Cruz's *autonomía* movement grew louder, particularly from the business, cattle-ranching, agricultural and land-owning elite, after the Morales government came to power in 2006, redistributed large tracts of state and privately owned land, and nationalised the gas industry. The conflict was often crudely framed in ethnic terms and underscored with prejudice, a clash between the people of the eastern lowlands and those from the *altiplano* (even though large numbers of the latter have migrated to Santa Cruz in recent decades in search of work). In a 2008 referendum more than 85 per cent of people in eastern Bolivia supported a call for greater autonomy. The vote was subsequently declared illegal and unconstitutional, though Morales did later grant the municipal authorities in the east powers similar in scope to the ones demanded.

As a result of this move, and the Morales government's wider support for Santa Cruz's hydrocarbon and agribusiness industries, tensions have eased somewhat. But they have not disappeared. A common view was summed up by an encounter I had at a restaurant named El Aljibe, based in a 19th-century townhouse whose exposed brick walls and wood-beamed ceilings all appeared to run at crooked angles. It was 12.30 p.m. and the restaurant, famous for its traditional *cruceño* cuisine, was full but an amiable waiter managed to squeeze me onto a table in the leafy courtyard, which was decorated with knick-knacks: tinkling wind chimes, vintage scales, rotary-dial phones, stopped clocks, irregularly shaped blue and green bottles, and a Roman-style water feature.

My dining companion was Theresa, who was in her late 20s and wore black-rimmed glasses and a sharp business suit. As tiny hummingbirds darted from flower to flower, she told me she was born in Santa Cruz and now split her time between the city and Barcelona, where she worked in finance. 'Santa Cruz is like Catalonia – everybody wants independence,' she said, as we ate *pastel de gallina*, a savoury-sweet chicken pie, and chunks of cassava with a fiery chilli sauce. 'We feel different here, much closer to Brazil. We do all the work, make all the money in Bolivia. But [independence] won't happen, we're too important to the country. Anyway it doesn't matter, it's all corrupt. Four people with the same name voting four times. All politicians are the same.'

After lunch I walked back to the Plaza 24 de Setiembre, whose name commemorates the date of the 1810 '*grito libertario*' ('cry for freedom'), when local forces turfed out the colonial authorities.

It was dominated by the 19th-century cathedral, a sandy-pink brick neoclassical construction with two bell towers that provided a sharp contrast with the churches in San Javier and Concepción. Silver-work from an abandoned mission church in the Amazon adorned the altar, while a collection of Jesuit relics, carvings and sculptures were exhibited in the museum, alongside one of the world's smallest books, a 7-mm volume containing the Lord's Prayer in a variety of languages. Outside the cathedral men in their 60s and 70s played closely-fought games at the chess tables, closely watched by a crowd of spectators. Similarly aged men in pressed black trousers, white jackets, and white naval-style hats wheeled around trolleys with flasks of coffee, while younger vendors cycled round with machines for juicing sugar cane fastened to the front of their bikes. A man in his 40s wearing a cap used his heels to inch his wheelchair from bench to bench, a small box of chewing gum for sale balanced on his stomach.

Two separate protests were being staged in the square, their respective areas demarcated by yellow police tape. One group had the green-and-white flags of the *autonomía* movement and placards reading: 'We denounce violations of the democratic system' and 'No to fraud.' The other was calling for greater recognition and rights for people with disabilities. Both sets of protesters appeared to have been in place for some time: mattresses rested on wooden pallets, strips of tarpaulin were rigged up to provide shade, cool boxes contained drinks and snacks, and a TV set was hooked up to a power line and tuned to an international football tournament. Everyone cheered when the final whistle blew and Chile crashed out.

***

A 20-minute walk south of the Plaza 24 de Septiembre beyond the Ramón Tahuichi Aguilera football stadium took me to a much smaller square in a quiet, middle-class neighbourhood of modern houses with tall perimeter walls. There were no chess players, coffee vendors or protesters in Plazuela Litoral, only a dog-walker exercising his poodle on the freshly mown grass. In the centre of the square was a rectangular monument made up of shiny black tiles. On its left-hand side a mural depicted a band of soldiers crossing a boulder-strewn river that ran through a rocky canyon, the setting sun illuminating their exploits. To the right was a long list of names and ranks, and a collection of Bolivian Army flags, crests and insignia.

Che Guevara is celebrated in street art and graffiti across Bolivia – and throughout South America – but this was the first time I'd come across a tribute to his captors. In 1966, 199 years after the Jesuits were expelled from the Spanish colonies in Latin America, the Argentine revolutionary arrived in the eastern lowlands. Although on the surface he had little in common with the priests of the Society of Jesus, Guevara had similarly ambitious plans for the region, which he believed would provide the launch-pad for a continent-wide uprising. It proved to be a fatal misjudgement.

CHAPTER 8
You triumph or you die

Che Guevara: Samaipata, La Higuera, and Vallegrande

When a middle-aged Uruguayan businessman travelling under the name Adolfo Mena González landed at El Alto airport on a flight from Montevideo on the afternoon of 3 November 1966, the immigration officials had little reason to suspect anything was awry. He told them he was visiting Bolivia as part of a research trip for the Organization of American States. In his passport photo he has a bald dome flanked with patches of grey-brown hair and a freshly shaved, rather rounded face. A slight squint is visible behind a pair of thick black-framed glasses, as if the photographer has caught him unawares. He is dressed in a neat but nondescript suit jacket, crisp white shirt, and tightly knotted tie with a chevron at the midway point. A smudged black thumbprint sits in the bottom right-hand corner, beside a scrawled signature. He looks like the manager of a provincial bank.

After collecting his luggage, González travelled down into central La Paz and checked into the Hotel Copacabana. Another photo, this time a self-portrait taken in his room, shows him seated on the bed, hunched over, with a paunch and a lit cigar in his mouth. There is something vaguely familiar but hard to place about the image. By the end of 1966, though, a distinctive mop of shaggy black hair and a beard had grown back, the suit was exchanged for military fatigues, and the González alias had been dropped for good. The unremarkable businessman from Uruguay morphed back into one of the most recognisable men of the 20th century: Ernesto Guevara de la Serna – better known as Che.

This was not the first time Che – a nickname derived from the Argentine term for 'hey' or 'mate' – had visited Bolivia. In July 1953, a year after the journey depicted in *The Motorcycle Diaries*, he and his friend Calica travelled north by train – in a first-class carriage – from the border town of Villazón to La Paz via Uyuni and Oruro. The pair checked into a cheap hotel and spent a month rambling across the city, dining with Argentine residents, hooking up with local girls, securing a pair of Venezuelan visas, and visiting a nearby mine. 'La Paz is the Shanghai of the Americas,' Guevara wrote in a letter whose content would not look out of place in the travel section of a Sunday newspaper. 'The widest range of adventurers of all nationalities vegetate and prosper in the midst of a colourful *mestiza* city that is leading the country to its destiny.'

But Che was also eager to explore the political situation in Bolivia, which 12 months earlier had experienced the National Revolution through which the broadly left-wing, mining union-backed Movimiento Nacionalista Revolucionario (MNR) party came to power. Policies introducing universal suffrage, land reforms, and a scaling-back of the army soon followed. In his letters, Che wrote about miners 'defending the revolution', marches by trade unionists, and 'torchlight' protests during which demonstrators fired rifles in the air. He also wrote, with a distinct flash of anger, about the treatment of indigenous Bolivians. Of a visit to the Ministry of Peasant Affairs, he noted: 'It is a strange place: masses of Indians from various groups in the Altiplano wait their turn to be given an audience. Each group, dressed in typical costume, has a leader or indoctrinator who speaks to them in their own native language. When they go in, the employees sprinkle them with [the insecticide] DDT.'

Che continued his travels and later met Fidel Castro in Mexico, subsequently helping him overthrow the dictator Fulgencio Batista during the 1959 Cuban revolution. He then served variously as the country's minister of industries, minister of finance, and president of the National Bank. Che also became a kind of ambassador at large, travelling to the Soviet Union and Eastern Europe to forge trade deals, and visiting New York as part of the Cuban delegation to the UN. In his speech to the General Assembly, he lambasted 'US imperialism', the treatment of Black Americans, the UN's approach to South Africa's apartheid regime, and, above all, US intervention in Latin America and the 'servile, sell-out' governments it propped up across the region.

Soon, though, he tired of ministerial work and international diplomacy. In 1965, he launched an ill-fated expedition to support a revolutionary movement in the Congo, before returning to Bolivia the following year. By this stage, the country was ruled by General René Barrientos, a former vice-president who helped lead a right-wing military coup in 1964, before claiming the top job himself in an election in the summer of 1966. He moved firmly against the left, exiling the leaders of trade unions and workers' organisations, slashing wages, sacking thousands, and overseeing a massacre of striking miners.

As the head of a band of around 50 predominantly Cuban and Bolivian fighters – the National Liberation Army of Bolivia – Che aimed to launch a socialist revolt that would quickly spread to its neighbours, draw the US into a conflict that would become a 'second Vietnam', and finally result in a continent-wide revolution. As well as the political situation in Bolivia, the country appealed because of its location in the centre of South America and borders with five other nations. Che also thought – mistakenly as it turned out – that the Bolivian Communist Party would be a useful ally. The first entry in his diary, later published as *The Bolivian Diary*, is from 7 November 1966, after he had arrived at the Ñancahuazú camp in the Andean foothills on the edge of the Chaco, around 260 km southwest of Santa Cruz. It opens, optimistically, with: 'Today begins a new phase.' Within 11 months, that 'new phase' came to a fatal conclusion.

***

On a busy street a couple of blocks south of Santa Cruz's old bus station I squeezed myself into the back of an idling *trufi* bound for Samaipata. The town, a two-and-a-half-hour drive southwest, would be the starting point for a journey retracing Che's final steps along the so-called Ruta del Che (Che Trail). I was keen to find out more about the legacy of his ill-fated campaign, which seemed on the surface to have some parallels with the Jesuit experience in Chiquitos: both were foreigners who arrived in eastern Bolivia with strong beliefs and ambitious plans, fell foul of the authorities, and have undergone, to varying degrees, something of a rehabilitation in recent years. Beyond the historical significance, I'd also been told the Che Trail was a spectacular journey in its own right.

After leaving behind the city congestion we skimmed the edge of Parque Nacional Amboró, a meeting point for three different ecosystems – the Amazon, Andean foothills, and the dry Chaco lowlands. Later the tarmac ran out and the *trufi* crunched onto a gravel road that ascended into a landscape of lush green hills, shallow rivers and groves of citrus trees. At 1 p.m. we reached Samaipata, bumping along narrow streets before grinding to a halt in the main square. Set in a valley an altitude of 1,650 m, the town was cooler than Santa Cruz but still pleasantly warm and the few people visible – a European backpacker nursing a coffee and gently strumming a guitar, and a local man taking a siesta on a bench beside a bed of purple flowers – appeared to be feeling the effects of a heavy lunch. Beyond the central blocks were cobbled streets that slowly turned to dusty tracks, and above the palm tree fronds and pinkish-brown tiled roofs were undulating green slopes, their bare, tawny summits dotted with lonely trees.

I checked into the budget Andorina Hotel, which had a vaguely new age vibe, no wifi, and a guest book that contained a list of things that make a 'real' traveller ('Real travellers chat with others, not sit looking at their tablets or phone' was one of the stern warnings). There were flyers advertising Spanish classes, yoga sessions, and volunteering opportunities. In the courtyard, beside a few giant cacti, a couple of fellow guests discussed a nearby Japanese-run garden where you could pick up 'blessed vegetables'.

I'd only planned to spend a single night in Samaipata before following the Che Trail south but kept conjuring up reasons to delay my departure. The town was incredibly welcoming: residents greeted me as they walked past and it was easy to fall into conversations. Given its size, Samaiapata was remarkably cosmopolitan. It received a steady stream of weekending *cruceños* and international travellers. A significant number of the latter subsequently decide to relocate long term, and there were now around 30 different nationalities among the town's 5,000-strong population.

As I sat on the terrace at Finca La Víspera, a bucolic Dutch-run ecolodge and organic farm on the outskirts, it was easy to understand how you could arrive for a week and end up staying for the rest of your life. Tranquil gardens were framed by verdant hills, a shifting breeze rustled a set of wind chimes and carried over the smell of cakes fresh from the oven, and a lolloping golden retriever rested at my feet. In the evening I was invited for a drink with Frank, a gregarious German who ran a local travel agency and helped to arrange my trip along the Che Trail.

Now in his early 50s, he originally came to Samaipata as a backpacker, fell in love, and decided to start a life here. Later we headed next door, to Cafe Latina, for dinner with my Che Trail guide Daniela, who was from Switzerland but, like Frank, had visited Samaipata as a traveller and fallen for the place. Over a steak and a few glasses of red wine from a local vineyard, restaurant owner Sylvain, who had relocated from France, told me about his forthcoming trip to India to visit Bodhgaya, where the Buddha found enlightenment.

Afterwards we headed out to La Boheme, a bar where seemingly the whole of the town had decamped to listen to live music, watch the football (bets on the final scores were scribbled onto scraps of paper and deposited in a glass), and drink round after round of the local Cordillera beer. I heard German, Turkish, Brazilian, British, Israeli, French, American and Australian voices, and several people spoke to me about the powerful but undefined 'energy' in Samaipata. 'Some people can't cope with it – it's too strong for them,' said Daniela. 'When I first came here I had to stay in bed for a week. It got too much and I needed to rest. It felt like I had the flu but I didn't have the flu. I still feel it, but I can cope with it now.'

***

The next day I caught a taxi from the main square to El Fuerte, an archaeological complex on the top of a pine-covered hill 9 km east of Samaipata. Named a UNESCO World Heritage Site in 1998, the area was first occupied around 300 CE by members of the Arawak-speaking Chané culture, later becoming a regional capital of the Inca in the 14th or 15th century. The site's natural defences and strategic value were clear – from its well-defended, 2,000-m-high perch there were near 360-degree views of the surrounding region – and it was easy to see why the Spanish, who briefly used it as a base in the 1500s, named it 'the Fort' (its Inca and pre-Inca names have sadly been lost to history). Yet El Fuerte was much more than a military site. A lower area was once an administrative and residential centre, and today contains a mishmash of ruins from various different eras, including the foundations of Spanish, Inca and pre-Inca homes, agricultural terraces, a market area known as the Kancha, and the remains of a plaza.

Above it was the focal point of El Fuerte, the Roca Esculpida (Sculpted Rock), a giant slab of red sandstone roughly 220 m by 65 m that stretched towards the cliff-edge, its ridged surface resembling a crocodile on the banks of the river, waiting to pounce on it prey. One of the largest pre-Columbian ceremonial structures in the Andes, its sides were covered with alcoves, niches that may once have contained idols, sets of geometric patterns, and numerous carvings of big cats, coiled snakes, and other zoomorphic images. Archaeologists have speculated that libations of blood or *chicha*, an alcoholic corn beer, may once have been poured down a series of zigzagging channels, which reminded me of some of the earthworks I had seen in the Llanos de Moxos earlier in my journey. Like Tiwanaku, erosion has taken its toll and a certain amount of imagination is needed to bring El Fuerte to life (though not so much imagination that you start to think that it was built by aliens as a runway to land spaceships, as some new age fantasists seem to believe).

***

The following day Daniela and driver Vladimir picked me up after breakfast. As we drove south past fields of mandarin trees and fences draped with folds of drying tobacco, she told me that although most travellers start their trips along the Che Trail in Samaipata, the Argentine revolutionary only made it as far as the town's outskirts. By July 1967, Che was physically drained, increasingly stressed, weak from hunger, and suffering badly without his asthma medicine. Despite a few successful engagements with the Bolivian military, there had been some costly defeats. His band of guerrillas – who never numbered more than 50 – were short on supplies and on the back foot.

Che made repeated calls for Bolivians to join his struggle. 'Today we make an appeal to workers, peasants, intellectuals, to everyone who feels the time has come to confront violence with violence and rescue a country being sold off in great slabs to Yankee monopolies, and raise the standard of living of our people,' he wrote in one public communiqué. Yet he failed to attract a single recruit from the Bolivian peasantry during his time in the country. As Jon Lee Anderson wrote in his exhaustive biography, *Che Guevara: A Revolutionary Life*, by this point in his mission: 'Che had barely enough manpower to get through each day, much less engage in political tasks of consciousness-raising and recruitment.'

On 6 July 1967, while Che rested, six of his men hijacked a truck and drove into Saimapata to buy food and medical supplies. After a shoot-out near the plaza they briefly occupied the secret police HQ, seized some small arms, and took 10 soldiers hostage – the latter were subsequently left alive but 'without any clothes' on the edge of Samaipata, Che noted in his diary. Overall, however, the mission was a failure. The men 'did not buy anything useful; as for medicines, nothing that I needed was obtained,' Che wrote. 'The action happened in front of all the townspeople and a crowd of travellers, so word will spread like wildfire,' he added. Daniela also told me an intriguing story, well-known locally but not mentioned in *The Bolivian Diary*. Apparently the men also purchased boots from a local cobbler. 'But whether it was because of his deliberate intention or because he was nervous, they ended up with only right-footed boots,' she said.

As we left Samaipata and its fertile hinterland behind, the road gradually gained altitude. Clumps of giant cacti reached out of thin, gritty soils, and uninhabited, scree-covered slopes loomed around us. A trio of condors glided on thermals, their white backs glinting in the sunlight. Turkey vultures, faster but far less elegant, chopped at the air with their wings. Electricity lines were bowed by bulbous mud-and-straw nests of rufous horneros, buff-coloured birds with sharp beaks. In the distance were green hills with sun-baked ridges.

When we stopped for lunch at a Chinese restaurant on the edge of the town of Vallegrande, Daniela explained why Che's guerrilla campaign failed to take hold in Bolivia. The country was one of the few in South America to have undergone a degree of land reform, which followed the 1952 National Revolution. Under the Agrarian Reform Law, forced peasant labour was officially abolished and large, unproductive feudal haciendas were broken up, with the land distributed to community-managed *campesino* federations, which subsequently became an influential force in Bolivian society. Although staunchly right-wing, President Barrientos pledged not to overturn the Agrarian Reform Law in return for the support of these federations.

In addition, the Communist Party of Bolivia proved at best unsupportive of Che's campaign and at worst actively hostile. As a result, the National Liberation Army of Bolivia attracted little local support; at its height Bolivians made up barely half of its members. Hunted by the Bolivian army, which was backed by both US military advisors and CIA operatives, Che's band of guerrillas was already in serious trouble by the time it reached Samaipata, and so it headed to the rugged terrain to the south.

We did the same after lunch. Vladimir, a calm if rather taciturn man, drove us out of Vallegrande and turned off the main road onto a dirt track that switch-backed up the Cordillera Oriental, an eastern range of the Bolivian Andes. When this yielded to a pebble-strewn track, he stopped the car and let down the tyres a little to provide more traction. Eventually, we reached the summit, a rocky ridge sparsely covered with pine trees. To the east, chains of broken hills collapsed into a valley bisected by the churning Rio Grande, which runs from the city of Cochabamba to Santa Cruz before flowing into the Amazon basin. There were no other vehicles, and only occasional signs of life. Every so often, we passed turnings for isolated villages, including the ominously named Salsipuedes Grande and Salsipuedes Chico. 'Salsipuedes means "Leave if you can",' explained Daniela. 'During bad weather, it's impossible to get out of the villages because the roads are too dangerous.'

Further on was the Boina del Che, a rock formation that vaguely resembled the revolutionary's iconic beret; someone had added a painted star to ram the point home. We stopped briefly in the largest village in the area, Pucará, which clings precariously to a mountain slope. There was an oversized plaza, a handful of simple shops, a sign asserting Bolivia's right to the sea, and not much else. Beyond Pucará a dirt road devoid of traffic continued past scrubland, potato patches, and ragged rows of corn, their heads starting to droop. Just before sunset, we reached the tiny hamlet of La Higuera, the centre of which was dominated by Che murals, statues and slogans. It was the end of the road for me and for him.

***

I spent the night at the Casa del Telegrafista, which was used at different times by both Che's guerrillas and the Bolivian soldiers pursuing them. Now a guesthouse, the building had changed little since the 1960s, when it was the local telegraph operator's house. There were stone floors, adobe walls, thick beams, and heavy wooden doors you had to flex your muscles to push open. The Casa del Telegrafista was run by a French photographer in his sixties named Juan, who had travelled throughout Latin America before – somewhat improbably – settling in La Higuera, drawn by the community's link with the mythology of Che.

After dinner we sipped a syrupy homemade coca liquor by the fire with Juan's girlfriend Manu, while their young son, a budding filmmaker, studiously recorded us on his camera until it was time for bed. Juan told us that some of Che's guerrillas were captured and left to die from their wounds – 'in agony, without medication' – in the courtyard in which we were sitting. 'Army generals and CIA agents also stayed here,' he added, showing me his collection of black-and-white photos of Che and his comrades.

In the morning we hiked down to the Quebrada del Churo, a steep-sided gully near the Rio Grande, following an overgrown trail riven with prickly plants. It was here Che was finally captured on 8 October 1967. By this stage, having been ambushed in La Higuera a couple of weeks earlier, Guevara's guerrillas were down to 17, exhausted and carrying only limited supplies, having suffered a series of gruelling attacks and ambushes. In his last diary entry, from 7 October, he noted that it was the 11-month anniversary of their 'establishment as a guerrilla force'. That night they set off under a 'slither of a moon' but came to a halt at 2 a.m. because one of the party – Chang, whose glasses were broken – could not see well enough to continue in the dark. Che listened to a report about the army's movement on the radio that he deemed a 'diversionary' tactic. His final words in the diary are prosaic: 'Altitude = 2,000 metres.'

The next day, at around 1 p.m. a firefight broke out between the guerrillas and a group of elite, US-trained Bolivian Army Rangers led by Captain Gary Prado. Eventually, after at least two of his comrades were killed, Che was shot in the thigh, with another bullet hitting his beret. As he tried to escape, he was captured. As Anderson wrote, Prado 'positively identified Che by his pronounced brow and the bullet scar near his ear – from the accident that had nearly killed him during the Bay of Pigs invasion of Cuba in 1961. Then he tied Che's hands with his own belt'. Caked in mud, near emaciated and unable to walk properly thanks to the gunshot wound in his leg, Che was helped out of the ravine by a pair of soldiers and taken to La Higuera.

We hiked back to La Higuera to visit the *escuelita*, a simple one-room building that functioned as the local school before earning notoriety as the site of Che's execution. It was bang in the centre of the hamlet, only a few metres away from several homes. They would have heard everything that went on inside, I thought. Local residents were divided, Daniela explained: some local families helped the guerrillas, others denounced them. Inside the *escuelita*, now a museum run by the community, the walls were covered with photos, maps of the campaign, newspaper articles, and messages from Che's admirers from around the world. The small selection of exhibits included the revolutionary's machete, a bloodied uniform, a rifle, ammo clips and bullets used by the guerrillas and the soldiers.

'I met Gary Prado once in Santa Cruz,' said Daniela. 'After they brought Che to the *escuelita*, Prado stayed up with him. He said Che was disillusioned at first but during the night they talked and he became more hopeful. Che thought the army would rather have him alive than dead. But on the morning of 9 October, Prado left to bring in the other guerrillas. When he returned around noon, he found that Che was already executed, apparently on the orders of the military high command in La Paz.'

In an interview with US TV network C-Span in 1989, Cuban-American CIA agent Felix Rodríguez, who was involved in the Bay of Pigs before travelling to Bolivia to help the army track down Che and his guerrillas, claimed he was the one who told Che of his impending execution: 'I told him, "Is there anything you want for your family?" So he looked at me, and you could tell very easily that there was a lot of sadness and sarcasm in his voice, when he said, "Tell Fidel that he will soon see a triumphant revolution in America." Then he changed and said, "And tell my wife to remarry and try to be happy".'

A sergeant named Mario Terán volunteered to do the deed and was told not to shoot Che in the face, so the army could make it appear he had been killed in battle. Che's last words were, reputedly: 'I know you've come to kill me. Shoot, coward, you are only going to kill a man.' The spot where he was shot dead at the age of 39 is now marked by the child-sized chair on which he sat for the last time.

Afterwards I walked around the hamlet, which is dotted with tributes to Che: a life-sized statue, dressed for battle, right hand raised to the sky, a cigar resting between his fingers; a large bust on a plinth decorated with Argentine, Cuban, and Bolivian flags, a white cross, and the message 'Your example lights up a new dawn'; murals and slogans on the walls of La Higuera's primary school, a stone's throw from the *escuelita*. Every October groups of Che's admirers travel to the hamlet to commemorate his death. More usefully for locals, Cuban doctors and nurses also regularly visit La Higuera to provide healthcare services, Daniela told me as we strolled to the outskirts.

From a ridge sprinkled with feathery white flowers we gazed across at a series of hills, dark green save for a few light patches where the foliage had been cleared for agriculture or snaking foot trails. They rolled like waves into the distance before crashing into the horizon. As I took out my camera and prepared to take a few shots of the landscape, a gentle breeze wafted across my face. I spun round to see a condor glide silently by, barely a metre above my head. Caught by surprise, I watched as it rode an air current before slowly disappearing into the hills.

***

The next morning we retraced our route back to Vallegrande, a low-key market town that played a key role in Che's posthumous story. After he was executed in La Higuera his body was strapped to the landing skids of a helicopter and flown to the Vallegrande's Señor de Malta hospital. There it was held in the morgue overnight, cleaned and washed by a nurse, and then laid out on a raised concrete slab in the laundry room. His eyes and mouth were open and it is said that he appeared almost to be alive. The resemblance with Jesus Christ, a particularly potent image in a devoutly Catholic town such as Vallegrande, was unmistakable (and subsequently captured in photos that travelled around the world).

'People say that the force of the spinning helicopter blades opened up Che's eyes and mouth during the flight from La Higuera,' said Angelina, a local guide who showed me round. 'Though it could have been the work of the soldiers who posed for photos with him.' Whatever the cause, locals flocked to view the corpse; some even cut off locks of his hair to keep as good luck charms. Today, the laundry room, which remained in use until the early 1980s, is once again a place for devotees, covered with messages in a variety of languages carved into the walls or graffitied in red. A bunch of red, pink, and yellow roses was propped up at the entrance.

The army chiefs decided to not to bury Che's body and thus create, in their view, a potential place of pilgrimage for his admirers; instead, it would be 'disappeared'. The hands were chopped off and the finger-prints used to confirm Che's identity. The rest of the corpse was then secretly dumped in an unmarked pit near what is now an airstrip on the edge of Vallegrande. There was no public confirmation of this at the time, of course. Instead, a tangle of speculative and contradictory rumours emerged claiming variously that Che's body had been burned, or dumped in the jungle, or spirited away overseas, or met some other gruesome fate.

After visiting the hospital, Daniela introduced me to another guide and Che expert, Gonzalo. As a 17-year-old, Gonzalo was part of the Bolivian-Cuban forensic search team that discovered Che's remains in 1997, after a retired army general, Mario Vargas, admitted his role in their disposal and revealed the location. 'I had no interest in him at that point – one of my friends was taking part and I just wanted to earn some extra cash,' said Gonzalo. 'But Che became my career.' The revolutionary's corpse was discovered in a 2-m pit. After being exhumed and examined at a hospital in Santa Cruz – where his teeth were matched with a plaster mould made a few years before his death – Che's remains were flown to Cuba. They now rest in a mausoleum in the city of Santa Clara – which Che and a band of revolutionary fighters captured in a decisive battle in 1958 – alongside those of 29 of his fellow guerrillas.

The site where Che was unceremoniously dumped is now home to the Centro Cultural Ernesto 'Che' Guevara, which was officially inaugurated by President Evo Morales on 9 October 2017, the 50th anniversary of his execution. After visiting the nearby Foso de Guerrilleros, a shady spot beside a murky green swimming pool and a field of grazing cows where the bodies of 12 of Che's guerrillas were discovered in 1998-99, we walked over to the complex. Inside was a mausoleum filled with evocative photos of Che. As a baby with his parents in Argentina; as a young man, smoking a cigar and reading Goethe; deep in conversation with Fidel Castro; in his Adolfo Mena González disguise. The neighbouring museum had first-hand witness accounts of the Bolivian campaign alongside quotes from Che, one of which seemed grimly appropriate: 'In a revolution, you triumph or you die.'

Until relatively recently, Gonzalo told me, many Bolivians had a negative image of Che, thanks to his portrayal by successive military dictatorships and right-wing governments. But under the presidency of Evo Morales these perceptions started to shift. Morales co-opted Che's image and was often depicted alongside him and former Venezuelan leader Hugo Chávez. 'For me, Che still has great significance,' Gonzalo added. 'He is a symbol of liberation.'

***

Although the Bolivian army wanted to avoid creating a place of pilgrimage for Che devotees, they inadvertently sparked a process of mythologisation and, somewhat ironically, commodification. Che's image, particularly Cuban photographer Alberto Korda's famous depiction of him in his trademark beret, has become part of popular culture, appearing on countless T-shirts, posters, and pieces of street art around the world. In some respects, Che has had a greater impact in death than in life. As Anderson wrote: 'Che endured ... as an almost mythical symbol of veneration. He inspired new generations of fighters and dreamers because of the revolutionary principles he represented – fearlessness, self-sacrifice, honesty, and devotion to the cause.' More than half a century after his death, regardless of his actual beliefs or indeed the basic facts of his life, Che remains an easy shorthand for youthful rebellion.

At the inauguration of the Centro Cultural Ernesto 'Che' Guevara, an event attended by thousands, including delegations from Cuba and Venezuela, Morales addressed the crowd. 'This is a historic moment, not just for me personally, but for all peoples who struggle for their liberation,' he said. 'To remember the 50th anniversary of Che's death is to remember the struggle for dignity and national sovereignty, and against imperialism.' Later, when he visited La Higuera, he told an Al Jazeera reporter: 'People die but their ideas never do. We are in different times now, times of democratic liberation, fuelled not by the bullet but by the ballot box and the vote.'

***

The decades after Che's death were a turbulent time in Bolivia. President René Barrientos – whose minister of the interior, Antonio Arguedas Mendieta, secretly sent a copy of Che's diary, along with his death mask and amputated hands, to Cuba – died in a helicopter crash in 1969. Bolivia remained largely under military rule until 1983, enduring a series of coups. Amid heavy competition, the most notorious dictator during this period was Luis García Meza. He came to power in 1980 in what became known as the 'Cocaine Coup', overthrowing interim president – and his cousin – Lidia Gueiler Tejada. (Tejada was only the second female head of state in the Americas after Isabel Perón in Argentina. She was also, incidentally, the cousin of American actress Raquel Welch.)

Meza was backed by a grisly coalition of drug cartels, neo-fascists, mercenaries, and Nazi war criminals such as former Gestapo chief Klaus Barbie, the 'Butcher of Lyon', who was responsible for the deaths of an estimated 14,000 people during the Second World War. He subsequently escaped to Bolivia, where he was reportedly involved in hunting down Che and organising paramilitary groups for Meza, among other nefarious activities.

Until he in turn was ousted by the army in 1981, Meza oversaw one of the most corrupt, repressive regimes in Bolivia's history – a title for which there is ample competition – with scores of people killed or 'disappeared'. In 1993, the Supreme Court convicted him in absentia of an array of charges, including genocide, murder, corruption, and armed uprising; he was also indicted for stealing and selling Che's Bolivian diaries, which appeared at an auction house in London with a $300,000 price tag in 1984. In 1995, he was arrested in Brazil and sent back to Bolivia to serve his sentence. Human Rights Watch described the conviction as historic: 'To the best of our knowledge, the conviction marks the first time in Latin American legal history that members of a de facto military government have been held to account for usurping power and violating constitutional norms.'

Throughout this period, demand for cocaine surged in the US and Europe. In response, coca growing expanded from the subtropical Yungas region near La Paz through the rainforest-covered plains of the Chapare. This sparked mass migration movements, violent drug-fuelled conflicts and – in the nearby city of Cochabamba – the kind of grassroots uprisings and social upheaval Che had hoped to bring to Bolivia a few decades earlier.

CHAPTER 9

Coca si

The 'war on drugs' and the rise of Evo Morales:
The Yungas, the Chapare, and Cochabamba

A persistent drizzle hung in the air as my *trufi* left the Villa Fatima neighbourhood in La Paz and headed out towards what has been dubbed the Camino de la Muerte – the Death Road. Northeast of the city at the Cumbre pass, the *altiplano* rears up to a height of 4,800 m before collapsing down through the subtropical Yungas valleys to the clammy lowlands of the Amazon. Along this route runs the Yungas Road, which descends more than 3,500 m in just 64 km. Some sections are barely 3 m wide, safety barriers are few and far between, and there are countless sharp bends and blind corners for drivers to contend with.

In the 1990s, hundreds of people died in accidents on the Yungas Road every year, giving rise to its macabre nickname and prompting the Inter-American Development Bank to describe it as the world's most dangerous road. This notoriety turned the Yungas Road, which was built by Paraguayan prisoners of war after the Chaco War of 1932–35, into a tourist destination, with hordes of backpackers signing up for cycling trips down it. A multi-million-dollar bypass around the most dangerous stretch opened in 2006, dramatically reducing the number of fatalities, but many drivers still opt for the old route. The edge of the road is marked – at a far higher frequency than any other highway I've travelled along in Bolivia – with small white crosses, extinguished candles and withered bunches of flowers, modest memorials to accident victims.

For all its hazards, the Camino de la Muerte is also one of the most spectacular roads in South America. It provides views of thickly forested, precipitously steep valleys and saw-toothed Andean peaks, as well as rivulets and waterfalls that sometimes splash across the road itself.

Shortly after starting its descent from the Cumbre pass the *trufi* was enveloped in a swirl of fog. The stoical driver slowed to a crawl, peering over the steering wheel, but unable to see more than 10 m ahead. It felt like we were travelling inside a cloud, a strangely peaceful sensation. The rest of the world disappeared from view and a hush settled over me and my fellow passengers. Several minutes passed before we pulled out into the sunlight and a sheer, 1,000-m vertical drop flashed into view through my window. Moments later a lorry braked sharply in front of us, before a motorbike carrying a family of five overtook us on the inside, clipping the wing mirror on its way through.

Eventually we reached the tranquil hillside town of Coroico, once a gold-mining centre, now an agricultural hub and holiday resort set at an altitude of 1,760 m. It has balmy weather, good-value guesthouses and restaurants, a friendly vibe, numerous hammocks and swimming pools to laze in, and panoramic views of knotted hills that slowly unravel as they tumble down the valleys. There are plenty of outdoor activities on offer – hiking, cycling, swimming, ziplining – but none are so compelling that you feel you have to do anything. Even the residents of the Madres Clarisas convent, who earn a few extra *bolivianos* by selling home-baked goods, are chilled. In the evening, I strolled down a narrow flight of steps and found a buzzer diagonally opposite a bar playing Bob Marley's 'Three Little Birds'. I rang it and after a short pause the door opened to reveal a counter, behind which sat a beaming elderly nun with a shock of white hair. 'Sorry, we've sold all the cakes and biscuits,' she said apologetically, 'but we've still got some wine.'

Thanks to the fertile soils and plentiful rainfall the focus of the Yungas, which run along the eastern slopes of the Andes, is agriculture. Many of the region's farmers have African-Bolivian heritage, descendants of enslaved people trafficked over in the 16th century to labour in Potosí's silver mines. Slavery was officially outlawed in Bolivia in 1825, but in practice continued for more than a century. After the silver mines declined, many Black Bolivians moved to the Yungas to work as farmhands on large haciendas in conditions that were often comparable to slavery. This situation persisted until the agrarian reforms of the 1950s, and today the estimated 35,000 Black Bolivians remain among the most disadvantaged people in the country.

I spent a couple of days unwinding in Coroico before heading out into the surrounding countryside, where terraces were cut into the hillsides and planted with coffee, bananas, cassava, guavas, papayas, and citrus fruits. I also found rows of bushy plants with straight, slender branches, oval-shaped, fern-green leaves, and reddish berries – coca, a far more valuable crop. Bolivia is the world's third-biggest coca grower after Colombia and Peru, with more than 255 sq km of land devoted to the crop, two-thirds of which is in the Yungas.

***

Coca leaves have been an important aspect of many South American cultures for millennia. A 2010 study in the journal *Antiquity* suggested they may have been used by people in the Andes for as long as 8,000 years. When chewed, coca leaves act as a mild stimulant and help to offset the effects of altitude sickness, stave off hunger, thirst and tiredness, aid digestion, and even suppress pain. They are rich in vitamins (including A, B1, B2, B6, C and E) and minerals (including calcium and iron), and relatively high in protein, carbohydrates and fibre when compared to other Andean fruits and vegetables. In addition, coca leaves have long been used in religious ceremonies, and as medicine, a form of currency, and a social lubricant, much as wine and coffee are in other parts of the world.

As many disappointed travellers quickly discover, chewing coca leaves and drinking coca tea does not produce a high per se. 'Chewing', in fact, is a misnomer: individual leaves, their stems removed, are placed in the inside of one cheek and largely left alone. An alkaline substance such as mineral lime is used to draw out one of the plant's principal psychoactive alkaloids, cocaine (the cocaine content of coca leaves is less than 1 per cent). After a while the musty, slightly bitter, grass-flavoured leaves form themselves into a saliva-soaked ball, puffing out the cheek in a squirrel-like fashion. They have a numbing effect on the mouth that always reminds me of a trip to the dentist.

When Europeans arrived in South America, they soon started to demonise the indigenous use of the coca plant. As Italian explorer Amerigo Vespucci who came to the continent in the early 1500s and from whose name the word 'America' is derived, wrote of the locals he encountered: '[T]heir faces and expressions were horrid; they chewed their cud like beasts, cheeks full of green herb.' In 1551, the Ecclesiastical Council in Lima condemned coca as 'diabolical'. Yet the Spanish authorities in what are now Bolivia and Peru began to soften their views when they realised the beneficial effects the leaves had on the productivity levels of those forced to work in the mines and fields. Colonial administrators took control of the trade in coca and usage duly increased, with miners consuming an average of 380 g of coca per week, according to some accounts.

Interest in coca leaves also began to grow beyond South America. The first English-language reference to the plant is believed to be Londoner Abraham Cowley's 1662 poem 'A Legend of Coca':

> Endow'd with leaves of wondrous nourishment,
> Whose juice succ'd in, and to the stomach tak'n
> Long hunger and long labour can sustain
> From which our faint and weary bodies find

> More succour, more they clear the drooping mind,
> Than can your Bacchus and your Ceres join'd.

In the 1850s, scientists managed to isolate and synthesise the plant's cocaine alkaloid, which was subsequently used to produce an array of drinks, medicines, tonics and other products throughout Europe and the US. Sigmund Freud championed the medicinal use of cocaine, wrote several papers and essays on the drug, and experimented widely with the 'magical substance', including on himself. 'I have been reading about cocaine,' he wrote, 'the effective ingredient of coca leaves, which some Indian tribes chew in order to make themselves resistant to privation and fatigue ... a small dose lifted me to the heights in wonderful fashion.'

One of the most popular coca products was Vin Mariani, a French wine that contained 211–253 mg of cocaine per litre. Adverts for the drink claimed that it 'fortifies and refreshed body & brain' and 'restores health and vitality'. Its fans included Thomas Edison, Ulysses S. Grant and Emile Zola. Pope Leo XIII carried a hip flash of the drink, awarded a 'Vatican gold medal' to its creator, French chemist Angelo Mariani, and even appeared on a promotional poster. The success of Mariani wine and other coca products inspired a pharmacist from Georgia named Dr John Stith Pemberton. In his search for an alternative to morphine, to which he had become addicted after suffering a serious wound in the US Civil War, he created Pemberton's French Wine Coca, whose original recipe included a mixture of cocaine and alcohol, as well as an extract from the kola nut, a caffeine-rich fruit from West Africa. It later became Coca-Cola, the world's best selling drink. Although cocaine and alcohol have long since been removed from the recipe, the drink still uses a coca-leaf extract named, rather banally, 'Merchandise No. 5'.

Although cocaine and cocaine-based products were legal and widely available in much of Europe and the US in the early part of the 20th century, the drug slowly fell out of favour, becoming associated with vice, criminality and ruin. US federal legislation in 1914 and 1922 stringently regulated and then banned the recreational use of drugs like cocaine and opium, with similar laws coming into force in Europe during the same period. In 1961, the UN Single Convention on Narcotic Drugs classified cocaine and coca leaves as illicit drugs. (Although as sociologist, historian and activist Silvia Rivera Cusicanqui has noted, the convention made an exemption for Coca-Cola. The company 'managed to get one single use for coca leaf included in Article 27 of the [convention]: "flavoring",' she wrote, allowing it to continue to use 'Merchandise No. 5' in its drinks.)

Despite being criminalised, cocaine use steadily increased in Europe and North America during the 1960s, before exploding as the 1970s wore on. This had a seismic impact on Bolivia, particularly on the Chapare region, which became a centre of coca production for the drugs trade, the site of a violent decades-long conflict, and the launchpad for Evo Morales, one of most significant political figures in South America in the last hundred years.

***

In the early 1980s, as Bolivia emerged from years of military dictatorships that combined repression with mismanagement and corruption, the country suffered a debt crisis and then a period of hyperinflation. In July 1985 inflation stood at over 60,000 per cent, at the time, one of the highest rates ever recorded. The following month Víctor Paz Estenssoro was elected president for the third time. Although he was a key figure in the 1952 National Revolution, which ushered in sweeping economic and social reforms, Estenssoro had since moved to the right. In an effort to tackle Bolivia's hyperinflation, he launched the New Economic Plan, a neoliberal programme that featured the input of a young Harvard economics professor named Jeffrey Sachs, who was acting as a government advisor.

The plan subjected the Bolivian economy to a bout of what became known as 'shock therapy'. Government spending was slashed, the currency was devalued, price controls were dropped, public-sector wages were frozen, and the whole economy was thoroughly 'liberalised'. At the same time, the international price of tin collapsed. The government partially dismantled Comibol – the public mining corporation set up under the first Estenssoro presidency – privatised mines and sacked around 30,000 miners. Sure enough, the New Economic Plan brought inflation down to manageable levels. Yet the medicine proved as damaging as the illness: Bolivia plunged into a cavernous recession and unemployment surged. (Sachs' shock therapy, meanwhile, was later applied to post-Soviet Russia and Eastern Europe.)

However, one part of the Bolivian economy was in rude health. Amid soaring US demand for cocaine, drug trafficking became a boom industry under the thuggish dictatorship of General Hugo Banzer (1971-1978). The short but highly destructive regime of Luis García Meza (1980-1981) was dubbed a 'narcocracy', so closely was it entangled with the international drugs trade.

During this period, coca cultivation – and drug production – expanded east from the Yungas across to the Chapare, a wide, tropical plain. In the geographic centre of the country and part of the Upper Amazon Basin, the region is blanketed with rainforests, interspersed with coiling rivers, lightly populated, and blessed with rich, fertile soils. As word of mouth spread of something akin to a gold rush – a 'green rush' is perhaps more accurate – tens of thousands of ex-miners (many of them ardent trade unionists), farmers hit by droughts and crop failures in the *altiplano*, and other unemployed people flocked to the Chapare to grow or process coca, whose price was soaring. Over the decade, the region's population more than quadrupled, with the vast majority of people working small-scale coca plots. Before long the Chapare was producing a third of Bolivia's crop.

***

I started my journey to the Chapare in Cochabamba, which lies to the southwest. My guide was Ariel, a gregarious guy in his mid-20s with faded blue jeans and a Ramones T-shirt. His friend Gabriel drove us out of the city and into the farmlands and market gardens of the Cochabamba Valley, long the breadbasket of Bolivia. Fields of vegetables, fruit, flowers, wheat, maize and other crops tended by *campesinos* and patches of land grazed by bony sheep and cattle were interspersed with small, busy towns, each one modestly prosperous.

In one village we pulled up outside an adobe-walled home with an oversized satellite dish balanced precariously on the corrugated-iron roof. Beside the front door was a white flag raised on a pole, signalling, Ariel informed me, that *chicha* was for sale. Inside, gnarled gourds were filled with the lightly alcoholic fermented maize beer from a big earthenware pot by a friendly Quechua woman in a white straw boater. Sacred to the Inca, it is still drunk across Bolivia (and elsewhere in South America) but *chicha cochabambina* is considered the best. Traditionally, said Ariel, as I sipped the frothy, gloopy, yellow liquid, women kick-started the fermentation process by chewing the milled maize and then spitting the softened result into a bowl, enzymes in the saliva having helped to convert the starch into sugar.

As we drove uphill, the scenery started to change, increasingly resembling the Scottish Highlands. The sky turned grey and mist fell. Laguna Corani, a steel-grey, loch-like reservoir, appeared to the west, and the surrounding trees were reminiscent of Scots pines. Strung along the road were trout farms and restaurants with ornamental ponds and humpbacked bridges. For lunch, Ariel suggested instead an unnamed, rickety roadside shack, where we ate delicious fried trout and chips. Prowling cats rubbed round our legs, ready to pounce on any scraps. Back in the car we crossed the final ridge of the Andes and the scenery changed again as we descended into the Upper Amazon Basin and the wide, flat, rainforest-covered plains of the Chapare.

We soon came to the first of several military checkpoints manned by heavily armed soldiers who thoroughly searched the boot of the car and our rucksacks, and carefully studied my passport, repeatedly comparing the photo with my face. A mirror with a set of wheels attached to its back and a broom handle fastened to its side was passed underneath the car to check for explosives. Ariel had forewarned me about this: the police and army in the Chapare tend to treat the few foreigners who pass through with suspicion. 'Don't worry,' he said. 'Yankee passports are more suspicious than British ones.' After a five-minute wait that felt more like an hour we were waved on our way. 'Of course,' continued Ariel, when we were out of earshot, 'the one thing worse than being mistaken for a drug trafficker is being mistaken for a Drug Enforcement Administration agent.'

***

A federal body charged with tackling drug trafficking and distribution in the US and overseas, the Drug Enforcement Administration (DEA) arrived in Bolivia in July 1986, reportedly at the request of President Víctor Paz Estenssoro. They subsequently launched Operation Blast Furnace, which lasted for six months and involved US army helicopters transporting DEA agents and Bolivian police officers on 'strike missions' to find and destroy cocaine laboratories.

Its impact, a declassified CIA assessment admitted, was at best mixed: 'Operation Blast Furnace ... has achieved considerable success in disrupting cocaine processing and trafficking operations in Bolivia since it began ... but these gains have been accompanied by virtually no arrests or drug seizures and may be only temporary.' The operation, and US involvement in the country more generally, proved unpopular in Bolivia and provoked serious political opposition.

As a result, Operation Blast Furnace was followed by the more secretive Operation Snowcap. This $80-million-a-year DEA counter-narcotics programme focused on Bolivia, Peru, and Ecuador and ran from 1987 to 1994. As a breathless article in the *LA Times* from the period notes, Snowcap's agents received 'special army training' and resembled 'Rambos. Camouflage fatigues, combat boots, black M-16 automatic rifles. Hard muscles, macho manners.' They were in the Chapare, it continued, to support the Mobile Patrol Unit for Rural Areas, or UMOPAR, a militarised anti-drug Bolivian police squad nicknamed 'the leopards'. Operation Snowcap was 'the first US anti-drug program that has assigned teams of DEA agents to live and work on a daily basis in the remote, rural beginnings of the long cocaine-trafficking trail.'

Under considerable US pressure, including threats to withdraw aid, Bolivia also put anti-narcotics legislation in place. In 1988, the government passed Law 1008, which permitted 12,000 ha of unregulated coca cultivation in the high Yungas for the Bolivian market, while rendering coca cultivation anywhere else in the country illegal. The law committed the government to eradicating at least 5,000 ha of 'illegal' coca a year, which escalated the violence in the Chapare. '[The] government militarized the … region with ensuing mass arrests, raids and murders. Coca growers responded by replanting coca in ever more remote and inaccessible areas,' wrote Silvia Rivera Cusicanqui in an essay for *ReVista*.

Under the law, harsh penalties were imposed for drug offences that, essentially, made little distinction between low-level dealers and cartel bosses. As Linda Farthing and Kathryn Ledebur noted in *Habeas Coca*, a report for the Open Society Foundations, Law 1008 'set disproportionately high sentences for drug-related crimes' and resulted in the imprisonment of 'many poor Bolivians at the lowest levels of the drug trade', often following years of pre-trial detention.

***

In theory, the ultimate targets of this US-led 'war on drugs' were men like Roberto Suárez, the 'King of Cocaine'. Born in 1932 in the city of Trinidad, he was the great nephew of Nicolás Suárez Callaú, the notorious rubber baron who I encountered earlier in my travels. Ruthlessness appeared to run in the family. In the mid-1970s, Roberto Suárez entered the cocaine trade, later boasting he made his first million dollars within seven months. He eventually became the biggest supplier to the Medellín cartel of Pablo Escobar – which controlled more than three-quarters of the global cocaine market at the time – and reputedly made over $400 million a year. At one point Suárez was producing so much coca he hired members of the Bolivian air force to ship it for him. 'His genius was … to gather most of his country's producers of coca and cocaine into one organisation, which he called "the Corporation" and which one author described as the "General Motors of cocaine",' his *Guardian* obituary reported.

The key to Suárez's success was securing high-level political and military protection. In 1980, following the election of a centre-left coalition led by Hernan Siles Zuazo that was perceived as a threat to the Corporation's activities, Suárez took part in the bloody 'Cocaine Coup'. He teamed-up with fellow drug traffickers, Argentina's Dirty War-era military dictatorship, Gestapo chief and 'Butcher of Lyon' Klaus Barbie, and a group of Nazi war criminals, fascists, Rhodesian mercenaries and paramilitaries named the Fiancés of Death. 'Together they decided to bring down the Siles government before it reached office,' wrote Dominic Streatfeild in *Cocaine: An Unauthorised Biography*.

'Realising that they would need a military figure of suitable standing to lead a successful coup, they [chose amenable army general Luis García Meza] ... Suárez had created the world's first "narcocracy".' Suárez even tried to influence the US government. In 1982, after his oldest son was arrested by the DEA, he wrote a personal letter to President Ronald Reagan: in return for immunity from prosecution, Suárez offered to pay off Bolivia's foreign debt, which totalled some $3 billion. The offer was not taken up. Although he may not have been able to exert his control on the president, Suárez was widely believed to have had political and intelligence service connections in the US.

With his hair slicked back, shirt unbuttoned to his chest, Suárez even made it into popular culture: Bolivian drug trafficker Alejandro Sosa, nemesis of Al Pacino's Tony Montana in the film *Scarface*, was inspired by his exploits. Back in Bolivia his philanthropic efforts earned him a certain amount of popularity and, like Escobar, he was viewed by some as a kind of Robin Hood figure. As Streatfeild wrote: '[Suárez] would dole out cash magnanimously, like a king, for suitable worthy causes. He rebuilt churches, surfaced roads and built schools. He handed out college scholarships.'

When the Bolivian police offered $10,000 for information on his activities, Suárez reportedly offered $20,000 for information on anyone who informed on him. In 1988, however, his luck ran out: his ranch was raided, he was arrested and an estimated 1.5 tonnes of cocaine was seized. By then one of the world's most wanted men, Suárez was convicted of drug trafficking and given a 15-year sentence. His cell in La Paz's San Pedro prison resembled a luxury apartment, complete with TV, fridge and several extra beds for visiting wives, ex wives, girlfriends, and his 18 children. Predictably, Suárez claimed to have found God in prison and displayed a poster of Jesus Christ on the cell wall.

After eight years, he was released and returned to his ranch, surrounded by cattle and bodyguards. Perhaps the most surprising element of Suárez's life is that he died of natural causes, just as his great uncle, Nicolás Suárez Callaú, had done. In 2000, aged 68, he suffered a fatal heart attack at home. Shortly before his death, Suárez told a TV reporter: 'The worst mistake I ever made in my life was to have gotten involved in cocaine trafficking.'

Suárez may have survived the 'war on drugs' relatively unscathed but many *cocaleros* in the Chapare were not so fortunate. Throughout the 1980s and 1990s, the UMOPAR acted with virtual impunity and was responsible for widespread human rights violations, including extrajudicial killings, excessive use of force, arbitrary arrests and detention, ill-treatment and torture, and clampdowns on peaceful protests, not to mention beatings, illegitimate searches and seizures, and even petty theft.

As Human Rights Watch noted in 1995, the US response was to simply dismiss the problem: '[The attitude] appears to reflect a determination not to be distracted from the principal goal of combatting drug trafficking, and a willingness to overlook human rights violations that arise in pursuit of that goal. When questioned ... about abusive interrogations by the Bolivian police, a senior DEA official [said] ... it is "not our job to interfere".'

But draconian legislation and heavy-handed policing failed to have the desired effect: according to some estimates, the Chapare was the source of as much as 25 per cent of the world's cocaine in the mid to late 1990s.

***

The situation in the Chapare deteriorated further when former military dictator Hugo Banzer was democratically elected president in 1997. Despite alleged links to drug traffickers in the 1970s, Banzer in his new incarnation set himself up as a staunch US ally in the 'war on drugs'. Taking a 'zero coca' approach, he wasted no time in launching Plan Dignidad (Plan Dignity). Backed by the US, the policy aimed to forcibly eradicate coca from the Chapare within five years, deploying the military in support of the police, striking hard at the livelihoods of *cocaleros* and provoking an angry response, especially when compensation payments for replacing coca with other crops were slashed.

There was a cycle of retaliatory attacks that claimed the lives of scores of coca growers, as well as military personnel and police officers. Amnesty International reported on incidences of soldiers and the police firing indiscriminately into crowds of protesters, *cocaleros* being arrested, assaulted and in some cases beaten to death, and human rights activists being harassed, intimidated and abused before being accused by government ministers of 'instigating violence'.

The brutality of Plan Dignidad – and a similar, albeit short-lived, forced eradication programme in the Yungas – was not even effective in its own terms, according to Farthing and Ledebur. It failed to meet 'its stated goals of destroying the coca crop or restricting the cocaine trade,' they wrote. 'Without any significant source of cash income, Chapare growers either fled the region or quickly replanted the leaf in spite of ongoing repression.' At the same time, coca production grew steadily in the Yungas, across the border in Peru, and in Colombia.

***

Six hours after setting off from Cochabamba, we followed the RN4, a highway that runs the breadth of Bolivia from the Chilean border in the west to the Brazilian frontier in the east, beneath a huge concrete arch marking the entrance to Villa Tunari, the biggest town in the Chapare. Canary yellow and raised on four legs, it bore the optimistic message 'Villa Tunari – Paraíso Etno-Ecotouristico' ('Villa Tunari – Ethno-Ecotourist Paradise') and was said to have cost a staggering $40,000, according to Ariel: 'At least, that's what the authorities claimed it cost.'

This was the most visible attempt to rebrand a town that had witnessed a notorious mass killing. In June 1988, as the government prepared to enact Law 1008, UMOPAR members opened fire on a group of unarmed *cocaleros* holding a protest march. Between 9 and 12 people – the exact number is still disputed – were killed and hundreds more injured.

Beyond the arch, a grassy bank lined with palms appeared in the centre of the highway, partially obscured by clouds of dust sent up by the near-constant traffic. The sides of the road were filled with *trufis*, buses, *moto-taxis*, lorries, and trucks, their drivers and passengers taking advantage of the ubiquitous petrol stations, mechanic shops, unkept guesthouses and food stalls shaded with plastic sheets, a few squawking macaws attempting to make themselves heard above the hubbub. There were also several large, open-sided restaurant-bars, mostly attached to empty hotels and offering views of the Rio San Matéo, respite from the sweaty humidity, and comprehensive menus featuring agouti (a rodent related to the guinea pig), peccary (also known as a skunk pig) and a bony catfish called surubi. These establishments were once frequented by *narcotraficantes*, who came into town to splash the cash, and later relied on trade from DEA agents and aid workers. But these days have long gone and the hotels and restaurant-bar have an abandoned, rather forlorn feel.

As the town's welcome arch suggested, there have been attempts to boost tourism in Villa Tunari and provide locals with alternative employment opportunities. Before it was expelled from the country in 2013, the US Agency for International Development (USAID) claimed to have spent almost $2 billion in the country over a 50-year period on a variety of schemes, including 'alternative development' programmes in the Yungas and the Chapare. *Cocaleros* were encouraged to switch to crops such as coffee, and funding was provided for infrastructure works and tourism projects. These programmes had only a limited impact, said Ariel, a view reinforced by a graffiti message I saw on walls throughout the town: 'No more USAID'. A few foreign aid agency staff sometimes passed through Villa Tunari, Ariel added, but many locals regarded them as little more than fronts for the DEA.

Nevertheless, it was possible to imagine a future in which sustainable tourism played a greater role in the regional economy. Despite the turbulence of the past 50 years – rapid population growth, intensive deforestation, and large-scale road-building, not to mention the wider ravages of the 'war on drugs' – the Chapare still has a wealth of natural beauty and offers a relatively accessible slice of the Amazonian lowlands. Villa Tunari could, perhaps, become something like a small-scale version of Rurrenabaque. It has an attractive river-and-foothill setting, good transport connections, and a small wildlife reserve on its edge. There are a few decent hotels scattered throughout the hinterland in picturesque locations, and a couple of Cochabamba-based tour companies run excursions to nearby national parks. Yet for the time being, visitors were thin on the ground. As I travelled through the region to see some of its fledgling tourist attractions, I only met one other foreigner, a German backpacker breaking a long bus journey with an overnight stay in Villa Tunari.

When I arrived at Parque Nacional Carrasco, a few kilometres south of town, the wardens told me I was the first person to buy an entry ticket in two weeks, even though it was, theoretically, the start of the tourist season. The park spans 6,226 sq km, reaching along the northern slopes of the Andes towards the Amazon, ranging in altitude from 300 to 4,000 m, and boasting cloudforests, rainforests, and grasslands. In the short drive from Villa Tunari the weather had closed in, turning the lapis-blue sky leaden. From a muddy track near the park entrance a pair of thin metal cables stretched high above the churning Río San Mateo, the river charging over a bed of jagged grey rocks. Rather reluctantly, I squeezed into a small, open-sided, manually operated cable-car with Ariel and one of the rangers. A young boy clipped himself to one of the cables with a carabiner and slid across in front, and we juddered along in pursuit.

By the time we reached the other side, the rain was pounding down. We trudged along muddy, riverine paths through a forest so thick with trees we could barely see a few metres ahead of us, crossed streams and clambered up hillocks and over smooth, slick rocks. The ranger told us the park sustained a dazzling array of wildlife – jaguars, tapirs, peccaries, 700 species of birds and more than 5,000 species of plants, many of them endemic. There were even rumours of uncontacted indigenous Yuracaré communities deep in the interior. But although the park was one of the most biologically diverse in the country, it was also under threat. Loggers, farmers, *cocaleros* and drug traffickers have taken advantage of the near-non-existent security to clear vast patches of the forest. But the section nearest Villa Tunari remained relatively pristine, the impenetrable foliage and undergrowth providing a veneer of protection for the time being at least.

Our target for the afternoon was the Cavernas de Repechón, a set of caves whose dank, fetid odour signalled their location long before we spotted them through the abundant foliage. Protected by a rudimentary fence that seemed a little unnecessary given the evident lack of visitors, the caves were home to a rare colony of guácharos, the world's only nocturnal, flying, fruit-eating bird. Also known as oilbirds, they are tan, chestnut, brown and deep red in colour, have hooked bills, and emit unsettlingly human-like shrieks and hoots. These cave dwellers are found only in the Caribbean and South America, and Carrasco is the southernmost point they reach. Peering into the inky gloom of the cavern, we were able to make out of several sleeping specimens before the stench drove us back. The next month, the ranger said, the guácharos would migrate north to Venezuela, navigating by means of echolocation and making eerie, rapid-fire clicks as they flew.

***

I spent the night as the only guest at Hotel La Puente, a simple lodge surrounded by forest and close to a collection of invigoratingly cool river-fed pools known as *pozos*, before setting off for Puerto San Fransciso. There Ariel and I boarded a motorised canoe, the paint flaking away from its hull, for a journey along the meandering Río Chipiriri, watching spider, capuchin, and squirrel monkeys frolicking in the canopies that lined the banks.

Afterwards, on the drive back to Villa Tunari, we stopped off in Villa 14 de Septiembre, a small town hacked out of the jungle and only just managing to keep the rampant growth at bay. Dense green foliage lapped at the rustic homes like an incoming tide and the trees were heavy with bananas and citrus fruits. *Trufis* and *moto-taxis* gathered in the centre, ready to transport people to towns such as Shinahota, once a hub for *narcotraficantes*, and Chimoré, a former HQ for coca-eradication efforts. The cheeks of the drivers bulged with coca leaves.

Villa 14 de Setiembre was where the political career of Evo Morales really started. He was born into an Aymara family of subsistence farmers in the village of Isallavi on the shores of – the now virtually evaporated – Lake Poopó in the *altiplano*. In 1980, when he was 20 and back home after studying in Oruro, side jobs as a baker and bricklayer, a spell as a trumpet player, and a period of military service, the region was devastated by El Niño-powered storms. His parents lost their crops, animals, and means of support. In dire straits, they – along with

farmers from across the *altiplano* and, in time, unemployed miners –
were forced to move, eventually settling in Villa 14 de Setiembre,
a 30-minute drive north of Villa Tunari.

There the family bought a plot of land and grew rice and fruits
before shifting to coca. It was an easy decision to make: coca
can be harvested four times a year and, as Martín Sivak noted in
his biography *Evo Morales*, a 'load of leaves (roughly 100 pounds)
[was] equivalent to 15,000 oranges' during this period. Alongside
farming, Morales founded a football team named New Horizon,
which soon won a local tournament. He also joined the local trade
union, initially becoming the sports secretary, responsible for
arranging matches and social events. The 'young ball player', as the
football-loving Morales was known, rose steadily through union
ranks, eventually becoming leader of an umbrella organisation, the
Seis Federaciones del Trópico de Cochabamba (Six Federations of
the Tropics of Cochabamba).

Morales and his colleagues responded to intensifying coca-eradication
efforts with protests, marches, roadblocks, occupations of municipal
buildings, and even hunger strikes, as well as confrontations with
police officers and soldiers. He was reputedly present during the Villa
Tunari massacre in 1988, returning to the town the following year to
speak at a commemoration ceremony. 'The next day he was beaten up
by a group of [UMOPAR] agents who, thinking he was dead, threw his
body in the mountains. An archive photo shows him on a stretcher,
seemingly beyond recovery,' wrote Sivak.

Morales saw the work of the *campesino* and *cocalero* unions as part
of a wider anti-imperialist struggle against the US, international bodies
such as the IMF and the World Bank, and a reactionary Bolivian elite
that had long excluded the indigenous majority. Coca, he argued,
was a sacred plant and a symbol of indigenous heritage and culture
in Bolivia. Cocaine, by contrast, was a US problem: 'We produce our
coca, we bring it to the main markets, we sell it and that's where our
responsibility ends.'

The *cocaleros* and their unions grew into a mass social movement
and potent political force, with Morales playing a key role. 'The coca
growers' organization burst into electoral politics following a
sweeping trajectory from local to national level,' wrote Cusicanqui
in *ReVista*. The unions mobilised *campesinos* in huge numbers,
negotiated for legal and legislative change, organised mass protests
such as the 22-day, 580-km March for Life, Coca and National
Sovereignty from the Chapare to La Paz in 1994, and won council,
mayoral, and finally parliamentary seats. In 1997, Morales was
elected to the Chamber of Deputies, the lower-house of the Bolivian

parliament, to represent the Chapare. Later he became leader of the Movimiento al Socialismo (Movement towards Socialism) party, commonly known as MAS.

***

On the journey back from Villa Tunari, Ariel talked about other grassroots movements beyond the Chapare that had aided Morales' political rise. One of the most important was in Cochabamba, which has a long-standing tradition of protest and direct action. In the city centre, we stopped at a hill surrounded by traffic-snarled roads. Colina San Sebastián was the site of one of the most famous episodes of Cochabambino resistance during the Bolivian war of independence, Ariel explained, as we followed a cobbled path from a gold-and-silver domed sports arena to the summit past statues, street lights, neatly-tended flower beds, elegant trees, and, somewhat bizarrely, car tyres planted upright in the grass.

In May 1812, as South Americans across the continent were fighting to free themselves from Spanish rule, Cochabamba came under attack from an advancing Spanish royalist army. With the men away fighting elsewhere in the region, Cochabamba's women – and children – took up the defence of their city. Led by a blind grandmother, the formidable Manuela Josefa Gandarillas, they armed themselves with sticks, saucepans and any other item that would serve as a rudimentary weapon. Ignoring calls to surrender, they fortified themselves on Colina San Sebastián, the tallest hill in central Cochabamba. Eventually, the women could hold out no longer and, on 27 May, hundreds were massacred. They became known as the Heroinas de la Coronilla, the Heroines of the Little Hill, and Mother's Day in Bolivia is celebrated every 27 May in their honour.

The summit of the *colina* had a monument dedicated to Las Heroinas. Beneath a cast-iron Christ were statues of steadfast characters, including one brandishing a cane above her head, and a carving depicting the women on foot holding off royalist soldiers on horseback. Beds of pink flowers surrounded the base and a plaque read: 'God and homeland. Here the soul of the women of Cochabamba was the secret of their heroism and virtue.'

It was a peaceful spot, with birdsong and chirping crickets muffling the engines and car horns from the busy roads below. In the distance, visible through hazy smog, the Cristo de la Concordia stood on top of a tall peak, his arms outstretched, as if bestowing the residents of Cochabamba with warmth and gifts. The pose is modelled on the better-known statue of Christ the Redeemer in Rio de Janeiro, though as Cochabambinos are keen to remind you, at 34.2 m (or 40.4 m if you include the pedestal) the steel-and-cement, 2,000-tonne Cristo de la Concordia is taller than its Brazilian counterpart.

Cochabamba has not lost the resoluteness of Las Heroinas. Local farmers played important roles in the radical *campesino* movements of the 1950s and 60s, and in 2000 the city's residents fought the Guerra del Agua, the Water War, a seminal moment for Bolivia and Morales' rise to power. Ariel was just a child when the uprising broke out but, from the way he described the events, it was clear it had made a lasting impression. (It also provided driver Gabriel with an acting opportunity: a few years earlier he had appeared as an extra in *Even the Rain*, a film about the Water War starring Mexican actor Gael García Bernal.)

The Water War had its origins in 1998. Amid spiralling inflation and stagnating economic growth, the IMF approved a $13-million loan to Bolivia with numerous conditions attached to it, notably the privatisation of 'all remaining public enterprises', which included Cochabamba's water agency, SEMAPA. In 1999, in a behind-closed-doors deal, the government agreed to sell-off the utility to Aguas del Tunari, a multinational consortium that featured the politically connected US construction-and-engineering giant Bechtel.

Water prices in Cochabamba subsequently rose significantly, prompting thousands of people to go on strike, take to the streets, erect barricades, occupy plazas and municipal buildings, clash with riot police, and blockade routes in and out of the city. President Hugo Banzer responded by declaring a state of emergency. In the brutal fashion for which Banzer was notorious, the army was sent in, curfews instituted, the rule of law curtailed, and shots fired. A 17-year-old student was killed and many others were injured or arrested, but the protests continued, sparking demonstrations in other cities, where they expanded to cover issues like poverty and low pay.

Eventually, people power triumphed and the government backed down. Aguas del Tunari lost its concession and a cooperative took charge of the city's water supply. 'The people have recaptured their dignity,' said Oscar Olivera, a trade unionist who helped to lead the protests and later won the Goldman Environmental Prize, 'their capacity to organize themselves – and most important of all, the people are no longer scared.'

***

The Six Federations of the Tropics of Cochabamba, and *cocaleros* more generally, played an important role in the Water War, which further boosted Morales' growing political ambitions and helped him expand his base of support. He was also aided by events in early 2002, when an attempt to shut down a coca market in the city of Sacaba, 18 km east of

Cochabamba, resulted in violent clash between *cocaleros* and the army that left six dead (two *cocaleros* and four soldiers).

This led to the 'embarrassing withdrawal of parliamentary privileges from Evo Morales, announced openly by US Ambassador Manuel Rocha, which merely added to the coca grower leader's popularity in the polls,' wrote Cusicanqui. In the 2002 presidential election, Morales claimed almost a quarter of the vote and MAS became the second biggest party in the country.

The following September-October the country was convulsed by the six-week Gas War. An estimated one in seven people joined protests against the government's plan to build a pipeline to export the country's huge natural gas reserves – a key element of the economy whose benefits, like silver and tin before it, eluded the vast majority of Bolivians – to the US via long-standing rival Chile. Led predominantly by indigenous, *campesino* and workers' movements and organisations, the protests called for the government to renationalise Bolivia's gas reserves, drop its neoliberal economic policies, and provide greater rights and representation for the country's indigenous majority, among other measures.

Instead they were met with repression. A state of emergency was declared and the military was sent into El Alto, a hotspot of the protests. Security forces committed multiple human rights abuses, killing around 60 people and injuring more than 400 others. Ultimately, President Gonzalo Sánchez de Lozada – who took power in August 2002, a year after Banzer's departure from office following a cancer diagnosis – was forced to resign. Commonly known as Goni and one of the richest men in the country, he fled to the US. These events helped to shape Morales' manifesto for the 2005 election, which called for 'oil and gas nationalization, the holding of a Constituent Assembly, land redistribution, defense of coca and the war on corruption,' argued Cusicanqui.

I was travelling through Bolivia in the run-up to the 2005 vote and the country was easily the most politically engaged place I had ever visited. Strikes, protests, marches, rallies and road blockades – jackknifed lorries and disused cars set alight were both popular tactics for stopping traffic – were near daily occurrences, even in small, out-of-the-way towns. Political posters, graffiti and slogans covered every available wall space, with 'Evo' and 'MAS' the dominant messages. It was clear that change was coming.

***

Morales won the 2005 election convincingly, gaining 53.7 per cent of the vote to become the first indigenous president in South America.

His victory was part of the 'Pink Tide', a wave of left-wing electoral victories that swept across Latin America in the early 2000s. In office he initially implemented a raft of broadly progressive economic and social policies that saw the percentage of Bolivians living in extreme poverty more than halve, GDP – for much of his time in office – grow by almost 5 per cent a year, and increased investment in education, healthcare and infrastructure.

Morales also moved away sharply from the US-led eradication-and-prohibition approach to coca. Instead he oversaw a policy commonly referred to as 'Coca si, cocaine no'. Under it, growers in places like the Chapare were permitted to cultivate small plots of coca, with coca unions tasked with ensuring everyone kept within specified limits, a participatory approach that was significantly less violent and repressive, cheaper, and more sustainable. Alongside efforts to increase the production of coca-based items such as teas for domestic consumption and export, there were attempts to tackle cocaine trafficking and production. But with continuing high international demand for the drug, not to mention large swathes of inaccessible terrain and long, lightly policed borders with Brazil, Chile, Argentina and Paraguay, this proved a nigh-on impossible task. Bolivia remains the world's third biggest producer of cocaine, the majority of it derived from coca grown in the Chapare, which is still dangerously entangled in the drugs trade.

The US, predictably, was unhappy with the Morales administration's approach. In 2008, President George W Bush blacklisted Bolivia – alongside Venezuela and Myanmar – for failing 'to adhere to their obligations under international counternarcotics agreements'. The following year, Morales expelled DEA agents from the country, where they had been present for more than 30 years, claiming they were involved in espionage. In 2012, the Bolivian government withdrew from the 1961 UN Single Convention on Narcotic Drugs in protest at its classification of coca leaves as an illicit drug. A year later, after a hard-fought lobbying campaign in the teeth of US opposition, the administration secured a major triumph, as a majority of member states voted to readmit Bolivia to the convention with a special dispensation recognising the practice of chewing coca leaves within its borders as legal.

In 2017, the government passed a new law that expanded from 12,000 to 22,000 ha the area that could be legally planted with coca, a policy that had informally been in place for a decade. The same year Morales revived a controversial plan to build a 300-km highway through the Chapare that would cut across the Isiboro-Sécure National Park and Indigenous Territory (popularly known as TIPNIS), northwest of Villa Tunari. When the scheme was originally proposed, it prompted fierce resistance and a 1,000-strong march on La Paz, during which indigenous protesters were attacked by the police. As nationwide criticism grew, the plan was put on hold, before later being revived.

As for the US, despite spending an estimated $1 trillion on the 'war on drugs', much of which was targeted at coca eradication, it remains the world's biggest consumer of cocaine, responsible for more than a quarter of the global total. Some five and a half million Americans – 2 per cent of the population aged 12 and older – used the drug in 2018, with purity levels rising and prices falling, according to the UN's 2020 World Drug Report. By contrast in Bolivia, 0.6 per cent of the population aged 15–64 were estimated to have used cocaine in 2018, with 0.2 per cent using cheaper cocaine base paste; consumption rates for both have risen in recent years.

Meanwhile, around a third of Bolivians regularly chew coca leaves and consume coca tea, sweets and, other products. As anthropologist and geographer Thomas Grisaffi wrote in his book *Coca Yes, Cocaine No*: '[Coca] is accepted across most sectors, regions, and ethnicities ... It is best thought of as a national custom, much like drinking tea is for the British.'

***

From Cochabamba I caught a bus 330 km south to Sucre, Bolivia's constitutional capital and the final stop on my travels. On the surface it is a place that has little in common with *cocaleros* and *narcotraficantes*, social movements and grassroots uprisings. Yet this refined city, the most architecturally beautiful in the country, if not the continent, embodies many of the recurring issues, themes and ideas I have encountered in Bolivia over the years. It is a place of ancient sites and little-known histories, unimaginable mineral wealth and rapacious tycoons, powerful indigenous identities and empire-shaking rebellions.

CHAPTER 10
A dinosaur stampede

The past and the future: Sucre

In a sunny courtyard, beside a statue of an indigenous archer raising his bow to the sky, a gaggle of primary school children in immaculate white-and-green uniforms were given a stern talking to about what they could and – more importantly – could not do in the Casa de la Libertad (House of Freedom). Stay with the group at all times, put your hand up to speak, and – above all else – do not touch a thing, their teacher told them: 'This is one of the most important buildings in Bolivia. It must be respected.' Her voice carried such authority I instinctively straightened my back and hurriedly stashed my phone in my pocket.

Facing the Plaza 25 de Mayo, the heart of the city of Sucre, the Casa de la Libertad dates back to the early 17th century. Now a museum and cultural space, it was originally part of a convent built for the Jesuits. A sturdy wooden door pockmarked with iron studs leads off the street into a cool stone hallway whose floor tiles have been worn smooth and shiny by centuries of footsteps. Beyond is a network of halls set around the courtyard, which is overlooked by a series of church spires that appear to be jostling for attention.

The school group and I were joined by a family of four from Santa Cruz, an elderly Argentine couple, and a middle-aged guide in a pressed white shirt. After nodding at the teacher, who directed an icy stare at her pupils until they quietened down to a dull roar, the guide explained in a hushed tone that Sucre was the site of the *'primer grito libertario de América'* – the 'first cry of American independence'.

In 1808, Napoleon invaded Spain, forced King Ferdinand VII to abdicate, and claimed the crown for his elder brother, Joseph Bonaparte. This sent shockwaves throughout the Spanish empire and boosted burgeoning independence movements across Latin America. In Sucre, the drive for change came from two key sectors: judges from the Real Audiencia de Charcas, an independent court based in the city that exercised jurisdiction on behalf of the Spanish crown over much of modern-day Bolivia, Paraguay, northern Argentina, and Uruguay; and the 'Doctores de Charcas', a group of students, graduates, and faculty members of the Universidad de San Francisco Xavier de Chuquisaca, one of the oldest universities in the Americas and a bastion of revolutionary thought.

On 25 May 1809, the judges and *doctores* overthrew the regional governor and formed a junta. They insisted their loyalty was to the king of Spain, rather than to Spain itself, and that as King Ferdinand VII had been deposed, Latin Americans should rule themselves – an effective declaration of independence. Some historians consider this the spark that ignited the wars of independence in Latin America, though others argue the first revolutionary stirrings were instead in La Paz or Quito in modern-day Ecuador. Moreover, there were many earlier uprisings led by indigenous peoples across the continent, such as the 1781 rebellion by Túpac Katari and Bartolina Sisa.

What is not in dispute is that the Casa de la Libertad was where Bolivia's Act of Independence was signed in July 1825 by representatives of provinces from across Upper Peru, a region spanning much of present-day Bolivia. The guide shepherded us into the Salón de la Independencia, which was once a Jesuit chapel, and along a faded blood-red carpet to a granite plinth topped with a gold-and-glass display case. It contained the original *acta de independencia*, which carried the date 6 August 1825, the guide explained, to commemorate the first anniversary of the decisive battle of Junín in Peru. As we took turns for a close-up look at the document, he recited from memory the opening passage: 'The world knows that Upper Peru has been, on the continent of America, the altar where the first blood of the free was shed and the land where the tomb of the last of the tyrants lies. The provinces of Upper Peru protest to the face of the whole earth, that their irrevocable resolution is to govern themselves.'

On the wall behind the plinth was a portrait of 'El Libertador' Simón Bolívar, after whom the newly independent country was swiftly named – 'If from Romulus, Rome; from Bolívar, it is Bolivia,' declared a representative from Potosí named Manuel Martín Cruz. Bolívar said the painting, by Peruvian artist Gil de Castro, was the closest likeness of him ever produced. Beside it were portraits of two fellow independence leaders, both of whom went on to become president of Bolivia: Antonio José de Sucre and José Ballivián. A few years earlier portraits of Katari and Sisa were temporarily hung above Bolívar, Sucre, and Ballivián, a nod to the oft-overlooked role played by indigenous South Americans in the anti-colonial struggle.

After providing brief but remarkably detailed biographies of the three men, our guide brought the tour to a close and thanked us for visiting with a gentle bow. The family from Santa Cruz, the Argentine couple and the teacher broke into a round of applause, swiftly followed by the children and me.

***

In a sweeping highland valley on the eastern edge of the *altiplano*, Sucre sits at an altitude of 2,810 m, which is really not that high by Bolivian standards. The region was controlled by the Inca and largely inhabited by Quechua- and Aymara-speaking communities until conquistadors overran it in the early 16th century. In 1538 (or 1540; the exact date is disputed), the Spanish founded the city that would become Sucre on the lands of the indigenous Yampara peoples. Since then it has been known variously as Charcas, Chuquisaca, La Ciudad de la Plata (The City of Silver), and eventually Sucre, thus earning it the title the 'City of Four Names'.

Within 25 years the city was home to the Real Audiencia de Charcas and the first bishopric in Upper Peru. As well as exploiting silver deposits in the surrounding area, Sucre became an administrative centre for the much larger reserves in Potosí, 160 km to the south. Soon it was the centre of Spanish political, economic and religious power in this part of the Andes. Many of Potosí's mine owners opted to live in Sucre, which offered a more comfortable altitude, a temperate climate and greener environs. On the backs of the enslaved indigenous and African people who laboured in the mines, silver wealth flowed into Sucre, funding the countless grand mansions, churches, monasteries, and municipal buildings that would later earn the city centre a UNESCO World Heritage Site designation.

As the 17th century progressed however, its power ebbed, as cities like Buenos Aires in what is now Argentina rose to the fore. After playing a key role in the struggle for independence from Spanish rule, the city was renamed Sucre (after Antonio José de Sucre) and made the capital of the new Republic of Bolivia, but political and economic influence continued to drift away. In 1899, following a brief civil war between conservative and liberal forces, the congress, presidency, and de facto capital status moved northwest to La Paz, though Sucre was allowed to retain the title of constitutional capital, as well as its possession of the Supreme Court.

Today, Sucre is the sixth biggest city in the country with a population hovering around 360,000. Although the drivers of political, economic, and social life in Bolivia increasingly appear to lie elsewhere, it retains a cultured, prosperous, middle-class air, with tidy streets and an unhurried pace of life. Downtown Sucre is a treasure trove of perfectly preserved 16th to 19th-century architecture. Laid out on an orderly grid system, it has an expansive square, the Plaza 25 de Mayo, in the centre, surrounded by a *mestizo*-baroque cathedral, neoclassical town hall, and elegant former presidential palace. Neighbouring blocks are filled with similarly impressive churches, chapels, monasteries, townhouses, and university buildings, their brilliant white adobe walls and red-tiled roofs gleaming in the sunshine.

The city's heritage is taken seriously: buildings in the historic centre must be freshly whitewashed each year – a uniformity of colour that has given rise to yet another nickname, the Ciudad Blanca, or White City – and modern constructions are banished to the outskirts. Along with its multilayered colonial and independence-era history, this architectural heritage could easily turn the city into something of a museum piece. Yet although in some respects rather conservative, Sucre also has a young, cosmopolitan feel, thanks largely to the crowds of students attending its universities. It also draws a steady stream of gringos. Scores of historic buildings have been turned into boutique hotels, B&Bs and hostels, there are numerous Spanish-language schools aimed at backpackers, and many Europeans have emigrated to the city to set up travel agencies, restaurants, bars, galleries, and other ventures.

Sucre's glorious Plaza 25 de Mayo is the paradigm of the Latin American square, especially on the balmy evening that followed my visit to the Casa de la Libertad. There was a slight breeze and a chorus of church bells echoing in the distance. The gardens were manicured, with 'don't step on the grass' and 'care for the plants' signs clearly adhered to, while the lower trunks of the towering trees were whitewashed for protection. The atmosphere was relaxed: teenagers embraced, children crowded round balloon and snack sellers, groups gossiped in the pavilion and ate chunks of the city's famous chocolate, and old men played cards and sipped *mate*, a herbal tea made from the leaves of the yerba mate plant, through metal straws known as *bombillas*. Beneath a statue of General Sucre, illuminated with red lights and with a statue of a lion at its base, a student showed off his break-dancing skills to a group of giggling admirers.

***

Beyond the historic centre are a couple of architectural curiosities, rare bursts of colour in the White City. In a leafy park near the stately Supreme Court is an Eiffel tower, a shorter and simplified take on the Parisian original, designed by Gustave Eiffel himself and installed in Sucre in the first decade of the 20th century. Standing around 12 m in height, roughly parallel with the surrounding treetops, it has a spiral staircase leading up to a viewing platform. The tower's iron frame had recently been given a thick coat of pumpkin-orange paint, a reaction, perhaps, against the strict planning regulations and uniform colour schemes in the city centre.

South of downtown Sucre, on the road to Potosí, is a far more outlandish construction, the Castillo de La Glorieta. During the 20-million drive an inquisitive taxi driver peppered me with questions, shooting off on wildly diverting tangents: 'How big is England?' 'How much were your sunglasses?' 'What's the oldest thing in England?' 'How many languages do you speak in England?' 'How much did your hotel room cost?' 'What music do you listen to?' I'd barely answered one question before another one was fired my way until eventually we reached La Glorieta, a kitsch fairytale-style castle seemingly built from the leftovers of assorted other projects. It was described by one of my predecessors on *The Rough Guide to Bolivia* as 'probably the most ridiculous construction in Bolivia, and a clear example of how wealth and taste do not always coincide'. I loved it.

Built over a seven-year period in the 1890s, La Glorieta was a vanity project for mining tycoon, banker, and diplomat Francisco Argandoña Revilla and his wife Clotilde. Overlooking a stream, the now-empty *castillo* is a huge, coral-pink wedding cake of a construction, with stucco busts of horses gazing down at visitors from the roof. I walked along a gravel path past garages and stables to a chapel with a 25-m neo-Gothic clocktower, an exact replica – albeit pink – of London's Elizabeth Tower, home of Big Ben. Taller still, at 45 m, is the yellow Russian-Byzantine-style Prince's Tower, which corkscrews out of the centre of the *castillo* like a minaret and is topped with a turquoise onion dome. It looks like a Hollywood take on *The Arabian Nights*. At the far end of the building is the sturdier, octagonal Princess Tower, complete with keyhole-shaped windows.

Outside the entrance of the *castillo*, now just a shell, is a statue of Francisco in his later years reaching out benevolently to a pair of stricken children. This was a tribute to his and Clotilde's work with orphans, which earned the pair the titles 'Princes of La Glorieta', bestowed on them by – coca wine-enthusiast – Pope Leo XIII during a trip to the Vatican. Hiram Bingham, who wrote about a visit to Sucre in his 1911 book *Across South America*, provided a slightly different version of the story. He described La Glorieta as a 'pleasure park', complete with summer houses, pagodas, and even a miniature locomotive – which turned out to be a 'small motor car in disguise' – that plied a railway line across the grounds. Much to his chagrin, Bingham was not able to actually enter the *castillo* but he did gain an insight into its owners after speaking to a local woman. 'It seems that [Argandoña Revilla] the head of the richest family in Bolivia ... decided to make a large donation to the Pope. Soon afterwards his

great generosity was rewarded with the title of "Prince of Glorieta",'
he noted.

Unlike Bingham, I was able to look inside La Glorieta, which was
taken over by the Bolivian army in the 1950s, four decades after the
death of the 'prince'. Although the facade is in good repair, much
of the interior is dilapidated after decades of neglect, with many of
the 40-plus rooms off limits. But enough of it has been restored to
remind visitors of the staggering wealth of Bolivia's mining barons
in the 19th and early 20th centuries. Much like their counterpart
Simón Patiño and his opulent Palacio Portales in Cochabamba, the
Argandoñas kitted out La Glorieta with ostentatious fixtures and
fittings from across the globe.

The rooms are a hotchpotch of different and often clashing styles:
wood, stone, and tiled floors; huge gilt mirrors; stucco ceilings; marble
fireplaces; Venetian stained glass; grand pillars topped with sculpted
leaves; a sweeping wooden staircase with a trail of dusty footprints;
and soft blue, terracotta, and cream colour schemes. There are portraits
of the Argandoñas in their princely garb as they meet the pope. On a
drawing room wall is a bust of a lion with a pineapple and a bunch of
grapes dangling from its mouth. Above it is a statue of what looks like
a hybrid between a llama, a donkey, and a gargoyle, augmented with a
set of golden wings.

In some respects La Glorieta's eclectic mix of clashing architectural
styles bear a resemblance to the *cholets* of El Alto. Yet it lacks their
grounding in indigenous identities, motifs, and beliefs – and indeed
practicality of use – instead appearing pompous, a conspicuous display
of wealth that looks overseas for inspiration.

Afterwards I wandered round the garden, home to massive palm
trees that appear to be in competition with La Glorieta's towers,
a dovecot, and several large ponds and fountains, now all dry. In the
grounds beyond is a military training school, which led to the surreal
sight of young privates with rifles and khaki fatigues being put through
their paces in the shadow of a pink pleasure palace.

***

Back in Sucre I joined the throngs at the counter of El Patio, which
has a reputation for serving the best *salteñas* in the city. After a bout of
gentle elbowing with my fellow diners, I was handed one of the piping
hot pasties, stuffed with chunks of beef, boiled eggs, olives and peas,
and wrapped in greaseproof paper. As I ate the *salteña* in the restaurant's
eponymous courtyard, sunlit and filled with bougainvillea, crumbs of
flaky pastry collected at my feet and rivulets of savoury-sweet sauce
trickled down my hands.

Afterwards, I hiked up to the Recoleta district, a steep 20-minute climb from the main square past historic churches, neatly tended plazas, and cobbled streets lined with classic Sucre homes – dazzling white walls, small balconies, overhanging terracotta-tiled roofs, and often the city's flag, a red 'cross of Jerusalem' on a white rectangle with a triangle cut out on the right-hand side. At the summit, near the 16th-century Franciscan monastery that gave its name to the district, a *mirador* offered panoramic views of the city, a sea of tiled roofs and church spires, with brown hills rising in the distance. It was populated by young couples, who nestled together, exchanged kisses and wandering hands, fastened padlocks to the fence to symbolise their love, and steadfastly ignored the vistas.

A short walk away, in a sombre colonial-era building on a narrow passageway, is the Museo de Arte Indígena, which highlights an aspect of Sucre's heritage, culture, history and inhabitants often overshadowed by the city's renowned architecture, well-documented place in South America's wars of independence, and cosmopolitan atmosphere. The location seemed fitting for a museum dedicated to the art and culture of two Quechua-speaking peoples – barely a stone's throw from a monastery founded with the express aim of converting indigenous peoples to Christianity.

The Museo de Arte Indígena is run by ASUR, an NGO that supports 'economic development projects derived from indigenous communities' own cultural experience'. Its focus is to help revive the traditional textiles of the Jalq'a and Tarabuco peoples, who live to the west and east of Sucre, respectively. More than a thousand weavers and embroiderers, female and male, have been supported by the programme, which boosts their income, showcases their work, and keeps alive historic techniques and styles.

The textiles exhibited in the museum are exquisite and remarkably varied. I saw colourful striped ponchos, shawls, tapestries, and *chuspas*, small bags for carrying coca leaves. The Tarabuqueño creations feature bright scenes from everyday life – farming, religious rituals, and festivals, as well as trees, plants, and animals – while the Jalq'a designs tend towards darker shades and supernatural imagery – gods, demons, fantastical beasts and subterranean realms. There were also ancient artefacts, fragments of textiles dating back as much as 2,000 years, including a Tiwanaku-era tunic made from the delicate wool of the vicuña.

In the courtyard I watched a female weaver from the town of Tarabuco, 60 km southeast of Sucre and famous for its Sunday market, which draws traders and artisans from across the region (as well as crowds of day-tripping tourists). Deep in concentration, she expertly manipulated the vertical loom in front of her, slowly bringing together green, blue, and purple threads to form a new image.

***

In the late afternoon I walked back downhill to the Plaza 25 de Mayo. As in La Paz, there were students in baggy zebra costumes, dancing energetically, gesticulating in comical fashion and helping (and occasionally hindering) pedestrians as they crossed the road. On the far side of the square, near the Casa de la Libertad, a protest march was underway. Led by a brass band, a class of primary school pupils dressed variously as syringes, purple germs, and lumpy pink tongues made their way along the pavement, waving and smiling. They in turn were followed by a group of adolescents aged 14 or 15, who carried placards and banners with slogans promoting safe sex and awareness of the dangers of HIV/AIDS. They stopped periodically to politely chat to passers-by and offer leaflets to idling motorists caught up in traffic.

Later, when I was home in London writing the opening chapters of this book, I thought back to those young people in Sucre. It was the autumn of 2019 and protests of a very different tenor and scale were breaking out across Bolivia. They had their roots in events that started during Evo Morales' first term in office (2006-09), when a new constitution was introduced – following a referendum in 2009 – that limited presidents to two consecutive five-year terms. After winning the subsequent 2009 election, Morales initially said he would not stand for the presidency again, but later changed his mind. In 2013, the Constitutional Court contentiously ruled he could run again as his first term took place under the previous constitution, which had different rules. This prompted heavy criticism, but Morales was duly elected for a third term in the 2014 election.

Two years later, he narrowly lost a referendum to change the 2009 constitution to allow him to run for a fourth consecutive term in 2019. Yet this proved only a temporary setback, as Movimiento al Socialismo (MAS) legislators asked the Constitutional Court to rule on the matter. In 2017, the court controversially scrapped term limits completely, allowing Morales to run again. This was met with widespread criticism in Bolivia and beyond. As Human Rights Watch noted: 'There is transparent hypocrisy in his argument that international human rights law bars the Constitution's term limits. In the past Mr Morales's administration has frequently contended that sovereignty should trump rights.'

The consternation fed into broader concerns about Morales' leadership style – including accusations of authoritarian tendencies – and his legislative programme. I recalled a conversation I had with a MAS supporter from El Alto in 2016. He praised Morales' policies, particularly the nationalisation of the oil and gas industries and increased social spending, but still voted against him in the referendum. He explained he was worried South America's first indigenous president would damage his legacy by staying in power for too long. 'We don't want a king here,' he said.

Despite these concerns – and criticism of his handling of recent devastating wildfires in eastern Bolivia – Morales appeared set to win a fourth consecutive term in the October 2019 election. But after the vote there were contested allegations of electoral fraud. Civil unrest spread across the country, with protests for and against the incumbent. Morales initially declared he had won by a sufficient margin in the first round of voting to render a run-off unnecessary, and warned 'a coup is under way, prepared by the right with international support'.

But he later said he would welcome an international audit of the results: 'I will accompany them and if there is fraud, the next day I'll call for a second round [of voting].' Meanwhile, opposition candidate and former president Carlos Mesa of the Comunidad Ciudadana party urged his supporters to 'defend the popular vote'. The violence on the streets intensified and there were mutinies by police officers. On 10 November, the Organization of American States (OAS) said the election result should be annulled because it had found serious irregularities (researchers from the Massachusetts Institute of Technology would later challenge the OAS's findings). Morales subsequently pledged to call a new vote, but opposition figures said the move had come too late, protests continued, and the commander-in-chief of the armed forces told journalists: '[We] suggest the president resign ... to allow for pacification and the maintaining of stability, for the good of our Bolivia.' In a televised address on the night of 10 November, the MAS leader announced his resignation as president and subsequently fled to Mexico. Vice-president Álvaro García Linera also resigned, as did the MAS presidents of the senate and chamber of deputies.

There was opposition to Morales from the left as well as the right, but it was the latter who filled the political vacuum after he departed. The conservative vice-president of the senate, Jeanine Áñez, declared herself interim president at a legislative assembly session boycotted by MAS. The contrast with Morales was stark: Áñez was an evangelical Christian who brandished a large leather-bound Bible and – in a subsequently deleted tweet from 2013 – had described Aymara New Year celebrations as 'satanic'. As MAS supporters continued to protest, the legislative assembly annulled the election result and scheduled a new one for May 2020. Áñez also set out to roll back many of the Morales government's economic, social, and foreign policies.

Amnesty International described the events that followed the October 2019 election as a 'social, political and human rights crisis'. It highlighted the repression of demonstrators, the excessive use of force by police and armed forces, and the targeting of journalists and civil society activists. In an August 2020 report, *Healing the pandemic of impunity*, the organisation said 'at least 35 people have died and 833 have been injured in the context of the protests' over the previous 10 months. Two notorious incidents occurred shortly after Áñez assumed the presidency: an estimated nine protesters against the interim government died during a march in Sacaba, near Cochabamba; and at least 10 people were killed at a blockade of the Senkata fuel plant in El Alto. 'The statements and evidence collected strongly indicate that the National Police and the Armed Forces used disproportionate and unnecessary force,' the report stated.

Amnesty International also said there were 'credible reports' of 'possible crimes and use of force' by MAS supporters during the post-election crisis. It highlighted the case of human rights activist Waldo Albarracín, who had long faced 'attacks, threats, stigmatization, as well as smear campaigns through public statements by senior officials'. Following the election, he was hit on the head with a 'blunt object' at a vigil and received threatening phone calls and social media messages, before having his house attacked and set on fire by MAS supporters, the organisation reported.

Áñez twice postponed the delayed general election, blaming Covid-19, but it finally took place in October 2020. This time there was no questioning the result: it was a landslide victory for MAS presidential candidate Luis Arce, a *paceño* from a middle-class family who read Karl Marx while he was at school, studied economics, worked for many years at the Central Bank of Bolivia, and served as finance minister in the Morales administration, where he was widely credited for his role in Bolivia's 'economic miracle', which saw an average growth rate of 4.8 per cent between 2004 and 2017, with millions lifted out of poverty in the process. He gained more than 55 per cent of the vote – Mesa, his closest challenger, won less than 29 per cent – and MAS secured majorities in both branches of the legislative assembly, a reflection of the party's widespread and resilient base of support.

Arce, who promised to boost social spending, introduce a wealth tax, and ensure justice for protesters killed while the Áñez government was in power, declared: 'We have now reclaimed democracy for Bolivia.' In February 2021, Supreme Decree 4461 was approved, granting an amnesty or pardon to MAS supporters detained for alleged crimes committed during the post-2019 election crisis. The next month Áñez and other former interim government officials were arrested on charges of 'terrorism' and other crimes. In August, she and her government were strongly criticised by an independent panel of human rights experts set-up by the Inter-American Commission on Human Rights. The Interdisciplinary Group of Independent Experts' 471-page report found the 'interim government came to power by sidestepping consti-tutional rules for presidential succession and persecuted opponents with "systematic torture" and "summary executions",' according to the Associated Press. It also described the Sacaba and Senkata incidents as 'massacres', and documented cases of sexual and gender-based violence against female detainees.

As for Morales, from whom Arce gently distanced himself, the former president returned to Bolivia following the 2020 election after almost a year in exile in Mexico and then Argentina. At the La Quiaca-Villazón border crossing in south east Bolivia, he was welcomed by thousands of supporters. 'As long as capitalism and imperialism exist, the fight goes on,' he told them.

***

My time in Bolivia was almost at an end but there was a final place I wanted to see before heading home. Ever since my first visit to the country, I've been captivated by Bolivia's multilayered history, particularly by the earthwork-builders of the Llanos de Moxos, the Tiwanaku empire, the Aymara nobles who built shrines around the Salar de Uyuni, and, of course, the Inca in Lake Titicaca and El Fuerte. But Sucre was a reminder that by focusing on the country's human history, I'd missed a huge part of the story.

The world's most important cement works – from the point of view of palaeontologists – are on the outskirts of the city. In the Plaza 25 de Mayo I boarded the Dino Bus, a double decker with a cartoonish image of a Tyrannosaurus rex on its exterior and impracticably low ceilings on the upper floor that forced me to bend almost double as I searched for a seat. We left behind the pristine whitewashed architecture and drove out to an industrial suburb just northwest of Sucre. The area was dominated by a tall grey-white cliff rising out of a large quarry, through which a stream of heavily-laden trucks chugged, while above tall chimneys belched plumes of charcoal-coloured smoke.

After paying the entry fee we made our way through the Parque Cretácico Cal Orck'o, which contained kitsch replica dinosaurs and pumped out deafening screeches, roars and howls, like sound effects from a horror film. At a viewpoint overlooking the looming cliff, which is known as Cal Orck'o, 'Hill of Limestone' in Quechua, we donned hard hats and goggles before being led down a steep trail to the muddy quarry floor by guide Juan José. Here we were rewarded with a close-up view of Cal Orck'o, which is around 120 m in height and almost a kilometre in length.

At first glance, the cliff appeared nondescript. But as my eyes focused, two indistinct indentations gradually formed themselves into a giant pair of dinosaur footprints. Then I spotted another pair, and then three more, and then more than I could count.

In total, the cliff has over 12,000 individual tracks from as many as 15 different species of dinosaur from the late Cretaceous period (68–65 million years ago), easily the largest and most diverse collection of its kind in the world. Cal Orck'o was originally flat, a bed of mud or sand covered with shallow floodwaters through which dinosaurs roamed, leaving behind their footprints in the soft earth. A volcanic explosion later covered the prints with a protective layer of ash that helped to preserve them. Further layers of sediments followed, eventually fossilising the prints. Around 25 million years ago tectonic movements forced the ground upwards.

'The earth folded like a giant accordion and created the Andes. This cliff is a tiny part of that accordion,' Juan José explained, the roars of the replica dinosaurs in the park above us just audible above the dull hum of the factory. It remained like that until the mid-20th century, when the Fancesa cement works opened and the hill was excavated, eventually leaving behind a near-vertical cliff. The dinosaur footprints were discovered by workers in 1994 and soon palaeontologists were flocking here from all over the world.

As he talked, Juan José led us up to the face of the cliff, which was riddled with cracks and crevices. We halted a couple of metres away and I fought to resist an almost overwhelming desire to reach out and put my hand in the centre of an oval-shaped print made by a sauropod, a giant herbivore with a long neck and tail, small head, and four trunk-like legs. Juan José said the biggest print at the site was almost 1.5 m in diameter, while another three-toed print belonging to a bipedal theropod closely resembled the trefoil leaves of the Adidas logo.

There are more than 460 footprint tracks, some stretching for hundreds of metres and many overlapping or criss-crossing each other. Some palaeontologists believe these are a snapshot of a stampede in which a gang of predators – including a young Tyrannosaurus rex nicknamed 'Johnnie Walker' by whisky-loving researchers – pursued their prey, with scavengers following in their wake, looking for easy pickings. 'These prints are from some of the last dinosaurs to roam the

Earth,' said Juan José. 'Some people like to joke that these dinosaurs saw the meteorite coming and started to run.'

Central Bolivia is rich in dinosaur sites – notably Parque Nacional Torotoro, whose arid valleys, canyons, and mountains are home to numerous fossils and footprints – but there is nowhere quite like Cal Orck'o. The government has declared the site a national monument and applied for UNESCO World Heritage Site status, but erosion remains a threat. Despite efforts to protect it, parts of the cliff have already crumbled away, wiping out series of footprints (though often exposing new ones in the process). Concerns have also been raised about the impact of the ongoing work elsewhere in the quarry.

As Juan José pointed out prints made by a titanosaur, a stocky sauropod that may have weighed as much as a double-decker bus, my mind started to drift. I thought back to the silver mines in Potosí, the rainforests of Parque Nacional Madidi, the iridescent *cholets* of El Alto, and the coca fields of the Chapare. With my flight home to London only a few days away, I felt I was leaving Bolivia having gained a deeper insight into the country, travelled to places rarely visited by foreigners, and glimpsed some of the challenges that lie ahead. I also felt a sharp sense of melancholy, the nagging concern I'd only skimmed the surface and exposed how much I didn't know. There are so many parts of Bolivia I still wanted to visit – from the Amazonian wilds of Parque Nacional Noel Kempff Mercado to the dry expanses of the Chaco. However far you travel, there's always further to go.

It was nearly 1 p.m. and the sun moved overhead, illuminating Cal Orck'o with a brilliant white spotlight. The footprints glowed, almost luminous. A tractor sent up spirals of chalky dust as it rumbled past, so close to the cliff-face the driver could have reached out and touched it. Explosions sounded in the distance, shaking the earth beneath my feet.

Key sources

Research for *Crossed off the Map* involved a wide range of books, newspapers, magazines, reports, research papers, websites, TV and radio programmes, and films, including the following.

Prologue: Bolivia does not exist

Dash, Mike, 'Run Out of Town on an Ass', *Smithsonian Magazine* (4 June 2012)

Chapter 1: Before Bolivia

Bingham, Hiram, *Across South America: An Account of a Journey from Buenos Aires to Lima by way of Potosí, with notes on Brazil, Argentina, Bolivia, Chile, and Peru* (Boston and New York: Houghton Mifflin Company, 1911)

Cholet – The work of Freddy Mamani, directed by Isaac Niemand (2018)

Cieza de León, Pedro de, *The Travels of Pedro de Cieza de León, AD 1532–50, Contained in the First Part of His Chronicle of Peru* (Hakluyt Society, 1883)

De la Vega, Garcilaso, *Royal Commentaries of the Incas and General History of Peru* (University of Texas, 1987)

Erickson, Clark L., 'Amazonia: The Historical Archaeology of a Domesticated Landscape', *The Handbook of South American Archaeology* (January 2008)

Fawcett, Percy Harrison, *Exploration Fawcett* (Hutchinson, 1953)

Gott, Richard, *Land Without Evil: Utopian Journeys Across the South American Watershed* (Verso Books, 1992)

Janusek, John Wayne, *Ancient Tiwanaku* (Cambridge University Press, 2008)

Mann, Charles C., *1491: The Americas before Columbus* (Granta Books, 2006)

Sarmiento de Gamboa, Pedro, *History of the Incas* (Hakluyt Society, 1907)

Chapter 2: The mountain that eats men

Bingham, Hiram, *Across South America: An Account of a Journey from Buenos Aires to Lima by way of Potosí, with notes on Brazil, Argentina, Bolivia, Chile, and Peru* (Boston and New York: Houghton Mifflin Company, 1911)

Cervantes, Miguel, *Don Quixote (Penguin Classics, 2003)*

Cieza de León, Pedro de, *The Travels of Pedro de Cieza de León, AD 1532–50, Contained in the First Part of His Chronicle of Peru* (Hakluyt Society, 1883)

Galeano, Eduardo, *Open Veins of Latin America: Five Centuries of the Pillage of a Continent* (Monthly Review Press, 1997)

Guardiola-Rivera, Oscar, *What if Latin America Ruled the World? How the South Will Take the North* (Bloomsbury, 2011)

'Episode 80: Pieces of Eight', *A History of the World in 100 Objects* (BBC Radio 4, 2010)

Flynn, Dennis and Giraldez, Arturo, 'Born with a "Silver Spoon": The Origin of World Trade in 1571', *Journal of World History* (University of Hawaii Press, 1995)

Izagirre, Ander, *The Mountain That Eats Men* (Zed Books, 2019)

Mann, Charles C., *1493: Uncovering the New World Columbus Created* (Vintage, 2012)

MacGregor, Neil, *A History of the World in 100 Objects* (Penguin, 2012)

Miller, John, *Memoirs of General Miller: in the service of the Republic of Peru* (Longman, Rees, Orme, Brown, and Green, 1828–29)

Temple, Edmond, *Travels in Various Parts of Peru: Including a Year's Residence in Potosi* (Philadelphia: E. L. Carey & A. Hart-Chestnut, 1833)

Weatherford, Jack, *Indian Givers: How the Indians of the Americas Transformed the World* (Fawcett, 1990)

Chapter 3: Tin kings and rubber barons

Fifer, J. Valerie, 'The Empire Builders: A History of the Bolivian Rubber Boom and the Rise of the House of Suárez', *Journal of Latin American Studies* (November 1970)

Geddes, Charles F., *Patiño: The Tin King* (Robert Hale Ltd, 1972)

Gladwell, Malcolm, *Outliers: The Story of Success* (Penguin, 2009)

Isherwood, Christopher, *The Condor and The Cows* (Vintage Classics, 2013)

Lehman, Kathryn, 'The Rapid of Hope and the Life of an Amazonian Boom-Town', *The Appendix* (18 November 2014)

Portman, Lionel, *Three Asses in Bolivia* (G. Richards Ltd, 1922)

Post, Charles Johnson, *Across the Andes* (Outing Publishing Company, 1912)

Vallvé, Frederic, *The impact of the rubber boom on the indigenous peoples of the Bolivian lowlands (1850–1920)* (Georgetown University, 2010)

Chapter 4: Flat white

Draper, Robert, 'This metal is powering today's technology—at what price?', *National Geographic* (9 April 2019)
Jacobs, Michael, *Ghost Train Through The Andes* (John Murray, 2007)
'Lithium', Friends of the Earth (2013)
Portman, Lionel, *Three Asses in Bolivia* (G. Richards Ltd, 1922)
Wright, Lawrence, 'Lithium Dreams', *New Yorker* (15 March 2010)

Chapter 5: Amazon primed

'August's fires in the Amazon are at their highest levels in a decade', Greenpeace (13 August 2020)
'Bolivia: Open Letter to President Morales on the fires in the Chiquitanía', Amnesty International (9 September 2019)
Chalalán Eco-lodge, Bolivia: Equator Initiative Case Studies, Equator Initiative, United Nation Development Programme (2012)
Fawcett, Percy Harrison, *Exploration Fawcett* (Hutchinson, 1953)
Ghinsberg, Yossi, *Lost in the Jungle: A Harrowing True Story of Adventure and Survival* (Summersdale, 2008)
Organized Crime and Illegally Mined Gold in Latin America, The Global Initiative Against Transnational Organized Crime (April 2016)

Chapter 6: The future is behind us

Bingham, Hiram, *Across South America: An Account of a Journey from Buenos Aires to Lima by way of Potosí, with notes on Brazil, Argentina, Bolivia, Chile, and Peru* (Boston and New York: Houghton Mifflin Company, 1911)
Cholet – The work of Freddy Mamani, directed by Isaac Niemand (2018)
Iyer, Pico, *The Man Within My Head* (Bloomsbury, 2013)
Lazar, Sian, *El Alto, Rebel City* (Duke University Press, 2008)
Núñez, Rafael E., and Sweetser, Eve, 'With the Future Behind Them: Convergent Evidence From Aymara Language and Gesture in the Crosslinguistic Comparison of Spatial Construals of Time', *Cognitive Science* (2006)
South American Handbook (Footprint Travel Guides, 1924)
Urbanization Trends in Bolivia: Opportunities and Challenges, World Bank (May 2015)

Chapter 7: Mission control

'Amazon fire tracker', Monitoring the Andean Amazon Project (2020)
Duguid, Julian, *Green Hell: Adventures In The Mysterious Jungles Of Eastern Bolivia* (The Century Company, 1931)
Ford, Kate, 'Two "ways of proceeding": damage limitation in the Mission to the Chiquitos', *Cultural Worlds of the Jesuits in Colonial Latin America* (University of London Press, 2020)
Friedman-Rudovsky, Jean, 'A Verdict in Bolivia's Shocking Case of the Mennonite Rapes', *Time* (26 August 2011)
Gott, Richard, *Land Without Evil: Utopian Journeys Across the South American Watershed* (Verso Books, 1992)
Županov, Ines G., and Fabre, Pierre Antoine (editors), *The Rites Controversies in the Early Modern World* (Brill, 2018)

Chapter 8: You triumph of you die

Anderson, Jon Lee, *Che Guevara: A Revolutionary Life* (Bantam, 1997)
Guevara, Ernesto 'Che', *Back On The Road: A Journey To Central America* (The Harvill Press, 2001)
Guevara, Ernesto 'Che', *The Bolivian Diary* (Harper Perennial, 2009)
'Shadow Warrior', *Booknotes* (C-Span, 30 October 1989)
The Trial of Responsibilities: The Garcìa Meza Tejada Trial, Human Rights Watch (1993)

Chapter 9: Coca si

Amnesty International Report 1999 – Bolivia, Amnesty International (1 January 1999)
Bolivia: Human Rights Violations and the War on Drugs, Human Rights Watch (July 1995)
Bolivia: The impact of Operation Blast Furnace: Summary, CIA (3 October 1986)
Cowley, Abraham, 'A Legend of Coca', *Six Books of Plants* (1662)
Cusicanqui, Silvia Rivera, 'An Andean Commodity and Its Paradoxes', *ReVista* (Fall 2011)
Farthing, Linda, and Ledebur, Kathryn, *Habeas Coca: Bolivia's Community Coca Control* (Open Society Foundations, 2015)
Grisaffi, Thomas, *Coca Yes, Cocaine No* (Duke University Press, 2019)
Gunson, Phil, 'Roberto Suárez', *Guardian* (4 August 2000)
Long, William R., 'Cocaine Patrol: Prowling Bolivia's Jungle With the DEA', *LA Times* (22 May 1990)

Nuland, Sherwin, 'Sigmund Freud's Cocaine Years', *New York Times* (21 July 2011)

Sivak, Martín, *Evo Morales: The Extraordinary Rise of the First Indigenous President of Bolivia* (St. Martin's Press, 2010)

Streatfeild, Dominic, *Cocaine: An Unauthorised Biography* (Picador Paper, 2003)

World Drug Report 2020, United Nations (2020)

Chapter 10: A dinosaur stampede

Bingham, Hiram, *Across South America: An Account of a Journey from Buenos Aires to Lima by way of Potosí, with notes on Brazil, Argentina, Bolivia, Chile, and Peru* (Boston and New York: Houghton Mifflin Company, 1911)

'Bolivia: A true commitment to human rights demands impartial and independent justice', Amnesty International (15 March 2021)

'Bolivia Should End Revenge Justice', Human Rights Watch (22 March 2021)

GIEI Bolivia: Informe sobre los hechos de violencia y vulneración de los derechos humanos ocurridos entre el 1 de septiembre y el 31 de diciembre de 2019, Grupo Interdisciplinario de Expertos Independientes, (23 July 2021)

Healing the pandemic of impunity: 20 human rights recommendations for candidates in the 2020 presidential elections in Bolivia, Amnesty International (20 August 2020)

Jacobs, Daniel and Meghji, Shafik, *The Rough Guide to Bolivia* (Rough Guides, 2018)

About Latin America Bureau (LAB)

Latin America Bureau (Research and Action) Limited (LAB) is an independent, non-profit publishing and research organization based in the UK. A registered charity, LAB provides news, analysis and information on Latin America, reporting consistently from the perspective of the region's social movements and poor, oppressed or marginalized communities – aiming to convey their voices to a wide readership across the English-speaking world.

Founded in 1977, LAB has published over 150 books and operates a lively website (www.lab.org.uk) and Facebook page (https://www.facebook.com/latinamericabureau/). You can sign up to receive the newsletter by clicking 'Subscribe' on the www.lab.org.uk home page.

Practical Action Publishing Ltd distribute all LAB titles, new and old. You can see the full catalogue at https://developmentbookshop.com/latin-america-bureau-titles. As well as print books, many titles are available in digital form and educational institutions can subscribe to individual chapters for course reading lists.

For more information, email contactlab@lab.org.uk

Index

CPSIA information can be obtained
at www.ICGtesting.com
Printed in the USA
LVHW081441040622
720515LV00012B/275

9 781909 014251

Crossed off the Map

Blending travel writing, history and reportage, *Crossed off the Map* journeys from the Andes to the Amazon to explore Bolivia's turbulent past and contemporary challenges.

It tells the story of the country's profound and unexpected influence on the world over the last 500 years – fragments of history largely forgotten beyond its borders. Once home to one of the wealthiest cities on Earth, Bolivia kickstarted globalisation, helped to power Europe's economic growth and trigger dynastic collapse in China, and hosted everyone from Che Guevara to Butch Cassidy.

The book also explores how Bolivians in and around the world's highest city, largest salt flat, richest silver mine and most biodiverse national park are coping with some of the touchstone issues of the 21st century: the climate emergency, populism, migration, indigenous rights, national identity, urbanisation, and the 'war on drugs'.

In its pages, award-winning journalist and travel writer Shafik Meghji illuminates the dramatic landscapes, distinct cultures and diverse peoples of a country that – in the words of one interviewee – 'was the building block of the modern world, but is now lost in time'.

'Meghji is a wonderful travelling companion, bringing to life a Bolivia rarely seen in such bright and beautiful light.'

Monisha Rajesh, author of *Around the World in 80 Trains*

'A thoroughly engrossing and informative look at a clearly underappreciated part of the world.'

Lyn Hughes, founding editor of *Wanderlust*

'Meghji skilfully unveils the layers of this complex society with candour and a warm curiosity.'

Noo Saro-Wiwa, author of *Looking for Transwonderland*

Practical ACTION PUBLISHING

LAB
LATIN AMERICA BUREAU

ISBN 978-1-909014-25-1

9 781909 014251